A FORGOTTEN LEGEND

A FORGOTTEN LEGEND

BALBIR SINGH SR.
TRIPLE OLYMPIC GOLD
& MODI'S NEW INDIA

PATRICK BLENNERHASSETT

$|$ N₁ $|$ O₂ $|$ N₁

CANADA

Library and Archives Canada Cataloguing in Publication

Blennerhassett, Patrick, 1982–, author
A forgotten legend : Balbir Singh Sr., triple Olympic Gold
& Modi's new India / Patrick Blennerhassett.

ISBN 978–1–988098–10–4 (paperback)

1. Singh, Balbir, Sr., 1924–. 2. Field hockey players—India—
Biography. 3. Olympic athletes—India—Biography. 4. India—History—
1947–. 5. India—Biography. I. Title.

GV1017.H7B54 2016   796.355092   C2016–900237–3

Printed and bound in Canada on 100% recycled paper.

Now Or Never Publishing
#313, 1255 Seymour Street
Vancouver, British Columbia
Canada V6B 0H1

nonpublishing.com
Fighting Words.

We gratefully acknowledge the support of the Canada Council for the Arts
and the British Columbia Arts Council for our publishing program.

for my grandmother,
a lover of books and discourse

"God has no religion."
~ Mahatma Gandhi

He has a spry jump to his step as he floats across the beige carpeting towards the podium. Back home across the Pacific Ocean, he walks slowly to a speech; calculating his movements, raising his guard, knowing half of each room he enters will be sufficiently filled with skeptics and naysayers. But here on this stage, he's a rock star, and after being introduced by Neha Buch, a bubbly 33-year-old female leader of a non-governmental organization, he looks like the president pre-elect. His smile unforced, his shoulders loose; surrounded by a glowing aura as he welcomes his listeners.

"Namaste," says Barack Obama, almost as if he's greeting friends at a party.

Here in the Siri Fort Auditorium of New Delhi, a cultural landmark that shows Bollywood films, hosts concerts, and stages plays, the forty-fourth President of the United States of America is more than happy to address this crowd.

He's flanked by two massive flags; one with red horizontal stripes representing the thirteen British colonies that declared independence from the Kingdom of Great Britain in 1776, and fifty white stars representing fifty states surrounded by blue. The other has three thick coloured horizontal bars in deep saffron, white and green. In the centre of that flag is the Ashoka Chakra, a circular wheel with 24 spokes, a prominent symbol in the Buddhist faith. The mood is electric, and you can tell Obama is feeding off the energy. Back in his US homeland, it's a bitter partisan battleground filled with vitriol and venomous hate. Here he's a welcomed dignitary, the leader of the free world, the most talked about visitor this country has had in decades.

"I bring the friendship and the greetings of the American people," he continues to uproarious applause. "On behalf of myself and Michelle, thank you so much for welcoming us back to India."

He thanks Neha for her introduction, and sets about outlining his coming speech to an auditorium filled with upper-crust Indian university students. Raised as part of the country's economic elite, they are born into affluence and offered chances most Indians can only dream of. Unlike Neha's speech, which touched on her own reservations about helping India's poor—concerns stemming from her personal fear of getting lice from members of the lower castes—this speech is going to articulate something different.

It's not about the rampant poverty plaguing every corner of India, rendering the country's human rights record into a shockingly dismal state. Nor is it about India's flagrant corruption, infecting its core, eating the nation alive from the inside out. Within the country's seemingly endless list of social ills: rape culture, a ghastly sanitation record, poverty, racism, sexism, a lack of basic necessities for most, Obama could easily cherry pick and lay waste. The US is no country club itself either; race riots, political bribery, a shrinking middle class and elected officials bought by major corporations with sinister invested interests means any finger-pointing idioms should be kept to themselves.

But this man is here for a different reason, to make a point about one issue, the issue of freedom, and to discuss the oppression that has the second-most populous country in the world in a chokehold.

But first, after he finishes with the pleasantries and some customary Hindi greetings, he proceeds to do what he's required to do during any foreign speech: sell America as the world's biggest trading partner. It's critical here at this moment in geopolitical time. Many think this nation will surpass China in global economic status, and with the Red Dragon suffocating under its own weighty expectations, there is no better time to pounce. Obama talks of the partnerships being formed between India and the US on this trip, during which he and Indian Prime Minister Nahrendra Modi shared a much publicized chuckle in a quiet rose garden in Delhi, the two at ease in each other's company, international leaders in a budding bromance.

"Of course, only Indians can decide India's role in the world," he says of a potential relationship between the world's largest democracy and one of the world's oldest democracies. "America wants to be your partner."

Then Obama shifts gears, slowly sliding into the real subject, his thesis, the specific issue of personal liberty. On January 25, 2015 Obama became the first US president to attend India's Republic Day celebrations. On that fateful day in history in 1950, India officially adopted its own constitution. It was the final formality in the establishment of a new country, one that had declared its independence three years prior. But in 1947, independence also meant a bloody Partition that descended over the country like a thick plague of ethnic hatred. Woman were raped, men were murdered, and hundreds of thousands were displaced—all in the name of religion.

Within the Indian Constitution was the promise and a personal pledge by Mahatma Gandhi himself of a nation built under the *idea* of secularism. However, the reality is muddied, and in a country where one religion forms the core identity and outright majority of the populace, secularism is more notion than custom, more idea than actual governance. History has marred India to its core, much like the Civil Rights Movement in the US, leaving longstanding scars that festered rather than faded with time.

Obama references his own personal hero, Martin Luther King Jr., stating when King was protesting racial segregation in the US, the human rights activist's guiding light was Gandhi and his non-violent resistance movement against British rule. It's a bridging moment between the countries' two icons, a way for Obama to express solidarity through similar pasts that took place continents apart.

But then this African-American man's tone shifts. Born in Hawaii to a white Kansas woman of English ancestry and a black father, a Luo from Nyang'oma Kogelo, Kenya, Obama becomes clinical with his words, removing his verbal scalpel and applying it like he's forced to do so frequently back home. Warmth is replaced with a more pensive, controlled demeanour. He digs deep, right to the heart of the matter. There's an itch this man of colour wants so badly to scratch, and it revolves around the idea of how differences can divide as much as similarities can unite.

While he's largely avoided referring to himself as a black man back home, here in India, he feels free to provide his own personal context. With the bitter taste of the race riots in Ferguson, Missouri still on his tongue, and the last gasping breaths of Eric Garner hanging in the collective air, Obama offers a quote that will be publicized in Indian papers across the country:

"Every person has the right to practice his faith without any persecution, fear or discrimination. India will succeed so long as it is not splintered along religious lines."

Referencing the very constitution he is there to celebrate, Obama jabs a proverbial knife into the crowd; not a shot at India, but a concession to how race and religion continue to segregate his own land, the one he is currently visiting and many countries in between. The crowd falls silent. Niceties dispensed with, Obama twists the blade unapologetically, speaking of how he himself has experienced racism countless times in his life; that his wife's lineage has roots in slavery, and that his grandfather was tortured by the British. He speaks of how under his country's constitution, all men are created equal, and should be treated as such—but aren't.

"Religion is written into our founding documents; it's part of America's very first amendment. Your Article 25 says all people are equally entitled to the freedom of conscience and have the right to freely profess, practice, and propagate religion. In both our countries, in all countries, upholding this fundamental freedom of religion is not only the utmost responsibility of the government, but also the responsibility of every person."

He leans forward ever so slightly, as if to address the crowd on an intimate level. His eyes search the room, making personal contact with India's young stars, the intellectual elite who have the daunting task of bringing this nation into the globalized twenty-first century. Then he offers up the most poignant words of his speech. None of them would appear in any paper anywhere within the sub-continent of Southeast Asia.

"Too often, religion has been used to tap into those darker impulses as opposed to the light of God. Three years ago, in our state of Wisconsin, back in the United States of America, a man walked into a Sikh temple and in a terrible act of violence killed six innocent people, Americans and Indians. And in that moment of shared grief our two countries reaffirmed a basic truth, as we must again today. That every person has the right to practice their faith how they choose, or to practice no faith at all, free of persecution and of fear and discrimination."

If a pin were to drop, every ear in this packed auditorium of a thousand would hear it. A once rowdy crowd slowly applauds, sounds of cheering a president is accustomed to now oddly muted. The hand clapping forced, the subtext of what this man uttered still unpleasantly bubbling to the surface, steaming atop the oven like a screaming kettle whistle.

★★★

Back across the Pacific Ocean in Glendale, Arizona less than a week later, the New England Patriots are basking in the snowfall of multicoloured confetti. Standing atop a podium in the middle of the field, quarterback Tom Brady, cheeks greased with eye black, sweat still dripping from his handsome locks, lifts the Vince Lombardi trophy in celebration. The crowd's applause crests as Brady's million-dollar smile gleams out across the North American continent. Having beaten the Seattle Seahawks and their suffocating defence, Brady stands atop the football world, his detractors dwindling by the second. He is celebrating his fourth Super Bowl title and third Most Valuable Player trophy. He has finally cemented himself amongst the game's elite, nabbing that elusive title that puts him in a different category of greatness altogether.

Journalists swarm Brady as he heads to the locker room to celebrate the win with his teammates. They want to know more about one of the greatest NFL players of all time. While Brady had previously won three titles with his Patriots, he'd also lost twice in the finals to the Goliath-slaying New York Giants, denting his stake atop the sport. Names like Joe Montana, wide receiver Jerry Rice and running back Jerry Brown were consistently mentioned as the greatest, but Brady was still largely a peripheral pick.

Now the Patriots quarterback has ceremoniously shoved his way into that conversation with a resounding victory. The discussion of the best of all time now has a new voice atop the mountain after Brady's team captured Super Bowl XLIX.

Reporters throw questions at him a mile a minute, shoving their microphones as close to his face as possible.

"Tom what do you say to the people who are calling you the best football player of all time now? Where does this put you in regards to your hero, Joe Montana?"

Brady, ever the humble professional and still months away from the residual blast of Deflategate, simply smiles, offering beautifully canned responses as he retreats to sip champagne and lick his wounds after an arduous season. But a few days later, the cover of *Sports Illustrated* revives the debate, posing a completely subjective question to which everyone is dying for a factual answer:

"After a Super Bowl win for the ages, the Patriots chiseled their place on the Rushmore of NFL franchises—and their quarterback staked his claim as the greatest ever."

The question about Brady is valid. But his statistics speak for themselves. He needs undertake no campaigning blitzes or public relations touring to make his case. For all their inconsistent babbling, the pundits have rightfully elevated him to the highest peak of this debate.

Trophies, records, and championships are all the San Mateo, California native needs to present towards the title of greatest of all time.

***

In the quiet suburbs of Chandigarh, India, an elderly man watches these two events unfold on the television in his living room. Two Americans, one a sitting president and the other a future Hall of Fame football star, waft around the room with his thoughts. A solemn internal discussion about race, and recognition, and how we stake our claim, cement our legacies atop countries and sports, and how we show respect to those who've achieved greatness amidst tidal-like adversity.

This man sits in a creaky wooden chair, his widowed daughter off to the left, cleaning the kitchen after dinner. His grandson beside him, half-heartedly watching, checking his phone, texting friends. The family's dog Amy, a playful golden retriever, snores after a long day of barking atop the house's rooftop deck.

This man's eyes are worn, his cheeks hidden behind a wiry white beard. He is tired after a long walk earlier in the day, a stroll in solitude through the nearby Fragrance Gardens. His knees get sore easily, so he sits at night, keeping his back straight to keep it from straining. He wonders if it's bedtime, if it's time to call an end to another long, hot day under the blistering Indian sun.

No one truly knows the thoughts in this man's head. No one knows whether or not he's currently wrestling with a serious, compounded notion of helplessness concerning the homeland he's poured his heart and soul into over some ninety years. But one thing is certain. As these two seemingly unrelated events unfold mere days apart in Fort Siri and Glendale, no man on the face of the planet is more linked to their resounding message. The script too well set, the characters too obvious. This old man cannot deny the undeniable connection between these conversations and his current predicament.

Of colour and creed. Of the greatest athletes of all time. Of the debates that rage through dinner tables in New Delhi, Boston, and everywhere in between. The clamouring continues, endless swirls of discussions in which rightful heirs slowly make their way to the summit through tireless discourse. But for this man, he remains anonymous amongst the masses. This old man sits quietly, alone except for his family members—wondering how he got to this moment of lonely internal reflection after a life of such remarkable history.

The Rooster Coop

"I guess, Your Excellency, that I too should start off by kissing some god's arse. Which god's arse, though? There are so many choices. See, the Muslims have one god. The Christians have three gods. And we Hindus have 36,000,000 gods. Making a grand total of 36,000,004 divine arses for me to choose from."

~ Aravind Adiga, *The White Tiger*

It is a writer's greatest fear, an entity completely and utterly ineffable.

Anyone who's spent an extended amount of time in India, or gone outside of the confines of its resorts and tourist track can attest to one thing with crystal, lucent clarity: the impossibility of adequately defining the country as a whole. India is the unanswerable question, inexplicable to the core, disorder its only defining trait or through-line. The more knowledge you acquire, the more confusing it becomes. Eloquence offers nothing. Nonfiction writers have tried and failed to pinpoint something with which they can equate the insanity, an anecdote or story that encapsulates India, that offers clarity amidst an infinite fog. Yet they always stumble, forever lost in the endless complexities of an indescribable riddle that defies logic yet somehow continues to exist.

It's only when you jump to the fictitious, fantastical side that any wordsmith gets remotely close to encapsulating the country in its entirety. In Aravind Adiga's 2008 award-winning novel, *The White Tiger*, which narrates India's class struggles amidst globalization through the eyes of a young village boy, Adiga sets an allegory for his homeland:

"Go to Old Delhi, behind the Jama Masjid, and look at the way they keep chickens there in the market. Hundreds of pale hens and brightly colored roosters, stuffed tightly into wire-mesh cages, packed as tightly as worms in a belly, pecking each other and shitting on each other, jostling just for breathing space; the whole cage giving off a horrible stench—the stench of terrified, feathered flesh. On the wooden desk above this coop sits a grinning young butcher, showing off the flesh and organs of a recently chopped-up chicken, still oleaginous with a coating of dark blood. The roosters in the coop smell the blood from above. They see the organs of their brothers lying around them. They know they're next. Yet they do not rebel. They do not try to get out of the coop."

India *is* this sensory explosion. Nothing short of maddening, every function of the human body flash bomb bombarded—smells, tastes, the smoggy haze of pollution, the literal crush of people, the dirt, the layer of dust and carbon dioxide coating the inside of the lungs. It's a never-ending pen of chaos, relentlessly pumping you full of emotions just by occupying the area around your skin. A beautifully messy country: organized confusion, downright overwhelming, simultaneously holding immense possibility and heartbreaking sadness.

While one percent of India's population reaps the benefits of a new economic boom, the rest are forced to jostle amidst the stuffy chaos of Adiga's coop. One point two billion souls, speaking more than 300 languages, some 450 million people living below the poverty line, half the world's outsourced IT services, 500,000 female infants killed each year due to illegal sex selection and abortion, the third largest GDP according to purchasing power parity, the third largest carbon polluter[1] and the largest number of illiterate people in the world.[2] A multicoloured, vibrant, culturally backwards beehive overflowing with smelly garbage,[3] economic honey dripping from its core and wavering on a thinly strung branch of democracy. A burgeoning superpower poised to take off like a rocket ship, or self-destruct in a glorious mess on the starting block.

In the summer of 2011, I spent a month in the state of Andhra Pradesh located in the southeastern portion of the country visiting a girlfriend. The area is known for its beautiful coastal scenery, religious temples, massive population per square foot, and overwhelming Hindu majority—roughly ninety percent of the population.[4] My time there was culture shock with the caps lock on. My ex had come over for a university social work practicum in the working class city of Chennai, and I spent a few weeks with her, visiting hospitals and city slums. Local social workers were trying to figure out how to properly test people for HIV/AIDS, but the culture was hugely condemnatory of sex before marriage—even the implications of getting screened were viewed as taboo or dangerous.

It's disheartening to hear doctors tell stories of trying to give condoms to patients who, despite being diagnosed with sexually transmitted infections, were still adamantly claiming they were virgins for fear of social expulsion even in private, confidential conversations. In a country where AIDS was running amok, killing at will throughout the village populations, young boys and girls flatly denied the contraceptives, eyes darting left and right to make sure anyone and everyone saw them refuse. I came home feeling defeated, wondering how one breaks from customs and traditions in such a fast-paced world. India was dealing with a legitimate conundrum faced by every religion today: how to combat rigid, downright suffocating traditionalism while helping its population deal with MTV-style problems like sexual activity and teen pregnancy. It was more harm than good; sex was done in secret and lied about profusely in public. The trip was one big clusterfuck of emotions, and by the time I left, I vowed never to return.

In the fall of 2014 I spoke to Ringo Dosanjh, a former colleague of my father. Ringo told me a story about his dad that I'd initially found interesting because of my previous travels to the country. He was wondering if I might return to India to further delve into what he felt was a case of serious injustice being done to his father.

I was instantly hesitant to even fathom going back, knowing full well I would be breaking a promise I'd made to my own sanity. A sour taste remained, the bitter reality of harsh third world life outside the Canadian bubble to which I'd grown accustomed still scratched into my memory. But as Ringo spoke, it became quite clear, quite quickly that this was a story I simply couldn't ignore.

Ringo wanted me to fly to Chandigarh, a city in the northern part of the country, to meet his father, a "forgotten legend". A three-time field hockey Olympic gold medalist nobody knew about. The story both intrigued and baffled me. This senior citizen was arguably India's most decorated athlete and greatest ever, yet Ringo said he lived in complete obscurity. Now in the twilight of his life, his family wanted someone with writing skills to transcribe his amazing story, to at least get it on record. They'd published an autobiography in 1977, but it did little to encapsulate the extraordinary existence his father had lived.

The cause of his father's anonymity was what started to keep me up at night. Why is this man not famous? Why isn't he a national hero, paraded around like Maradona, trotted out for national events like Pelé or ensconced in some cushy executive role like Michael Jordan? Why aren't there multiple flowering biographies floating around of him? Field hockey was India's go-to sport for much of its existence, pre-dating Independence in 1947. Only in the past decade has it ceded the crown to cricket, and done so grudgingly. Why has this man's own country forgotten him? Nothing added up.

It made no sense. In most nations, heavily decorated retired athletes were overly inflated showmen and women, attending elaborate jersey retirement ceremonies, making money as broadcast correspondents, or serving as sports franchise ownership tycoons. Is this a self-imposed silence to make some type of political statement? And in a country like India where they worship heroes like Gods and elevate Bollywood stars to incredible heights, using them to hawk hair gel and cell phones, why is this man not burnt to a crisp from the Indian spotlight? Or was this something else, some sort of strange conspiracy at work?

I was a small-time author paying the bills as a local journalist. I'd been to India before, and had written many stories on South Asian immigrants who'd settled in B.C.'s Lower Mainland through *Business in Vancouver* magazine,[5,6,7,8] so I felt adequately comfortable mulling over the idea on a professional level.

Within any true blue reporter is the desire to uncover a massive story, to overturn a rock and watch the bugs scatter in all directions—to expose a Watergate scandal or bring down a corrupt official with nothing more than a great piece of penmanship. My ego was pining for the chance to investigate a real meaty conflict, to throw aside mundane days of interviewing boringly polished local politicians for something bigger, something grander. This was my chance to put a dent in the world, a chance to rewrite history rather than just cover it.

I told Ringo I would go, cover what I saw, and see what came of the entire experience. Little did I know what I was getting myself into, that the story and this man would end up consuming me in a quest to unfurl the truth, to peel away an issue eating India from its core and lead me deep into a religious rabbit hole of a country with a sixth of the world's population.

Of course the initial response to my trip was muted at best, and all the preliminary signs I received were negative. Friends and family worried for my safety: stories of foreign journalists captured and publicly beheaded by ISIS, who'd specifically called out Canada on numerous occasions, were front and centre in the international media cycle. Back home, tensions in the Middle East had heightened fears of terrorism. While I'd done my research and traveled to the country before, news of Al-Qaeda reportedly preparing for a major attack in India did nothing to quell my own internal hesitations.[9]

I knew the chances of capture or dying in an attack were slim, but as I wrestled with the decision, the news media whipped my fears into a bubbly froth. The last thing I wanted to do was end up as some political pawn, forcing my girlfriend and family through arduous months of unthinkable stress while I suffered through my own Hell as a western captive in overseas hands.

I wouldn't be traveling as a tourist; I would be on an official Journalist Visa. If detained, captured, or kidnapped, the deck would be stacked against me. My girlfriend was supportive, but she had a few tearful moments as I explained the regional threats India faced on a daily basis: proximity to its arch-nemesis Pakistan; shelling in Kashmir;[10] and four countries within a few hundred kilometres that offered serious threats to my life if I set a foot in.[11]

I would be making this trip solo, with nothing more than a laptop, recorder and blind faith that I could avoid becoming a statistic or breaking news headline about another journalist killed or kidnapped abroad. I would have no security detail, or be operating inside a heavily fortified green zone. I would be out professionally in the third world with no ties to a corporation or organization with international branches in India, and little more than my own knowledge and expertise to guide me through this daunting maze of unpredictability.

In its 2013 year end report, Reporters Without Borders ranked India 140th out of 179 countries in terms of media freedom, as the country "is at its lowest since 2002 because of increasing impunity for violence against journalists and because Internet censorship continues to grow."[12] This was not Canada where I could interview and investigate with literally no fear of personal harm.

But the opportunity was too compelling to dismiss. A chance to meet an Olympic hero, to break from the tourist track and interview locals about a mysterious story in a far-off land. The journalist inside me overpowered any human instincts, forcing me to research as much as I could about the subject and country, knowing the more committed I became, the tougher it would be to say no. My younger sister, ever the level-headed sounding board of our family, summed it up rather eloquently after I rang her for counsel:

"All I know is that you might regret going, but you will surely regret not going."

So I picked up a Journalist Visa through the Indian Consulate via an outsourced application company called BLS International Canada (the irony that my Indian visa application was outsourced to another outfit wasn't lost on me). From the moment I learned of the story to the day my flight departed was less than a month. My crash course on India's social underbelly and her all-encompassing rooster coop was about to begin.

On November 7, 2014, I vacated the pristine first-world comforts of Vancouver, flying through Heathrow Airport. An eight-hour layover, eighteen hours in the sky and thirteen time zones later, I landed at Indira Gandhi Airport, just south of New Delhi, India's capital. My bags were two hours late and I couldn't use any of the washrooms on the Air India flight from London because they'd all been sufficiently defiled, so it was safe to say I was in a state of functioning hysteria when I finally touched down.

It's here at Indira Gandhi Airport, in my semi-delirious state that I'm picked up by Kabir Bhomia, a 35-year-old moderate Sikh Indian with a finance degree who had at one time worked for the

ICICI Bank in Johannesburg, South Africa. He's sporting a fishing hat and speaks fluent English. His accent shades of Indian, British and South African somehow all rolled into one as he welcomes me to his homeland.

Kabir's *nanaji*, my mother's father in Punjabi, is the grandson of the forgotten legend. He's in charge of organizing his schedule and occasional local appearances. Kabir looks after his elderly grandfather while acting as his pro bono public relations manager while he's between jobs trying to figure out his own career path. Bhomia returned from South Africa to help his mother care for his father—a former pilot in the Indian Air Force—who succumbed to Parkinson's Disease a few years ago. Kabir is my handler for this trip, my in to the 20-plus interviews I'll end up conducting as I traverse hundreds of kilometres in the northern portion of the country in the span of 14 jam-packed days.

Kabir's a smart, educated man in a country full of rampant illiteracy and ignorance. His sensible attitude and fluent English quickly become sanity saviours in my times of need. In public Kabir largely abides by strict social norms; in private he lets loose on his country with a vitriol for which he makes little apology. Voicing his displeasure with the city, almost under his breath as if the twenty-two million souls that populate the world's fourth largest metropolis[13] might be listening in.

"I *hate* Delhi."

He's tall for an Indian at six-foot-one, and has a propensity for staying up late texting female "friends" on his phone, and then sleeping through breakfast. His scattered nature appears to have him in an endless mental and physical swirl, pacing rooms as he fiddles with his phone. Yet this only adds to his oddly charming manner. He's a sweet, polite, single man in India, looking after his family while being pressured to start his own.

The family is pushing for something else, too. They've started a PR campaign to bring Kabir's elderly grandfather, this forgotten legend, into the spotlight. They're tired of his anonymity and fed up with his status as a regular citizen and retired pensioner with a fixed income; most multiple Olympic gold medalists make a living attending events, doing public appearances, or giving paid speeches at the very least, parlaying their fame into legitimate post-playing day careers. Kabir's elderly relative was doing none of this, his only income a meagre government stipend, earned via decades of backbreaking public service, which had initially been revoked upon retirement and only reinstated after a lengthy court battle with his employer, the Punjab Sports Department.

Why would this family even need to campaign for him? You'd think he'd be flooded with daily calls to endorse products and back corporate campaigns, pushed and pulled around, his legacy squeezed for every last penny as friends and family milked his accomplishments for gifts and handouts. India is a consumerist's dream—products can be marketed to approximately a billion eager buyers. And according to Kabir, this gold-medal winning Olympian loved nothing more than to preach the importance of the country's youth and tout India's promise as a nation. He is a marketing firm's dream, ripe and ready for the talk show circuit, press tour and billboard campaign.

But none of this was happening.

Money didn't appear to be the problem. That is, the family wasn't doing this because of dire financial strain, they were making ends meet. The house they all lived in was paid off, and Kabir's deceased father had passed on a government payout after his death. In a world of ulterior motives and back alley scheming, this appeared to be a straight-ahead push with honourable intentions: the elder statesmen of their family had been getting the short end of the stick and they wanted change. But they were spinning their wheels, flat-out stuck in the muddy ditch, and at wits end.

Dhyan Chand—a Hindu from the state of Uttar Pradesh—was getting all the press. Another field hockey star, long since deceased with an inferior resume, was an international sporting god. There's the Olympic-sized, Major Dhyan Chand National Stadium in Delhi,[14] and another arena named after him in Lucknow, Uttar Pradesh.[15] Multiple god-like statues have been erected across the country in his name and there is talk of the Bharat Ratna, India's highest civilian honour,[16] and a biopic by Bollywood mega-mogul KJo (Karan Johar) in the works.[17]

There's also the Dhyan Chand Award,[18] given out by the Government of India; Hockey India's Dhyan Chand Award[19] and countless articles and news media clippings about his amazing legacy both at home[20] and abroad.[21] India has even made its National Sports Day, August 29, the same day as his birthday.[22]

Although Chand passed away thirty-five years ago, his legacy appears to be growing.[23] He is a household name, widely regarded as field hockey's greatest athlete.

And yet, he is undeniably *second* best. When you stack the two Indian field hockey stars' statistics and accomplishments side by side, the elderly Sikh comes out on top. Chand won his three consecutive golds before the Second World War claimed two consecutive Olympic games. At the time, field hockey was largely a showcase of British Raj supremacy. After India became an independent nation, birthing Pakistan in the process and essentially quashing the British Raj team—replaced partially by Great Britain—competition was fierce, and India still dominated the game. For a North American comparison, take football's Joe Montana, Terry Bradshaw, and Tom Brady. All three have won four Super Bowl titles. However, Bradshaw is almost never mentioned as one of the greatest players of all time, while Montana and Brady are consistently atop the debate.

Why? Any football junkie knows Bradshaw was an adequate quarterback who played great in big games, but the real reason the Pittsburgh Steelers won all those Super Bowls was the team's rough and tough Steel Curtain defensive line, thus he rarely gets mentioned in the debate. Similarly, Chand won his medals because he was the best player on an already dominant British Raj squad. In contrast, newly independent India won three Olympic gold field hockey medals because one man's play elevated his squad above other powerhouse nations like Great Britain and Pakistan, who sought to beat the Indian team *specifically* for political reasons.

So far in the Bhomia family's PR campaign for their elder statesman, the only success they've had is getting their grandfather quoted and featured in local Sikh-friendly newspapers and featured on local Punjab friendly television shows. They've also managed to create a Wikipedia entry and a Facebook page with about 700 followers. It's safe to say that while the family is adamantly trying, they're wholeheartedly failing.

But as I'm slowly finding out, this is not simply a case of national forgetfulness, but something more concerted, possibly sinister at work, as Kabir's mother Sushbir tells me the night I meet her.

"This is a crooked world."

Kabir, ever the explanative enthusiast, likens his mother's quote to something Jawaharlal Nehru, India's founding father and first Prime Minister once said: "The problem with India, is Indians."

But before I can start uncovering the various pieces of this mystery, I have to physically get to Chandigarh. This means the vehicular veins of the world's most crammed country, stuffed full, every corner of the coop packed wire tight with uninterrupted pandemonium. For every square kilometre of land in India, there are almost 400 people trying to eke out a living where the average person makes less than an American dollar a day[24,25] with a life expectancy lower than North Korea, Bangladesh and Venezuela—which has the second highest murder rate in the world.[26,27]

With my life in my driver's hands, Kabir and I cram into his dusty 2007 Skoda Octavia to wade through the masses. Delhi's traffic is horrifically dangerous; car accidents are rampant, a minute-to-minute occurrence. Crash rates in India are some of the highest in the world, only China has more reported accidents.[28] An influx of cars bought by the burgeoning middle class, and high levels of drunk driving, lack of police enforcement, and poor road conditions make the nation's tangled roads a breeding ground for motor vehicle-related fatalities.

As I sweat my way through a steam pot mug of an afternoon, I find myself bracing against the doorframe, praying to Ganesha that we don't get side-swiped by a jam-packed rickshaw, or crushed against a concrete divider by an overflowing commuter bus. Delhi is laid out as a spider web of disconnected transportation grids, mixing old and new routes in irregular, sporadic patterns as the metropolis sprawls outwards in all directions like shattered glass. We're heading along Dwark Road to Sector 4, where Kabir has a third-floor flat in the Shri Badrinath Apartments complex. It's a relatively new but poor working class neighbourhood of beige coloured high-rises in one of Delhi's countless boroughs. Here townships are divided into numbered sectors, meaning you don't live in the west end or downtown; you live in Sector 4 or Sector 15.

The purpose of our detour is so Kabir can pick up some supplies to bring to Chandigarh. More importantly, he's showing me his 1982 Royal Enfield motorbike, purchased from a guy in Agra for around $1,000 US. He has yet to break this news to his mother and he tells me this information, quite comically, is off the record. Laughing, he says that his Enfield is a source of great pride, but like a temperamental girlfriend.

"She's quick to let you know how she's feeling."

Having motorbiked throughout various foreign countries in my life, it's my first chance to bond with Kabir through common interests. By the end of the trip, we're as close as two people can get, and to this day, I consider him a good friend, a like-minded soul I met on the other side of the planet.

After packing some clothes and downing a Kingfisher beer, we set out towards the airport, back on Dwark Road, linking up with National Highway 8 through what feels like eight different merge lanes all coming into one.

One does not visit Delhi; one experiences it. Packs of gaunt street kids with bloodshot eyes paw at the car window, yelling for spare change. The mix of sewage and diesel fumes infest the nostrils, traditional Bhajan music blares over loudspeakers, the sound cutting through the incessant honking. There's a concerted effort as a Westerner to avoid having a panic attack here. Delhi comes at you fast, and hard, and if you're not ready for it, it will overwhelm you almost immediately.

We merge onto India Gate, a massive roundabout and memorial for the undivided Indian Army soldiers who died in the First and Third Anglo-Afghan Wars. The Amar Jawan Jyoti, the flame of the immortal soldier flickers through the car window as we crawl north along Outer Ring Road, which runs parallel to the Yamuna River. This is the largest tributary of the Ganges, itself one of the largest rivers in the world. The Yamuna is rife with garbage and pollution; a septic dumping ground at many points, giving off a stink one might liken to mould growing in someone's basement that's somehow been liquefied.[29] This river is literally choking on filth as various forms of waste have left it inhospitable to anything that dares enter.

A nasty, dry chest cold compounded by a runny nose smacks me across the face as we get on the 7 RCR (Racecourse Road). Voice goes hoarse, body chills overtake and the sweats begin. I try to nap, but I'm violently shaken out of a doze every time we're forced to swerve lanes to avoid an accident in the form of a spastically moving rickety truck or dilapidated scooter. Throughout the course of my trip I will battle this resilient virus, which hangs onto my lungs like a suckerfish, fed by the deeply polluted air[30] and arid, pollinated winds.

Luckily, we're embarking on this journey on a Sunday afternoon. The gridlock is suffocating—as opposed to downright asphyxiating, and I'm told things could be a lot worse, we could literally be standing still for hours on end. We spend more than a few stoplights inching forward while every motor vehicle, alongside forms of transportation I didn't know existed, such as four-plus riders on one makeshift scooter or a dozen people packed inside a rickshaw, all jostle for position at the starting gate. Kabir, ever the experienced Indian driver, shifts us from first to neutral as he explains the appalling state of Delhi traffic.

"If you want to avoid the rush hour, you basically have to drive between midnight and five in the morning. Other than that, you're pretty much screwed if you have to get somewhere at a certain time. If there's an accident, or some type of a VIP, it's even worse."

Sure enough, potbelly police officers drag out rustic roadblocks on wheels before a roundabout and we're forced to sit tight for a good fifteen minutes. Apparently this is a common occurrence in Delhi, where politicians get presidential treatment to avoid the notorious traffic, solving the problem for themselves while making it exponentially worse for everyone else. There are laws in place that allow pretty much every type of diplomat to use a siren on his car,[31] but it quickly becomes clear that the only way you're avoiding gridlock is if you can actually play God and get the cops to stop it for you.

What if I actually needed an ambulance in Delhi? I'm currently running a mild fever and if I took a turn for the worse and needed medical attention, I'd be screwed, forced to waste away as my first aid responders sat stuck in immovable traffic jams. Kabir says this is just the tip of the iceberg when it comes to the many issues plaguing Delhi's transportation sector including an over-crowded metro system.[32] Regular cars are now known to sport all sorts of sirens and lights to try and avoid the gridlock. He tries to explain the origins of the problem, but in my delirious state, his sarcastic words escape me, my notes at this point reduced to poorly scribbled gibberish:

"There is a hangover from the old colonial days still in vogue in which having a red beacon on top of your car signifies that you are a VIP—very idiotic person—who isn't bound by the traffic rules, etcetera, which govern the common [folk]. In Hindu, that translates to 'AAM,' which, if translated back into English, is 'mango' people."

Later, when I sleep off my fever and replenish the fluids I've drained from my body, I learn that 'mango' is a typical Hindi word for common people, slang terminology I hear a few times throughout my trip.

Our drive continues north from Delhi along the Grand Trunk Road. Technically this highway runs all the way from Afghanistan to Bangladesh. The road itself serves as a cultural roadmap and historical timeline of the area, dating back to the Mughal Empire of the early sixteenth century.[33] In Rudyard Kipling's 1901 novel, *Kim*, the author fawns over it in the way only a British Raj novelist could: "A wonderful spectacle", he writes, that "runs straight, bearing without crowding India's traffic for fifteen hundred miles—such a river of life as nowhere else exists in the world."

Times have changed. While there are patches of decent thoroughfare, today the Grand Trunk Road is mostly cracked, pothole-filled concrete in need of serious upgrades. We pass multiple resettlement colonies,[34] half abandoned, slightly dis-coloured brick-and-mortar buildings crammed together like leftover Legos and dubbed adequate housing. Kabir says the people inhabiting these high-rises are "working poor mangos", meaning they have windows with no glass and nothing more than running water—but they also have jobs.

India's slums are well documented, yet the oxymoronic jux-taposition of the dire poverty within the media spin of the coun-try's tech boom is on display more blatantly than I imagined. Beside shiny high-rise towers, whose multinational corporate logos like eBay and Intel glimmer in the sun, are mountains of rotting garbage and abandoned, decrepit buildings. Kids climb and play on them, mothers rummage for food and mangy dogs look for safe places to hide.

In India you bear witness to some of the worst levels of poverty and the lowest quality of life on the planet. In his 2006 account of the country, *In Spite of the Gods*, Edward Luce described life in Delhi's slums as "people living in conditions that ought to have disappeared long ago." He interviewed a group of women in the area who'd gone through unthinkable horrors:

"One had visited the police station to register a case for rape. She was taken to one of the cells and raped again by those to whom she had turned for help. Another had lost a child who was playing outside on the street when he fell into a channel and drowned in the sewage . . . A widow had been trying and failing for years to obtain a certificate proving her husband had died in order to benefit from a small state pension. She could not afford the bribe that would secure the certificate."

Even the 2008 Academy Award-winning movie *Slumdog Millionaire*, set in Mumbai's slums which shows kids getting their eyes burnt out to garner more sympathy as beggars still manages to downplay how barbaric life is in this country's ghettos. In the face of such misery, I'm reminded of a 2012 *Vanity Fair* piece on Mukesh Ambani's Mumbai skyscraper mansion,[35] said to have cost $1 billion US. It features 400,000 square feet, 27 storeys, a 168-car garage, and a "snow room" that simulates actual snowfall conditions. Ambina's wife Nita is a self-described philanthropist. While wealth inequality is nothing new, in India it takes on a heightened level of absurdity. The nation's high number of billionaires is alarming, record-breaking disproportionate to most first world countries,[36] and India is also home to a staggering third of the world's poorest people.[37] Here, the word "poor" takes on a whole new meaning. Patrick French further outlined the daily atrocities plaguing India in his 2011 non-fiction book, *India: A Portrait*:

"A bride was burned to death in Jodhpur on the orders of her mother-in-law because her family had not delivered a dowry. In Imphal, an unarmed young man was shot by police commandos, execution-style, only paces from the state assembly. A widely syndicated newspaper photograph showed a mentally ill girl tied to a post on a grimy city street while her mother went to work each day. A journalist reported from Patna that children had replaced oxen on the farmland of Raghubansh Prasad Singh, the rural development minister: in an accompanying photo, little boys dragged a heavy plough across a sodden field . . . In Rajasthan, girls were injected with a cattle hormone to bring on puberty prematurely, so they could be sold to brothels in the United Arab Emirates. Dozens of handicapped children in Gulbarga were temporarily buried up to their necks in a garbage dump during a solar eclipse in the hope their disabilities might miraculously disappear. Several families in a village in eastern Uttar Pradesh were massacred because they came from the wrong caste."

On the northern outskirts of the city, we hit the town of Bhalswa Jahangir Pur, passing a water treatment facility with rusted pipes, worn fences and wild dogs running through its grounds. Ninety-seven million Indians, almost equal to the entire population of the world's twelfth most populous nation—the Philippines—do not have access to clean drinking water. Twenty-one percent of the communicable diseases contracted throughout the country are caused by unsafe drinking conditions.[38] I clutch my bottled water tightly, trying to stay hydrated. The blasting sun gives little relief; the tainted, air-conditioned air clogs my nose and lungs.

Next is a vast field of rustic power lines, kids and pedestrians walking through the labyrinths of steel and cords. Housing erected underneath the structures, a game of cricket off to the side of one row. The state of electricity in India is one of frayed, disjointed webs; a patchwork of networks, and a glaring problem that can be summed up in a few staggering statistics: 300 million people in the country have no access to it, many more get it sporadically, and poor wiring and negligible safety standards kill thousands through electrocution each year. Of the world's 1.3 billion without access to power, a quarter of them are here in this country.[39,40]

We drive through Murthal, Sonipat, and Panipat beside an elevated expressway. Unfinished and abandoned highway upgrades shoot spikes of rebar into the air like jagged teeth. As we drive, Kabir's speed-talking me through a local history lesson. He speaks of PM Modi's Clean India campaign (Swachh Bharat Abhiyan),[41] in which public shaming is meant to stop littering. On the surface, it seems almost simple-minded. But when you watch kids rummaging through oil-stained garbage and playing atop mounds of God-knows-what, it's more than apparent levels of trash are a serious crisis in India.[42] Sandwiched between buses, cars, and pedestrians, who dart across the road in some deadly real-life version of Frogger, Kabir nails me with a thesis statement, a mantra about this inexplicably complicated country:

"India is proof that God exists."

At first I don't get the reference.

"With all this chaos," he continues, "how would India ever exist without him?"

In Karnal, about four hours north of Delhi, we stop for tea and a bread omelet at a *dhaba*, a highway inn with convenience stores and an outdoor kitchen. There are fruit-fly riddled mangos and cow dung cakes for sale, but I pass on the local cuisine and sip a hot coffee, trying to remain alert. It's here I first realize I'm an outsider, or *gora*, Hindi for white person. Goras are not a common sight in this area, we are in the real India, well off the country's tourist track. Eyes follow me wherever I go. The attention is uncomfortable but manageable, and I make sure to keep multiple sight lines, to stay out of tight spots, and avoid the massive crowds. This mental strategizing allows for the illusion of safety in a country where safety measures appear to be whimsical theories rarely adhered to in practice.

I relieve myself in what will be the first of many highway rest stops where I literally try not to touch anything. While it may seem overtly Western to feel so disgusted in a third world bathroom, mounds of actual crap rotting on the floor around the toilet at one stop force me to dry heave on the spot. Sanitation might seem like an odd social ill on the surface, but after stepping on human feces multiple times, it's clear this is yet another serious issue with little end in sight.[43]

The sun sours a beet red, cutting a swath through the polluted air like a dusty brushstroke. We race past Ambala, Zirakpur, and finally arrive in Chandigarh. It's been a little less than seven hours of driving, but my body and mind ache like it's been weeks at sea. I've been moving across the globe continuously for more than twenty-six hours, and even though it's close to 35°C outside, I've started to shake with chills. I can only afford two weeks in India to solve the mystery of this vast country's forgotten legend. I can't waste time being sick or sleeping much if I want to understand what's going on behind this monstrous veil.

Chandigarh's beauty lies in its ability to appear somewhat relaxed and, in certain lights, almost first world. Known as the "The City Beautiful", it's the only city in India that is the capital of two states—Punjab and Haryana. India's states are divided up much like they are in the US, holdovers from pre-Partition lines drawn in which British Raj divided up the land into provinces. Chandigarh was also the first planned metropolis in the country, designed by Swiss-French Architect Le Corbusier.[44] This means the infrastructure lends itself to traffic flow instead of impeding it at various dangerous choke points. Though the population numbers more than a million people, it does not appear as Indian as the rest of India. Motorbikers wear helmets, cars obey stoplights, and the streets are relatively garbage-free and well maintained. In the bustling coop, it is a quiet corner of the pen.

Shortly after 9PM we reach the Bhomia residence: a two-story, four-bedroom estate with a gated fence. The house is decidedly middle class, even for North America, with its maze-like layout of square footage. Running water, clean toilets, showers, decorative collectibles, photos and religious paraphernalia abound. It will become my home for the next week or so, my only real sanctuary amidst the chaos and physical clutter of this country.

In Chandigarh, I'm less than a day's drive from the infamous India–Pakistan border, where a suicide bomber killed close to 50 people at the Wagah crossing a week before my arrival.[45] Both the Pakistani and Indian military hold daily parades and flag-flying ceremonies on their respective sides. The event draws crowds of hundreds, even thousands on the weekend when this attacker blew himself up amidst the mass of people. There's daily shelling in Kashmir to the north, a conflict that has raged since 1947, led to all-out war in the 1970s, and still has India and Pakistan looking like they might just break into another full blown international conflict at any moment.

To the east is the edge of the great Himalayan mountain range. Although I can't see the mountains because of the smog, the thought that I am extremely close to the highest point on the planet crosses my mind more than once. I'm blatantly far from home, worlds away, at the mercy of a land brimming with culture and history. The reality of the situation settles in, letting me know just how far I've globe-hopped for answers to a very peculiar question.

Inside the Bhomia residence, I meet Sushbir, Kabir's widowed mother. Like any good matriarchal figure in a household of men, she peppers me with questions about my personal comfort level and makes endless offers of hot tea and sugar cookies. Her kind eyes sparkle behind wire-rimmed glasses, and she twists her hands, accentuating her words as she speaks. Her flatbread *parantha* stuffed with boiled potatoes becomes my go-to dish at every meal, and she commands her kitchen like any good workstation, alternating between conversations and the *tawa*, a frying pan used for cooking.

But it's the third inhabitant of this house I've traveled to the other side of the planet to meet.

His name is Balbir Singh Dosanjh. He is most commonly known as Balbir Singh Sr., to distinguish himself from multiple other Balbir Singh field hockey players who came after him. He is a 91-year-old Indian field hockey centre forward with three Olympic gold medals, a Guinness World Record, and an Olympic Record to his name. He is a devout Sikh in a predominately Hindu country. He is a self-described secularist and nationalist. He stands five-foot-nine and has the lean frame of an athlete, even at his advanced age. He speaks softly, vocal chords worn after nine decades on the planet. He wears a *pagg*, the traditional Sikh turban, his beard is icy white and he is extremely polite, at one time literally offering the shoes off his feet to me when I appear in the living room sock-less.

He is this country's greatest athlete, living or deceased. He was the dagger in the heart of Great Britain at London's 1948 Olympics, leading an independent India to its first medal as a sovereign nation mere months after Gandhi and company navigated an ugly, bloody road to India's freedom through Partition; just one of many iconic, amazing stories concerning his life I will learn about.

His existence has all the makings of a Hollywood—or more fittingly—Bollywood film. But not only is the phone not ringing off the hook, it's not ringing at all. Although Singh Sr. is painfully humble, this is not sufficient reason for his complete anonymity.

More confusing still, he's fallen into obscurity in a country trying its damnedest to create a sporting culture.[46] This misguided attempt was nowhere more apparent than the 2010 Commonwealth Games, held in Delhi. Plagued by corruption, inadequate infrastructure—including a bridge that collapsed shortly after construction—countless delays, missed deadlines, threats of boycott by some member countries, and even an outbreak of dengue fever, the event highlighted the country's epic failure to promote itself on the grandest of scales. [47,48]

Singh Sr. did not receive an invite to these games as a special guest, let alone complimentary tickets to a match. Though, by any historical measure, he probably should've been running the Queen's baton in the stadium during the opening ceremonies.

In 2004, the Indian men's field hockey team was training in Chandigarh for the upcoming Summer Olympics in Athens. One afternoon, they went for a jog in the Fragrance Gardens. Singh Sr. was out walking with his grandson Kennedy, who now lives in Sydney, Australia. The whole team ran by him. Not a single member recognized the proverbial Michael Jordan of their sport. Only after Kennedy stopped captain Dilip Tirkey, who was bringing up the rear, did they clue in.

Surely the country's best field hockey players would know one of the men responsible for bringing India to international sports stardom with his goal-scoring prowess? Sure, it was a while ago, but with the internet we're uncovering forgotten heroes of the past everyday. With all the talk of globalization opening India up to new forms of media, why hasn't Singh Sr. been uncovered from the sand? A buried diamond, rife for superstardom, or at least state dignitary status, ready to sound the horn for a country filled with international potential.

Why is this the fate of Balbir Singh Sr.?

THE YOUNG VANDAL

"Oh, we want a new breed of men before India can be cleansed of her disease."

~ Sarojini Naidu, Indian poet

Massive legs pump like oiled, muscular piston heads. The horse gallops across the dusty fields of Vehari Tehsil. One of the hottest places on the South Asian sub-continent, it's an arid, dusty dirt that chokes the airways. Steam particles smeared across the horizon, the sun beats hard upon this land, baking it intensely with no sign of relief. Adjacent to the windy Sutlej River, it's a largely barren spot between what is now Multan to the west and the highly militarized India-Pakistan border to the east.

Atop this rare Marwari horse, with its inward curving ears, is a small boy, turban bobbing up and down on his head as he holds tightly to a set of reins. The wind in his ears is all he can hear; he loves the breakneck pace, the freedom speed offers. The boy snaps his wrist towards the rear, whipping the back of the horse with the leather strap, yelling for him to pick up speed.

"Yah!" He screams in Urdu.

His uncle Karam Singh taught him how to ride out here in the larger Multan district. Karam was a *patwari*, a government official assigned to the rural areas. Karam would let his pre-pubescent nephew ride out into the searing sun, making rounds on what they called the "village beat." Children from nearby huts would dart out to meet him, screaming with laughter, chasing the young boy as he rode bareback on the humongous, sweat-drenched beast.

He loved the independence of galloping so fast, of watching the plains whip by at a feverish pace. An adrenaline junkie from birth, the ability to reach speeds of 40 kilometres per hour on an unpredictable animal was right up his alley. Karam would help him up on his horse, tell him not to do anything too stupid, give the horse a slap on the behind, and send them off.

One day, returning from a long ride, the boy slowed the horse to a canter at a nearby irrigation ditch. He brought the animal to the edge and let it slurp up the lukewarm liquid. Dismounting, he dipped his head below the surface for his own relief. The unblocked sun relentless, cracking the dirt on the ground. There was little shade other than the occasional cluster of flowering trees over small streams feeding into the mighty Chenab River.

After his horse quenched his thirst, signalling his intentions with a neigh, the boy wrapped his hands around its neck and jumped on. He was readying the reins when a ghastly figure of a towering man darted from a plot of bushes by the irrigation ditch.

Startled, the boy tried to take off, but the man grabbed the reins and stopped him.

"Where do you think you're going?!"

The man was portly, gruff; wearing tattered clothes with villainous eyes full of intensity.

Flash-frozen with fear, the boy did not answer. His uncle had told him about thieves in this area. They would steal horses, ride them west and sell them in the city of Multan.

"Get off the horse!" shouted the man.

Thoughts swirled around the young boy's head. If he dismounted, he risked danger, possibly death. But if he tried to gallop away and failed, he might meet a similar fate. He looked into the eyes of this burly man, the smell of filth wafting into his nostrils.

The horse had no saddle, so there were no stirrups to kick. The man was growing impatient, and was about to grab the boy and yank him off the horse's back.

Then, with one swift motion, the boy jabbed his hand, fist closed except for thumb, right into the soft belly of the animal. The horse let out a high-pitched squeal, reared back, and took off like a rocket. The boy wrapped his hands around its neck, closed his eyes, and held on for dear life.

After a few moments, he unclenched his eyelids and looked back. The man had been thrown from his feet and had rolled into the muddy waters of the irrigation ditch. He flung curse words in Urdu after the fleeing horse. Astride his steed, the youngster's heart fluttered and thumped against the inside of his chest cavity with thunderous intensity. He couldn't help but let a smile crack from the corner of his lip.

country: a small village named Haripur Khalsa, in the Jalandhar district which is now part of the Punjab state of India. Home to a mountainous hilly region known mostly for agriculture and vast plains and fields, it sits some 600 metres above sea level, close to Islamabad and Abbottabad, which are today part of Pakistan.

The British Punjab Province, in which the majority of India's Sikh population lived prior to Indian independence in 1947, is an area of environmental extremes: humid temperatures during the day dropping to single digits at night. A healthy monsoon season is hoped for every June or July, but periods of crippling drought periodically ruin entire fields of crop cycles. The northern part of the Punjab is rife with rivers and tributaries, water rushing down from the mountainous regions where snowstorms are a common occurrence. The southern portion is a relatively flat landscape of fertile soil, trees, and shrubbery. It's a place at the beck and call of Mother Nature, its vegetation much like its people, struggling and surviving amidst a volatile, sometimes violently unpredictable climate.

At that time, Haripur, Punjabi for "area of God", had a population of just a few hundred, a melting pot of Muslims, Sikhs and Hindus, all living together in relative harmony. Their cultures and religions meshed on a daily basis; a largely uncontested land inhabited by simple farmers and their kin. There was no power, electricity or running water. Families lived in clay brick huts with wooden roofs covered in straw. There was one well in the centre of the village, from which everyone gathered drinking water.

The conditions were harsh, and many villagers died of malnutrition, disease, or in accidents. Children in Haripur were known to eat dirt, a condition known today as geophagy. Used as a digestive aid or supposedly to help cure calcium deficiency in women during childbirth, it's a largely abolished practice that still takes place in extremely poor rural areas.

On Dec. 31, 1923, a midwife aided Singh Sr.'s mother, Karam Kaur, in birth. In the Sikh religion, the middle name for all females is Kaur, or princess, and all men are Singh, or lion. That Singh Sr. knew the exact date of his birth was unusual for the time. His official birth record lists October 10, 1924, the earliest date his family could get to a city to register him. Calendars were scarce at best, and most villages followed the seasons. Sometimes birth records were knowingly delayed to give children a head start in growth and development. But New Year's Eve was a celebrated day, and as Karam sweated on the *manji*, a woven bed, pushing with all her strength, she gave birth to her first child—a beautiful, healthy baby boy.

Karam was a stunning woman, with long, flowing hair, loving eyes and soft, dainty features. She wanted nothing more than to be a mother, to raise children and offer them the best life possible. Her head wrapped in a scarf, she hid herself mostly out of respect and to shelter her skin from the relentless sun.

While the area was poor, it was rich in culture. Singh Sr. tells stories from before his time, legends of beautifully decorated weddings and massive festivals to which every creed was invited. He remembers that all three major groups—Hindus, Muslims, and Sikhs—would help one another in times of need. Crops were shared, cattle passed around, and the local economy ran largely on the symbiotic notion of community. Little coin or gold was flashed. Haripur was largely an area governed by the notion of sustainable agriculture. In describing it, Singh Sr. closes his fist, to signify unity.

That all changed after 1889, he says, when the British slowly squeezed the area within the vice of the Raj, the Hindi term for "rule" or "kingdom". The Indians refer to the British imperial strategy as "divide and conquer"; the Brits mapped out the area according to religious majorities, laid the groundwork for segregation, and deliberately watered the seeds of racism that still plague the country to this day.

Singh Sr. is adamant about one thing: the source of the strife he's spent his entire life battling.

"The British," he says, shaking his head, his voice matter of fact. "They created the problem."

The Dosanjh family are descendants of Bhai Bidhi Chand, a Sikh warrior who was also a religious preacher during the time of Guru Hargobind. Bidhi was one of the five Sikhs chosen to accompany Guru Arjan on his journey to Lahore where he was martyred in 1606.

His father was Sardar (which denotes nobility) Dalip Singh Dosanjh, a freedom fighter with links to some of the independence bombings against British rule that took place in the early 1900s. He was tall and athletically built, with a long dark beard and unforgiving blue eyes; an intimidating figure physically and mentally. In his son's memory, this patriarchal figure towers over him. An outspoken critic of British rule, Dalip was adamant this English annexation had no place in the South Asian portion of the continent. His disdain was particularly rooted in the segregation of colonization, the way the white interlopers sought to divide villages that were doing just fine without outside interference.

"He was an active member," says Singh Sr. of his father's resistance work. "He was in and out of jails, imprisonment with hard labour more than once. Six months at a time, sometimes. He was very involved in the movement."

His father had been politically mobilized against Raj rule by Bhagat Singh, a Sikh Indian and revolutionary who was one of the key figures in the Hindustan Socialist Republic Association.[49] They were one of the first organized groups to push for India's independence from the British Raj[50] in the early days of the twentieth century, and kickstarted what would become a long and arduous push for sovereignty. Before his death, Bhagat Singh—who was something of a Che Guevara for the Punjab—employed guerrilla warfare tactics against the British. In some of his photos, he wears the stylized fedora he used to blend in, making him look like a Prohibition Era–style mobster, or a character from Boardwalk Empire. Bhagat is most famous for the 1928 assassination of John P. Saunders, the assistant superintendent of police for the Punjab area, an act carried out with two other members of the movement. Bhagat was later tried in a court case that made international headlines and executed by hanging in March of 1932.

Whatever connection Singh Sr.'s father had to the early independence movement has been lost to history. He did not speak to his family much about his political days, leaving them to guess how deep his involvement was, and how close he actually was to people like Bhagat Singh. One suspects that if he spent more than a few months on a few separate occasions in jail, that this probably was not a passing hobby, but an issue very close to his heart he might have been willing to die for.

Singh Sr. barely saw his father during his early childhood in Haripur. He remembers only a few instances when Dalip would return home. This led the young boy to seek attention elsewhere. His squirmy nature and inability to sit still are familiar traits that mirror biographies of other famous athletes. Today, he might be diagnosed with Attention Deficit Hyperactive Disorder and placed on calming, addictive medications, but back then, children such as Singh Sr. were inexplicable problem kids.

One day, against his mother's wishes, he crawled atop his family's mud hut, pulling himself up by the loose straw. He made it to the top, but his feet, now slathered in slippery clay, caused him to tumble to the ground. He hit the dirt with a glorious thud—and probably a concussion to boot.

A young Louis Zamperini, who went on to compete in the 1936 Berlin Olympics, was a local terror in Terrance, California before he found his calling—track and field. Singh Sr. was no different. He could not sit still, even for a moment.

Singh Sr. quickly became a mischievous ringleader for a gang of local kids, and got into all kinds of trouble. His mother, ill-equipped to deal with such a rambunctious soul, could do little to stop her son's frenetic attitude. Her only ploy to slow him down was to lure him inside with fresh butter and *jaggery*, a cane sugar treat. But it was hopeless: the boy would soon dart back out, now even more energized on a sugar high.

Every day, packs of youngsters followed him around, all of them getting into mischief: terrorizing farm animals, ruining crops, and driving families mad with their antics. They played games, such as *kabaddi*, a traditional Indian wrestling sport. Singh Sr. remembers the sounds of flute and *ektara*, a string instrument plucked with one finger, which they would strum as they traversed the land looking for mischief to occupy their time.

Without proper schooling, in a village where male farmers spent long, backbreaking hours tending crops, discipline was hard to come by. A village of mothers could do little to quash a pack of young boys. Females were scarce in general, with girls often dying shortly after birth (often due to infanticide). In India's largely chauvinistic society, having a boy was cause for celebration; giving birth to a girl was treated like a funeral. Without proper direction, Singh Sr. could've easily fallen victim to a number of ills plaguing children during that time such as inadequate education and death from accident. The development of one usable set of skills to find a lifelong low-paying job could've been the end of what would become an extraordinary life, but his father would make sure this was not his fate.

In the blink of an eye, this poor Sikh boy seemingly destined for nothing but hard rural labour, had his life spun 180 degrees. In 1928, shortly after Bhagat assassinated Saunders, Singh Sr.'s father left active political duties behind and moved the family to Moga. Singh Sr. was five years old. His only concern was leaving the friends with whom he'd grown accustomed to spending his days.

Moga was a village located about 85 kilometres southwest of Haripur. Singh Sr. remembers the move was not a discussion, nor was there time to say goodbye. He transformed in an instant from farm child to small town boy, the transition a swift kick in the proverbial midsection. Suddenly he was surrounded by pedestrians, pavement, concrete and buildings. He'd never heard the radio before, or experienced a hot shower.

Like many cities in the Punjab state, Moga had a relatively high literacy rate compared to the rest of the country. It was a far cry from Haripur, and the move would give Singh Sr. a better chance at a better life.

In retrospect, Singh Sr. believes his idealistic father had an about face sometime during his childhood days in Haripur. The realistic part of Dalip knew trouble was brewing in the area. Wanting to change the course of his family, and particularly the life of his only son, he moved them east in hopes of a more prosperous life.

"He wanted me to focus on my education," says Singh Sr. "He wanted me to get an education and become something. To do something with my life other than work on a farm."

He speaks highly of his father, out of love, but more a sign of respect. His father was a strict man who disciplined him frequently. Singh Sr. tells the story of how, shortly after they moved to Moga he hit a young sweeper boy from the so-called "untouchable" caste dusting around the dorms. Dalip beat his son until he was black and blue, then sat him down and told him to never subject someone to punishment that cannot hit back—regardless of his caste, colour, or creed. While the beating itself sent a mixed message, somehow Singh Sr. understood. Dalip then grabbed his son by the scruff of his neck, walked him back to the *Harijan*, Hindi for untouchable, and made him apologize on the spot.

The other boy didn't know how to respond, he'd never been apologized to before in his life, especially from what he believed was a higher caste. He simply nodded sheepishly and continued his work, worried somehow, he might meet a similar beating. But Singh Sr. kept his word, and said it was a defining moment for him and the shaping of his ethical values.

While the Indian constitution of 1950 abolished the mistreatment of the *Dalit*—a Sanskrit word roughly meaning untouchable believed to be the first iteration of the widely used term—abusive practices are still rampant in India. The legacy of enforced segregation remains a festering blister, dating back hundreds of years in the country, a black mark smeared right across India's human rights record.

In traditional Hindu society, *Harijan* status was associated with occupations that were regarded as ritually impure, such as leatherwork, meat butchering, or removal of garbage, animal carcasses and human waste. These jobs were thought to pollute the individual, and this pollution was considered contagious—making all bodily contact with a *Harijan* a risk. Ignorance led to fear; disease killed at will during this time, and to the uneducated, a *Harijan* was the producer of germs and/or viruses, rather than harbouring them because of filthy working conditions.

As a result, the so-called untouchables were banned from most forms of social life. Physically segregated from the surrounding community, they could not enter temples or schools, and were required to stay outside the villages. Other castes took elaborate precautions to prevent incidental contact or to even go anywhere near them at times.

In defiance of these Hindu norms, Singh Sr.'s father was not a subscriber to the caste structure like some Sikhs, however it was still a widely accepted norm. Rather, he followed in the footsteps of Gandhi, who originally tried to rename the members of the lowest class *Harijan*. Sadly, the term, which initially meant "Children of God", soon became yet another derogatory way to describe the group.

Singh Sr. himself followed in the footsteps of his father's ideals, and credits his incredible self-control to him. He neither smoked nor drank and only now has a glass of whisky each night at his doctor's recommendation.

"He was Sikh by birth," he says, reflecting on Dalip's life. "Nationalist and secularist by choice. I followed him, in his footsteps."

Upon arrival in Moga, the family struggled to find accommodations. Singh Sr. and his mother were forced into a women's hostel, while Dalip went out in search of work. Before long, the educated, well-read former freedom fighter found employment as a teacher at the local missionary school—Dev Samaj High School. He also took in other family members as siblings to Singh Sr.; Sushbir, Singh Sr.'s eldest daughter, was in college before she learned that his father's sister was actually her cousin.

Having settled, Dalip and Karam enrolled Singh Sr. at Dev Samaj, in *kachi*, which is similar to kindergarten class. His mother was illiterate, so she also took classes and completed a course in adult education.

During that time, the area was under loose Muslim rule, so teaching was done in Urdu, the traditional Muslim language. However, Singh Sr. says all languages were fairly similar at the time, making it easy to switch back and forth between spoken Urdu, Punjabi, and Hindi. He can still speak and write all three fluently. His command of multiple languages is impressive as during his formative years he was never considered a star student.

In recalling his school days, Singh Sr. tells a story that sheds light on the tough mentality he brought to the field hockey pitch. At the age of five, while horsing around after school on the monkey bars at the *akhara,* a sand field used for sports training, his friends dared him to see how far he could leap. A born competitor, Singh Sr. swung farther than any other. In fact, he swung himself so far, he flew *off* the grassy area—right onto hard dirt.

The result was a dislocated elbow. Petrified by the thought of his father's strictness, Singh Sr. didn't tell him about the injury. Instead he suffered through weeks of excruciating pain. He tried everything to fix his arm, dabbing mustard oil on it and wrapping it tightly in a cloth in the hopes that cutting off circulation to the joint would somehow magically heal it. Finally, he went home to Haripur to visit his mother, who returned to the village to prepare to give birth to her second child. She noticed he was sipping his soup cumbersomely, using his left hand.

An embarrassed look crept across Singh Sr.'s face.

"She said, 'What is wrong with you?' And I said, 'I think my arm is broken.'"

Karam rushed her stubborn son to an elderly lady a few doors down who knew how to set bones. After a few sessions, his arm was set properly in a cast and the recovery finally began.

Those journeys back to Haripur for the summer months left Singh Sr. with mixed feelings. His closest childhood friend Sucha stayed in the village, and it was wonderful for the boys to reunite. However whenever Balbir would return, Sucha would have little time to play. He was part of a farming community, and spent almost every waking moment taking the cattle out into the fields to graze, working until sunset alongside his father and uncle.

Sucha was not alone. The kids Balbir had grown up with in Haripur, the sons of farms labourers and shepherds (mostly Jat Muslims), had largely settled into a simpler rural life. Children in the village did not attend school, and thus remained illiterate. And reminders of India's caste system were everywhere. Singh Sr. and the Dosanjh family were against any sort of loosely based or strictly adhered to caste system because of Dalip, thus he treated his friends like social equals in both public and private.

Through his words and deeds, his punishments and speeches, his father had rubbed off on him. The boy would not adhere to strict social norms, no matter the ramifications.

When Singh Sr. joined the Haripur kids out on the vast fields where they would play while tending cattle, the caste system blurred and faded regardless. Only in the company of elders did unhealthy social norms truly come into play. Children, like anywhere in the world, had yet to shackle themselves with such debilitating social structures.

Sadly, the move to Moga did little to deter Singh Sr.'s mischievous nature. He'd found a new group of kids to play with, older boys who let him tag along because of his appealingly reckless nature. He'd climb high into fruit trees, sitting some twenty feet up in the air on the tallest branch, so far up that even some of the other youngsters begged him to get down. He'd scale the rickety wooden fences at Dev Samaj, get up onto the roof of the school, and dart across the dusty concrete as other students watched in awe. His body needed to move, as if some type of metaphysical leash was trying to rein him in when all he wanted was to break free.

One day a seven-year-old Singh Sr. left the household unannounced to go swim with his new friends. They headed towards a nearby canal where the buffalo grazed. The boys dipped their unspooled turbans into the tadpole and insect-infested water, thinking they could filter a clean drink through the cotton. Singh Sr.'s mother, worried he was lost for good, cried profusely until he got home. But it was not uncommon for him to leave unannounced and return some hours later; his inability to sit still meant he wandered off onto the land more than once without leaving any kind of indication as to where he was going and when he would come back. This son hid most of his deviations and pranks from his father, fearing physical punishment, and pushed the burden onto his loving mother, who refused to give him up for beatings.

Eventually, like many restless children looking for something to latch onto, the wandering boy filled with mischief found his calling, a passion that would make the exuberant boy from the

Punjab sit still—and win him three Olympic gold medals in the process.

★★★

The new household in Moga was directly across the street from Dev Samaj. From the front, he could see the field hockey pitches located out back behind the classrooms. From as early as he can remember, he watched the games from the courtyard. In a rare show of stillness, he'd sit quietly, listening to sticks crackle like kindling, the tough leather ball whipping hard across the field, tenacious players galloping after it like a herd of unruly animals as they yelled and screamed, kicking up dust in all directions.

His mother watched, dumbfounded. Could this be her spastic, uncontrollable son, sitting cross-legged like he was meditating? But her boy wasn't finding divine intervention through religious reflection. He'd found a different deity to follow, though the teachings of India's most famous sport—field hockey—were not far from doctrine itself.

"My first love since childhood," Singh Sr. says, smiling.

He recounts his almost maniacal love for the game in his autobiography, *The Golden Hat Trick: My Hockey Days*—published in 1977. As told to Samuel Banerjee, a sports editor who is now deceased, Singh Sr. describes the sport like a womanly figure:

"She reciprocated my sentiments. Our love grew. She was constantly with me to light my days; her dazzling charm enlivened my dreams."

The Moga boy's iconic story of infatuation with the sport, retold in a few local newspaper articles we look over during one of our nightly whisky sessions, goes as follows: while watching a field hockey game, a ball rolled all the way off the pitch and landed at his feet. He picked it up, examining the circular object, only to have it snatched away by a teenager. That was when Singh Sr. noticed his father watching. Expecting Dalip's stern demeanour in full force, the boy figured he would be punished for interfering with the match. But that was not the case.

Shortly after, on his fifth birthday, he received the most important present of his life. Once again, the patriarch of his family had found a way to steer his child in the right direction.

"My father bought me my first stick," says Singh Sr. "And the rest is history."

He darted from home straight onto the field, his little legs barely able to keep up with his excitement. Immediately he joined a game, running, galloping back and forth until he felt as if his tiny lungs were about to burst. That night he came home exhausted. His mother, peering around a corner, saw her normally fidgety son sleeping like a log. She sighed in quiet relief, for her boy—and for herself. Her son had left her falling apart at the seams. Now he'd discovered a channel for his endlessly physical nature, a conduit for his unguided mischief.

When he awoke the next day, his rambunctious soul now had a purpose, and one purpose only—field hockey.

★★★

Kulbir Sidhu is a longtime friend of Singh Sr.'s and a retired deputy commissioner from the Ajitgarh suburb of what is now Chandigarh. Sidhu's father Ajmer and his uncle Ishwar both taught Singh Sr. at Dev Samaj. Here, Kulbir says his friend laid the groundwork for what would become an incredibly illustrious career, playing for hours on end in the blistering sun, slogging through the rainy season when the mud would make the fields almost unusable. Singh Sr. loved the game, and he became extremely good, extremely fast. He also loved competing. When one game would end, he'd hop over to the field and join another as fast as he could.

"His medals were won on that playground," says Sidhu. "That was where he learned to play the game the way he did. He spent the better part of every day there for years while he was growing up, my father said."

If you look back on the life of any great athlete, somewhere in their early years you can pinpoint the essential practice time that signals the start of a meteoric rise. Malcolm Gladwell outlined this theory in his 2008 book *Outliers: The Story of Success*, arguing that expertise is achieved through 10,000 hours of practice. Michael Jordan, after being cut by his high school basketball team, took to the court alone and honed his skills through endless days of shooting. Pelé spent his childhood training in the slums of São Paolo, juggling a homemade soccer ball he took everywhere with him.

Singh Sr. was no different. Once he had that stick, every available hour was spent playing, practicing, or sleeping—sometimes with the stick. He talks of setting up bricks and shooting balls at them for accuracy. He used to hit the ball against a wall on an angle, and then chase it down to fine tune his trapping skills. He'd bounce the ball on his forehand, counting taps to a hundred, then let it drop halfway to his feet before whacking it on goal. He practiced so much he garnered a reputation around the area as something of a vandal.

"At that time, there was no window that was safe from my ball," he says with the slightest of smirks.

His father punished him every time he broke a pane of glass, but never took his son's stick away or told him to stop practicing. In retrospect, Singh Sr. realizes his father's stern outer shell hid a warm, loving, thoughtful interior. While he was tough on his son, it was always with good intentions. As a boy, he feared his beatings, but he understood that they would only come if he brought them upon himself.

And now the boy had a purpose, a calling, a channel for his energy. Singh Sr. had taken to his nation's sport, one of the few remaining positives of an ugly foreign rule.

The British first came to India in 1612, during the days of the East Indian Company. What began as a set of discrete trading interests in Southeast Asia morphed into outright control in 1858, after citizens of India rose up in protest against the Company's corrupt practices. The 1857 uprising, called the Indian Mutiny by the British and the First War of Indian Independence by Indian nationalists,[51] led to almost two years of intermittent violence and cost millions of dollars. In its wake, formal British rule was established under the Raj.

Sikhs, while still a minority, were one of Great Britain's strongest allies until the independence movement started. However, the British also feared them: their soldiers were known as experienced killing machines, and had historically been the continent's first line of defence, geographically speaking, when conquerors rode south from the mountains. Sikh men are known for being big and burly, as compared to shorter, leaner Hindu and Muslim men. Life on the farm and in rural areas meant labour was compounded by protein rich diets, crafting generations of males who look like all-pro running backs or rugby players.

In the early years of the twentieth century, the political tensions that had helped precipitate the uprising against the East India Company now helped consolidate India's nascent nationalist movement, uniting men such as Singh Sr.'s father (before he left political life) from a vast array of scattered tribes and kingdoms against a common enemy. That enemy was frustratingly inchoate: Raj rule never encompassed the entire landmass of the sub-continent. Around two-fifths of what is today India, Pakistan, and Bangladesh continued to be independently governed by more than 560 large and small principalities and kingdoms, some of whose rulers fought the British during the First War of Independence, but with whom the Raj entered into treaties of mutual cooperation.

Singh Sr. explains the situation more bluntly: the British thought they were better or more educated than the natives, and thus rule was deemed a natural progression towards order and civility. Deep divides were created along political, religious and socioeconomic lines, separating those who still supported British rule, as it was advantageous for them specifically, and those who sought independence because of prejudice and poor social standing. This meant a block in any city could contain Muslims, Sikhs and Hindus who were alternately for, or against, rule. All these tensions helped to chop the wood and light the fire for India's descent into a bloody Partition comprised of civil war and religious riots upon the granting of Independence in 1947.

Luckily, the Singh family lived in an area somewhat void of direct imperial oppression. At this moment in time the Punjab region was relatively calm compared to areas closer to what is now the India-Pakistan border, and to lands further south where outright Hindu majorities were starting to impose their will on other religious minorities. Divides were blurry, and within the town of Moga, life was relatively progressive, albeit still incredibly conservative. Female births were usually hidden or mourned; infant girls sometimes smothered. The land was largely ruled by corrupt government officials who responded only to bribery, and politicians—be they Anglo-Indian, Sikh, or Muslim—whose sole purpose was to stay in power by any means necessary. This included violence, intimidation, and sometimes murder. Moga was far from a utopia but given the circumstances, livable to say the least.

Dalip had found shelter from further oppression by working in the missionary school. The family was able to fly under the radar at a time when their patriarch's past might have put a target on his back. A smart, self-educated man, Dalip was fast realizing the tremendous changes that were about to confront the nation. But he kept his opinions to himself, focusing instead on his teaching career and raising a large extended family under one roof and one set of ideals.

The lasting effects of colonialism on India have been incisively chronicled by many, including the Nobel Prize-winning author V.S. Naipaul, one of the world's preeminent minds when it comes to shedding light on the bitter taste British rule left in various countries. Two of his nonfiction travelogues about the country speak volumes via their titles alone: *India: A Wounded Civilization* and *India: A Million Mutinies Now*. Imperial rule didn't just leave a scar on India. It ultimately created a country unable to shed the spectre of its past.

"Now it can be argued forcefully," writes Naipaul in *A Million Mutinies Now*, "that the idea of secularism in India has never been much more than a slogan; that the very fact of religious block voting proves this to be so; that the divisions between the communities have by no means been subsumed in a common 'Indian' identity; and that it is strange to speak of nationalism when the main impetus in present-day India comes from regionalist, separatist political groups."

While religious discussions are largely taboo in everyday Indian culture, talk of field hockey is rampant. Simply head to any newspaper, television or radio station, and you'll find a plethora of Sikh, Hindu and Muslim journalists who will talk your ear off when it comes to the country's most storied sport.

Prabhjot Singh, a Sikh, the editor-in-chief of the PTC News Channel in Chandigarh and formerly the editor-in-chief of the *Tribune* newspaper, is an esteemed and established sports journalist who's extensively covered field hockey in India. He spoke about India's lengthy history with the sport—one of the few positive legacies of British colonialism—from his station headquarters.

"The British when they came over, they brought three sports with them," he said. "The first was golf, which was for royalty. The second was cricket, which was for the rich. And the third was field hockey, which was for the poor."

Indians took to field hockey, Prabhjot said, because British army stations were usually positioned outside of the cities, in the areas of urban sprawl where the poorest people lived. The Indians watched the soldiers playing and ended up taking to the game. The British soldiers, mostly men on tour from the home-land, were less abrasive than their Anglo-Indian counterparts, who lived permanently in country, and were more than willing to engage in a colourful game of harmless shinny with the locals. They offered sticks and lessons, inviting their neighbours to participate. The deep roots of field hockey in India's history are most evident in events like the Beighton Cup, an Indian club field hockey tournament started in Calcutta in 1895, which still runs to this day.

Prabhjot, a walking-talking encyclopedia of Indian field hockey history, says that the British army men probably had no idea that their innocent offer to play alongside the Indians would lead to such a passionately adored sporting pastime. Field hockey became a national craze that would both elevate the prestige of the Indian athlete around the world and signal the country's downfall when the sport switched to Astroturf fields in the late 1970s. In the blink of an eye, the equipment changeover left the

Sports Authority of India and the India Hockey Federation (now renamed Hockey India after a crippling corruption scandal) dumbfounded and dated as more industrious nations erected artificial pitches to keep with the times.

But these changes were decades away. Back at Dev Samaj in the heart of Moga, the school had three field hockey pitches divided by age. The youngest would play on one, the oldest on the other two. Young and impressionable but an exceptional athlete, Singh Sr. found himself on the big kid's field in no time, grinding it out with boys three or four years older. However, he did not yet play centre forward, the position with which he became synonymous.

" 'Go and stand in goal' they would say to me," recalls Singh Sr. Eager to please and filled to the brim with energy, he valiantly took up the position.

In the late 1920s and early 1930s, goalie padding consisted of newspapers tied around the shins, and perhaps a glove of some sort. No helmet, no chest protector. Balls, weighing almost six ounces, hard as a rock and hitting speeds of well over 100 kilometres an hour, were stopped with the body. Singh Sr. says welts and bruises were a daily occurrence, but essential to a team's triumph. Some days he would return home to his mother, who would turn her son's body around like a carousel in horror, pointing out fresh wounds. At first, she thought he was being bullied. But she soon found out her son's scars were self-inflicted and a desired pain.

Each day, this tiny boy stood in net and took his punishment, putting his body on the line for the team. His sacrifice didn't go unnoticed. It wasn't long before his ability to literally take a shot had graduated him to fullback, or deep defender. He then proceeded to make a name for himself stopping the other team's scorers, smothering forwards and starting proficient counterattacks of boys sometimes a few feet taller and three years older. It didn't matter where you put the young Singh Sr.; he would quickly master and dominate the position.

During the first half of the 1900s, field hockey was at the height of its popularity. British colonization had made it the premier sport of Southeast Asia, spreading across the region like wildfire. While in recent times the game has become known internationally as a woman's sport, earlier in the century it was played only by men. Its historical significance cannot be overstated. From its first inclusion in the Olympics in 1908, through the height of the British Empire and up until the end of the Second World War, field hockey was arguably the world's most famous pastime. In terms of sheer numbers of players and fans, it still ranks regularly in the top five to this day. To many, it was and still is religion, and for many Sikhs, it was second only to religion in terms of personal duty.

Rajdeep Singh Gill is the former director general of police for the Punjab, the president of the Basketball Federation of India and also a family friend of Singh Sr.'s. He's currently semi-retired and lives in a large two-story mansion with multiple servants in an upper-crust area of Patiala, just south along the national highway from Chandigarh.

Gill says it was during the young Singh Sr.'s time at Dev Samaj that the mental foundation of Sikhism was laid, for both his father and Singh Sr. "It is a way of life as much as it is a religion," he adds.

Sikhism originated in the mid-1500s through the teachings of Guru Nanak, the religion's founder. It's one of many religions that originated from the Indian subcontinent over the years, the other most notable faiths being Hinduism, Jainism and Buddhism.

Sikhism follows ten gurus, passing on teachings until the final guru, Gobind Singh, died in 1709. Sikhs worship from the Guru Granth Sahib, their holy book, which was ordained by Gobind. The Guru Granth Sahib began as a book of hymns, but soon expanded to encompass various written passages, two of which are held in common with almost every major religion: this text is the holy word of God, and spiritual enlightenment can be found by reading it.

In the modern Bhomia household, Sushbir is by far the most spiritual and religious of its three residents. She subscribes to common ideas like "positive energy" and the notion that "everything happens for a reason," but does not seem overtly devout to Sikhism *per se*. In her summary of the religion, she discusses how "the word Sikh means 'disciple of God', who follows the writings and teachings of ten gurus." There are also fifteen commandments, the central tenants of the faith, much like Christianity and Islam. Sushbir translates them for me one night while she prepares a dinner of homemade butter chicken:

1. "Only one God, present everywhere; God is truth. There is no deity, no idol worship. Follow the ideals of gurus, accepting the perpetual guidance of Sikhism."

2. "Equality for all."

3. "Make an honest income."

4. "Share earnings, one-tenth towards the needy."

5. "Avoid the five sins: pride, lust, greed, anger and attachment."

6. "Do not believe in superstitions."

7. "Practice meditation."

8. "Do not use intoxicants."

9. "No stealing and no killing."

10. "Regard any other than one's spouse as brother or sister (no adultery)."

11. "Don't sacrifice animals."

12. "The Five Ks."

This one I have to get her to explain. The Five Ks are five articles of faith that Sikhs are supposed to wear at all times, as commanded by Guru Gobind Singh. It's these five items that make Sikhs so instantly recognizable. The first is the *kanga*, a comb to be used for the hair that symbolizes cleanliness; the second is *kesh*, which means keeping your hair long, as God intended—hence the turban worn by men. The third is the *kurpan*, a short dagger worn to symbolize a duty to protect those in trouble. Then there's the *kara*, an iron bangle (bracelet) worn as a reminder to use one's hands for good intentions, and finally the *kacchera*, a loose-fitting undergarment made for battle.

While Kabir used to sport a beard, bracelet, and turban, he shed them when he took his banking job in South Africa. He says that he plans on growing his beard back again and sporting a turban when he reaches middle age. Singh Sr., on the other hand, while not spiritually religious, is very traditional when it comes to abiding by the faith's rules. He wears the turban, and even the *kacchera*, on a daily basis. He combs his beard and keeps his turban in immaculate condition, a testament not only to his religion but to his disciplined style of life.

The other tenets? Sushbir continues:

13. "Worship God."

14. "That Sikh beliefs do not contradict science."

15. "Everyone is welcome from all religions within the Sikh Gurdwara."

This inclusivity is crucial to Sikhs. Turbans and long beards are also worn by Muslims, and the uneducated observer may well lump the two groups together, though they are completely separate and opposed to one another on many cultural and religious grounds. This incorrect equivocation was especially common in the wake of the Sept. 11th terrorist attacks. In the aftermath, American Sikhs were improperly targeted as Muslim or Arab terrorists, resulting in more than 700 incidents of violence,[52] including a mass murder at a Sikh temple in Wisconsin.[53] Referenced in Obama's speech at Fort Siri, an American white supremacist walked into a Sikh Gurdwara in Oak Hills, Wisconsin with a semi-automatic pistol and murdered six people. Less than a year after the Sept. 11 attacks, the atrocity showcased a blatant lack of understanding for the various faiths outside of North America, grouping distinct creeds into one all-encompassing, racist "Arab" stereotype.

Or more recently, after the Paris attacks carried out by ISIS jihadis, a Canadian Sikh journalist was photoshopped to look like a Muslim terrorist, forcing a Spanish newspaper to issue a formal apology for republishing the horrible gaffe.[54]

The religious history of India encompasses a myriad of religions, and it would take a mountainous pile of books to chronicle the various creeds flowing through every corner of the subcontinent. One thing, though, is clear: Hinduism is the outright majority, and while India is labeled a secular nation, it is in fact a country of Hindus, who make up 80 percent of a nation of over a billion people.[55] The world's third largest religion behind Christianity and Islam, Hinduism has no unified text or singular holy book such as the Bible or Koran, and the faith has gone through multiple reinventions in the course of its lengthy history, which dates as far back as 800BC. It's labeled a fusion religion with diverse roots and no single founder or central figure; while it's largely practiced, it's rarely adhered to with any underlying sense of uniformity.

Speaking from the living room of his house, Gill—himself Sikh—talks about the rich history of the faith he shares with Singh Sr. Sikhism becomes the foundation of one's existence, he tells me, teaching not only history but a way of life in which honour and dignity come first and foremost.

"You are taught to have a simple lifestyle, a high moral fibre. Sacrificing yourself for the greater good. This is the way [Singh Sr.] was raised."

At Dev Samaj, Singh Sr.'s field hockey prowess had him on the pitch with the oldest kids, playing a central role in thwarting the opposing team's attacks. He was young and pre-pubescent, but fierce beyond his age. What he lacked in size he made up for in ball pursuit. He was tough as nails, but fair and sportsmanlike above all else. The more people I interviewed about his overall playing style, the more I found myself likening him to one of those guys you love to have on your team, but hate to play against.

Many of his friends told me he never received a single caution or penalty (field hockey uses red and yellow cards much like soccer) during play. Although it's a tough stat to believe and literally impossible to verify, Singh Sr. searches his memory when asked to confirm, then diverts the conversation, his voice customarily humble, "I think this might be true, but it is not the point."

Soon Singh Sr. graduated to Dayanand Mathuradas College. He'd purchased a tennis ball to train with, and using his stick, he'd hit it against the wall at close range, trying to corral it when it bounced back. It moved much faster on the rebound than a field hockey ball, adding another element to his game: lightning fast reaction time. The tennis ball also brought relief to Singh Sr.'s mother and father for a short time, as the soft outer shell rarely broke windows.

It was now 1936 and a twelve-year-old Singh Sr. had been hearing stories about Nazi Germany on the radio. Hitler had become dictator of the country two years prior, sending shivers and shockwaves through the European continent back home for many Anglo-Indians. Britain seemed to have even bigger problems to deal with than an Indian independence movement in which Gandhi was amassing daily support for a growing sovereignty push. What would soon be known as the Quit India Movement came to a head at the worst possible point for a country dealing with a dictatorial leader who was also gathering a much different type of support in his own country.

The Nazi regime famously took control of the 1936 Olympic Games in Berlin and attempted to use the international event to showcase Germany's power. To their dismay, many athletes made statements against Hitler's tyrannical regime, hijacking the games under the idea of sport as a unifying beacon of peace. African-American Jesse Owens won four gold medals in defiance of German propaganda pushing Aryan superiority, and middle-distance runner Zamperini—his story made famous by Laura Hillenbrand in *Unbroken: A World War II Story of Survival, Resilience, and Redemption*—ran a final lap of 56 seconds, catching the attention of Hitler himself.

There was another team in Berlin, the British Raj's field hockey squad, with an equally impressive star. Led by Chand and a jumbled mix of ethnic and Anglo-Indian players, the team beat Nazi Germany in the final 8-1, once again giving the proverbial middle finger to a racist dictator hell-bent on creating an Aryan race of white supremacists. Chand scored a hat trick in the gold medal game, giving the Hindu star his third consecutive gold medal and cementing himself as the world's greatest field hockey player.

Back home in Moga, the now 13-year-old Singh Sr.'s body was starting to take shape, and the Grade 9 DM College student was anxious to take his game to the next level. He was already dominating, and he wanted a new level at which to compete.

One night, he headed to the local theatre with his friends to watch a movie. Singh Sr. was not much for flicks; even then, he preferred to be on the pitch practicing or playing in a heated match, games so competitive they were only stopped by the setting sun.

Regardless, there wasn't much media available to Singh Sr. He knew the Olympics were going on, and he'd heard stories of a dark-skinned Hindu with short, neatly combed hair taking the field hockey world by storm with his wizardry on the pitch. But he had yet to see any actual footage.

Before the movie started, a newsreel rolled across the screen of the outdoor theatre. Singh Sr.'s eyes shot up. He became motionless; his body froze with excitement.

The video opened with a clanging bell, the Nazi Political Party logo etched into its metal surface. It was the opening ceremony for the 1936 Berlin Olympics. Superimposed behind it was a bird's eye view of the Olympic stadium in the German capital. The shot cut inside to raucous cheering from the crowd. Various flags were raised as trumpets played the Horst-Wessel-Lied, the Nazi party's anthem, and the crowd offered up the Nazi salute as multiple countries' athletes made their rounds on the track.

As he watched the Germans emphatically salute their leader, Singh Sr. wrinkled his nose, confused—he wasn't sure what was going on. However when a group of dark-skinned British Raj athletes made their way into the stadium dressed in suits, he knew what was coming. In fact, he could barely contain himself.

Hitler gave a speech, declaring the Games officially open, and then the video cut to the British Raj team on the field hockey pitch. Chand, in white shorts along with his teammates, cut back and forth with the ball, sending his defenders retreating backwards. With his brother Roop Singh feeding him beautiful passes, Chand was unstoppable, potting three goals against the Germans.

In a rickety outdoor movie theatre in northern India, Singh Sr. watched Chand play with unblinking eyes, transfixed by his country's Olympic hero, an Indian atop the field hockey world. Eyes looking halfway to the stars above the giant black and white screen, the young Sikh who hoped to blossom into a star himself was searching for an idol.

Immediately after watching the movie, which Singh Sr. paid so little attention to that he can't recall what it was about, he darted home and tried to practice in the dark. It was futile, but he went to bed with dreams of emulating his newfound hero, scoring goals on the world's largest stage, of representing his country and wearing its colours as he burst with pride like his new idol—Major Dhyan Chand.

He slept with his stick that night, clutching the wooden handle tight between his fingers. He'd found his calling. He had a singular, determined goal. And the rest, as they say, was about to become history.

MAKING OF A LEGEND

"India is not a nation, nor a country. It
is a subcontinent of nationalities."
~ Muhammad Ali Jinnah

By 1940, Singh Sr.'s father Dalip had shelled out a small fortune replacing windows around Moga. His son, now a teenager about to graduate from DM College, had begun to deeply frustrate him. He didn't want to take away the young boy's great passion, but the cash-strapped teacher was going broke relinquishing portions of his paycheque to the unforgiving landlords who came to his doorstep, holding white field hockey balls as evidence.

Having mastered whacking a tennis ball, a pubescent Singh Sr. reverted back to the real thing as he added weight and strength to his frame. This meant days of hammering the hard ball against a brick wall, developing what would become an internationally lethal shot. Dalip's wife Karam had little sympathy: her husband had bought the stick and ball for their only child, so it was his burden to bear. In the end, Dalip continued to pay up, as patient as a father could be, and Singh Sr. sheepishly crept around the house, hiding behind corners as if trying not to disturb a bubbling volcano.

Overseas Nazi Germany had ruthlessly overtaken Denmark, Norway, Holland, Belgium, and France, moving the chess pieces for the Second World War into place. India's independence movement was also pushing to a head, led by the iconic, charismatic, and deeply humble Gandhi who himself would live on in memory as one of mankind's most celebrated icons of peace. Behind Gandhi was his protege, a more pragmatic heir apparent Jawaharlal Nehru—who would become India's first and longest serving Prime Minister. There was also the outspoken social rights lawyer Sardar Vallabhbhai Patel, and the scholar Abul Kalam Azad, who along with Gandhi and company strongly denounced Nazi Germany. Their non-violent resistance movement would one day birth the Indian National Congress—the dominant political party that has largely led the country from independence up until the election of Modi.

True to form, the independence movement's denunciation was made with one massive stipulation: Gandhi and his followers would not participate in the war unless India became its own sovereign nation. The demand was a clear attempt to leverage their cause at a timely historical moment. It drove a further wedge between Gandhi and the All Indian Muslim League, led by Muhammad Ali Jinnah, initially an ally of the independence movement who would break from its goals to create Pakistan. Jinnah supported the Allied Forces campaign outright, and throughout the period of time, grew distant from Gandhi and Nehru in particular—a personal spite between two London educated lawyers fuelled by personal jealously and cemented by religion.[56,57]

British impatience was growing, the tension exacerbated by the bending of the fragile imperial bond just when it looked like Hitler might take Europe for good. As Germany flash-burned its way across the continent, the Allied Forces began to converge, trying to stop the Nazi dictatorship in any way possible.

On Sept. 3, 1939, Britain declared war on Germany. Many Indian men loyal to the British Raj were deployed to fight. But in the Punjab province where Singh Sr. and his family lived, discontent towards British rule was no longer hidden in the shadows. Independence was openly debated. Sikhs, Hindus and Muslims alike were tired of being told what to do; their forced service in the war accentuated the point that they were not in control of their own destinies. Many local men, following in the footsteps of former independence fighters such as Singh Sr.'s father were adamantly opposed to serving a ruling power and heading overseas to die for one they were fed up with in the first place. Indians were perishing in a war they knew little about, nor had any real personal stake in.

In Moga, Singh Sr. was now sixteen years old and fully grown, a boy in a man's body. Puberty had come, sprouted him up a few inches and packed kilograms onto his frame. He was no longer the tiny boy on the older kids' pitch. Now he was a quintessential powerhouse, able to rub opponents off the ball, strong but agile. Local scouting reports saw few pitfalls, other than the fact that he was a Sikh in a predominately Hindu country. Of course, none of that concern was ever written down. In India, the field hockey world has long been controlled by Hindus; while the Punjab has produced some of the finest players of all time, each was forced to go through their own personal hell to make a name for themselves.

As a ferocious fullback on DM College's top squad, Singh Sr. lifted the team to multiple inter-college tournament wins in the area. Though he was years younger than his teammates, he was ahead of his developmental curve, not only playing with the big boys but dominating them as one of his team's indisputable stars.

When it came to the classroom, however, he was far from extraordinary. At the start of 1941, he failed his intermediate exam. Distraught and fearing punishment from his father, he climbed onto the school's roof and sat, watching his own house, a hundred yards away across the field hockey pitches. He feared his father would not let him continue playing. He sat on the roof for more than seven hours—and his absence ignited a panic. Scores of neighbours set out on foot, scouring the railway tracks looking for him. It wasn't uncommon for someone to go missing in those days and disappear completely; be it the climate, the volatile political scene, or the general scarcity of safety measures, life in Moga was still relatively harsh.

Singh Sr. watched the chaos unfold from afar, saw people gather at his doorstep, ready to start a search party. His cousin and good friend, Darshan Singh Dhesi, yelled his name over and over as he searched the school grounds, but still Singh Sr. did not come down. His lips started to dry; he was thirsty and his stomach rumbled for food. The sun beating down on the concrete made him sweat profusely, beads descending to the ground and frying in the heat.

At last his mother broke free from the group, fearing the worst. She started running up and down the streets, flailing her arms, calling her only child's name. Finally Singh Sr. relented; he could not bear to see her endure another bout of stress in his name. He climbed down off the roof, head held low, and lurched home across the field. His mother came running, showering him in hugs and kisses.

"Oh my son, I am so glad you are okay!" she said as she inspected him once again.

She was so relieved to see her son that she neglected to ask where he'd been. His father, not wanting to destroy his wife's fragile peace, did not punish Singh Sr. However, he demanded that he take his exam again and pass.

What made Karam's situation so much more precarious was that she had given birth to a daughter a few years after Singh Sr. Named Kulwant, the little girl was nicknamed Sita because of her beautiful appearance. The family did not care that they had given birth to a female, and celebrated her arrival progressively—even defiantly. Friends and neighbours were perplexed when, in accordance with tradition, Karam and Dalip brought them candy and flowers to celebrate the birth, but being polite, they did not raise much protest. Dalip was an imposing figure at over six feet, a principal-like man who towered over most inhabitants of Moga. He had a bombastic voice, and was well equipped with education and book smarts when the townsfolk descended into disagreements.

But sadly, at the age of three, Sita succumbed to pneumonia. Medications at that time were local herbs and spices, and these did nothing to quell the baby's fever. She screamed and cried for days before her death.

Distraught, Karam mourned with her deceased child overnight before finally gathering up the courage to offer the body up for burial and start the process of moving on. Singh Sr. says she did not become pregnant after Sita's death, a rather odd occurrence in a time and place when no form of birth control or contraceptive was available. But his mother appeared finished in terms of producing offspring, and her young son's fate as an only child was thus sealed.

In the wake of Sita's death, Karam's concern for her son increased tenfold, and his disappearance left a hole in her she knew could never be filled unless her son returned.

As the monsoon season ended in Moga and spring blessed the land once again, farmers in the Punjab scrambled to plant cauliflower and maize crops for the upcoming harvest. The town also hosted the local spring Basant Memorial Hockey Tournament. Held at the school grounds of Dev Samaj, the tournament was part of a larger local gathering. Everyone in the city came to watch the best local field hockey players compete. Elaborate feasts, flower petal-lined walkways, large colourful drapes looping overhead sheltering attendees from the searing Indian sun. A yearly tradition, the event is not only a gathering but a celebration of another season passing. And what better way to celebrate than by playing boatloads of field hockey.

Singh Sr.'s elder cousin, Darshan, put a team together to compete in the oldest youth group. Although he was by far one of the team's best players, Singh Sr. was also the youngest. And when it came time to solidify the line-up, the position choosing invariably went top to bottom.

"They were all older players than me," recalls Singh Sr. "They wanted to play fullback. And I wanted to play fullback; they said, 'No, I'll play fullback.' And I said, 'That's my position; where should I play, then?' And Darshan said, 'Today, you are a centre forward'."

Singh Sr. had been dreaming of this day. He'd remembered the newsreel of Chand, a young centre forward in his prime, dancing through German defenders at the 1936 Olympics in Berlin. The memories took on a new sense of clarity as news of Hitler's blitzkrieg war across Europe streamed into Moga via radio and newspaper. Chand had defied an imposing figure, walking fearlessly into the lion's den and emerging with a gold medal for the British Raj. Little did Singh Sr. know that he would one day get the chance to emulate his hero on a similar stage.

But first, there was the Basant Memorial Tournament. Singh Sr. took to the pitch to start the first game, lining up at centre forward. It was a foreign position for his body, but his mind was more than ready.

Dressed in cleats, a white handkerchief covering his bun instead of a turban, he stared across the line at the other team's fullback. Singh Sr. knew his opponent's tendencies better than his own; he'd been playing the position for more than three years, mastering the skills of thwarting centre forwards' attacks. No one knew it yet, but a goal-scoring clinic was about to descend on Moga like a monsoon in the middle of spring.

Mere minutes into the first game, Singh Sr. had already collected a hat trick, sending opposing teams into strategic disarray as this unknown teenager gutted them from the inside out.

"Cover him!" they yelled in panic.

"Who? The kid?!"

"Yes, the kid! The one scoring all the goals!"

Two days later, the youngest player on Darshan's team proudly hoisted the championship trophy for his undefeated squad. He was the tournament's leading goal scorer, having scored a hat trick or more in each contest. The sound of his stick wapping balls into the nets and snapping the mesh echoed through the town's gossip chains.

"Did you hear about that boy Balbir?" the whispers asked. "He scored so many goals for Darshan's team; they won the whole tournament because of him."

His teammates crowded around, in awe of their young compatriot's talent. One of the eldest put his hand on Singh Sr.'s shoulder.

"They said 'Now you are a centre forward'," Singh Sr. recounts proudly. "From that day on, I never played fullback again."

Singh Sr. cherishes his Olympic gold medals, secreting them away in his room and only revealing them on special occasions. But if you ask him what his favourite trophy is, he points to a small brass cup sitting on the coffee table in the living room of his daughter's home. The room is filled to the brim with the plaques, memorabilia, and honorary medals he's received during his lifetime—oddly, the vast majority not from his own homeland. Reaching among them, Singh Sr. picks up the brass cup, which is no bigger than a saltshaker, and holds it like cherished Olympic gold.

"This is my favourite trophy," he says with a smile.

Even as the Second World War ravaged Europe to the west, and Gandhi gathered national steam towards a final push for independence in India, the young Punjabi boy was the talk of the region. Singh Sr. had arrived. In field hockey-mad India, this meant a great deal. It was his first taste of fame, and he handled it humbly, telling everyone that his victory would not have been possible if his teammates hadn't fed him such perfect passes, right in the slot.

On the streets after the tournament, Darshan, who would go on to a career in education as a principal in Punjab, eagerly took credit for lining his younger cousin up at centre forward. While Singh Sr. was shy, Darshan had the makings of a modern-day sports agent, using Singh Sr.'s fame to score free meals and bypass lines around town.

"He was less modest than me," says Singh Sr. in his trademark tone of understatement.

Darshan was seen as a managerial genius; his cousin's multiple goals had punctured defences like a pencil punching through paper. When I ask Singh Sr. how many goals he scored in the Basant tournament, he replies almost in embarrassment:

"It is many; however we won, which is the most important thing."

His selfless nature is an ideal character trait for a hero. However, in India, the sporting culture promotes showmanship, bravado and ego. Those who are willing to sell themselves end up getting most of the credit—Darshan's adjacent fame proving the theory. But no one could deny the power of goal scoring.

Watching tapes of Singh Sr. score, his trademark celebration is to have none. After potting a ball into the net, he quickly turns and starts jogging back to centre to line up for the ensuing face-off. A few times he cracks a small smile, but mostly he focuses on congratulating his teammates for passing to him. In a world of bravado, his play is void of selfishness.

Watching that fateful Basant tournament with a keen eye from the sidelines was a stout man named Rattan Singh. He was a professor at Sikh National College Lahore, and like a seasoned scout, he'd developed a knack for plucking exceptional field hockey players from outlier areas. It was an easy job finding Singh Sr., a 16-year-old competing with boys a year or two older yet still winning top honours as tournament MVP.

Rattan sought out Singh Sr. after the tournament and asked him if he would be interested in attending Sikh National College, known for its impressive field hockey teams. In the Indian system at that time, grade school ended at Grade 10 and students would complete an additional two years at a college school before formal university. Located in faraway Lahore City, which became part of Pakistan after Partition, the area was at that time the largest undivided metropolis in the Punjab area.

"I was thrilled because I loved hockey and it was an honour to be invited to join a college," says Singh Sr. "I wanted nothing more than to play field hockey. My father wanted to make sure I focused on my schooling, though."

Although he was a master on the pitch, he was in jeopardy of failing his Grade 10 exam. He would have to take the test again to attend Sikh National College. His father said he would give him his blessing if Singh Sr. promised to pass the test—which he did—and then kept up with his homework while at Sikh National College. At the start of 1941, Singh Sr. made the trip to the big city of Lahore to further his athletic dreams.

At that time, Lahore was a mesh of diverse religious backgrounds. Now the capital of a devout Muslim country, back then it bustled with an endless array of cultures and creeds. The city was the largest Singh Sr. had ever been to, and at first he found himself in awe of the volume of people.

On the pitch, however, he was unflappable. He started his first game for the college at centre forward, and scored almost immediately. It was more than apparent that he was a special talent. Rattan had obviously made the right choice, as the Sikh boy quickly made a name for himself on a new set of pitches.

In 1942, the British Raj came looking for soldiers. Many of Singh Sr.'s friends at Sikh National College left to join the Army, Air Force or Navy. By the end of the Second World War, an estimated 2.5 million Indians would fight as part of Britain's military forces, while back at home the Quit India campaign was being fuelled by a jailed Gandhi.[58] Japan's military reach could've easily extended to the doorsteps of the Indian border from the east, and Britain was eager to solidify its hold on Southeast Asia amidst growing calls for independence. It was a tight spot politically for everyone, but Raj rule ended up winning out through sheer force. The British detained close to 100,000 Indians to quell independence-related uprisings, but in doing so further ignited a call for a new, sovereign nation free from outside Anglo-Saxon oppression.

Singh Sr. was reluctant to enlist. His father's eyes had told him a different story of what it was like to participate in war, to battle against men for ideals such as freedom and liberty. Luckily, his play on the pitch absolved him from fighting. He'd already led the reserve team to the 'B' League Championship, competing with various colleges around the western portion of the state. The next season, he followed that up by winning the far more prestigious 'A' League Championship. Goal after goal, tournament win after tournament win; thanks to their young star, Sikh National College was soon the premiere school in the region, and Singh Sr. got another taste of celebrity.

The morning after winning the 'A' League Championship, the principal announced to the whole college that Balbir had brought them to a new level of prestige. He was the Johnny Football of his class, the quarterback, the popular kid, and everyone wanted to be his friend. If anyone was going to be kept from the war, it was Singh Sr.

He stayed in the college's hostel on the first floor, rooming with other boys, taking intermediate classes such as English and Economics. But Singh Sr. looks back on it now and is quite candid about his studies, saying, "My mind was always elsewhere. It was on the pitch."

Word of this talented teenager was spreading throughout Punjab. He was a natural, selfless goal scorer—if such a thing is even possible. Kulbir Sidhu, whose father Ajmer was Singh Sr.'s teacher and headmaster, said his humbleness remained, even as everyone around him stroked his ego.

"He was already a professional at that time," recalls Sidhu. "From as far back as my father can remember, he said he was never one to take credit for his own actions on the pitch. The team always came first."

But Singh Sr. was also in danger of failing his final examination of the year. Luckily, he was saved by an unlikely hero. Due to a shortage of beds at his university, a Master's of Science student at the Engineering College was rooming in the dorm beside Singh Sr. Through the grapevine, he heard rumours that Singh Sr. was going to bypass his final exam, head home to Moga for the summer, and thus circumvent the whole graduation process. His family had grown understandably weary of his aptitude for flunking big tests, and Singh Sr. figured the best way to solve the problem was to ignore it.

That was not to be. The Master's student "literally grabbed me by the ear and dragged me back to my dorm room," Singh Sr. recalls, smiling sheepishly.

His name was Kirpal Singh Gill, who later retired as chief engineer of Punjab, and he forced Singh Sr. to stay at the dorm for thirty days to study with him. From sun up to sundown, they worked in the garden. Kirpal's commitment to his schooling rivalled Singh Sr.'s prowess on the pitch, and this led the young athlete to a revelation: to succeed, he needed to apply the same vigour to his studies that he brought to field hockey. Of course, the strategy worked, and he passed. He never saw Kirpal again, but to this day he thanks him endlessly for saving him from failing yet another grade.

With Singh Sr. released from intermediate schooling, it wasn't long before a bigger and better school came calling for the Sikh phenomenon.

Khalsa College, a large university in Amritsar—just east of what is now Lahore, Pakistan's capital city—is housed in a massive complex that sprawls across 300-plus acres.[59] The building, which features six wings, is beige, a dusty discolouration that remains palace-like in appearance to this day. Built in the Indo-Sarcenic Revival architectural style, it's strongly influenced by traditional Indian and Mughal schools of architecture. In person, it has the mystique of any ancient building: the floors creak with character, the walls warped by decades of rain damage. The sparse lighting gives it a ghost-like feel, even though it's stuffed to the brim with children and teachers. Built in 1892 by the British, it's produced a who's who of Sikhs over the years: former chief minister of the Punjab Pratap Singh Kairon, former chief election commissioner of India, Dr. Manohar Singh Gill and musician Rabbi Shergill.

Aside from its vast academic facilities, Khalsa College is also home to a gym, a cricket stadium, and—of course—acres of field hockey pitches. Sardar Harbail Singh, a noted athlete who played with Chand and would go on to coach India at the 1952 and 1956 Olympics, was a physical education teacher and athletic director at Khalsa and an undying student of the game. Devoutly religious, he had a stout physique, thick beard and steely eyes.

In 1943, during one of the smaller inter-college tournaments in Lahore, Harbail came looking for a certain player he'd been trying to reach for months. A young Sikh centre forward who scored with ease, a growing boy who evoked memories of Chand. The Hindu legend's career was being truncated by the world war, which would eventually claim two consecutive Olympic games.

After watching him play, Harbail offered Singh Sr. a scholarship on the spot. In a certain way, the recruitment was a long time in the making. A few years prior, just after Singh Sr.'s glorious showing at the Basant Tournament, his cousin Darshan had coaxed the Sikh centre forward to go to Amritsar to try out for Khalsa. Too young at that point to compete with players in their late teens, the 16-year-old went unnoticed. However, Singh Sr. vowed he would be back. Now he was—in full effect.

When Singh Sr. went home to tell his father however, the news was not all good. He didn't know that Harbail had long since taken notice of him, and had been writing letters to his household asking for permission to enlist the teenager at Khalsa College. His father had thrown the letters out without telling his son. Singh Sr. had barely passed his Intermediate Exam, and his father refused to let him go to Khalsa, wanting him to stay in Lahore where the onus was on studies, not on the pitch.

"For him," says Singh Sr. " 'No' means 'no'. There was no questioning him. I did pass my intermediate exam at Lahore, but he still said no. He still wanted me to stay at Sikh National College at Lahore."

Singh Sr. was devastated. Khalsa College was another notch up the field hockey ladder, and he wanted nothing more than to play for them. He went back to his dorm room, despondent and sullen, sure that he was missing his one chance to suit up for one of the country's most prestigious athletic universities. What if Lionel Messi, a short Argentinian kid with growth hormone deficiency, had never been offered the chance to join Barcelona FC's youth program? Or if Lisa Leslie had never been coaxed onto the basketball court while in middle school, later joining a boys' team in Grade 8 which gave her further confidence? Singh Sr. was at a similar critical juncture in his career, he needed the care and attention to take him to the next level.

Singh Sr. spent a long, cold night lost in thought, wondering if his lack of assiduity in the classroom had finally spelled disaster for his burgeoning career on the pitch.

The next morning, he sulked around, moping, carrying his body like it had been drained of vitality. He dared not defy his father's strict orders, but his beating heart would not relent. He knew his life was to be played out on the pitch, not in a classroom.

But then his father had another inexplicable change of heart. On some level, Dalip must have known his son's path lay in sport, not the classroom. He went to Darshan, who had famously moved Singh Sr. to centre forward in the Basant tournament, and bought him a ticket to go to Lahore, where he could give Singh Sr. the good news. Darshan promptly hopped on a crowded bus—then a luxurious form of travel—and made the rigorous trek from Moga to Lahore along a cracked, pothole-laden road, arriving later that day.

"I was so happy," says Singh Sr. "At first, I was confused to see Darshan come all that way. Then when I heard the news he was bringing, I was a very happy boy."

Khalsa College showed both their prestige and their desire to have Singh Sr. onboard. They sent representatives from the team to collect his things at his dorm room in Lahore and promptly took them northeast to Amritsar.

"They said to me as I was leaving," recalls Singh Sr. " 'Please come up to the university when you can and then left, just like that."

Singh Sr. hopped on a train and made the trek to the religious city, which is also home to the Golden Temple, a famed centrepiece of the Sikh faith. Known locally as the Harmandir Sahib, it was created by the fifth guru of Sikhism, completed in 1604 and today is a major tourist attraction, which thousands of people visit on a daily basis. Singh Sr. felt immediately at home at the school, and was in awe of its prowess and his new mentor.

"I never knew what systematic coaching was until I joined Khalsa College," he wrote in his autobiography. "The men in Amritsar saw themselves as 'human engineers' building men through ideas and ideals, giving purpose to their lives by planting tiny seeds of principle and wisdom. And among them Harbail stood out as a towering figure. His involvement with the game was complete. He stressed on the total development of man— body, mind and soul—and high on his list of priorities were the physical, mental, emotional, social and spiritual aspects of life."

Harbail was also a devout Sikh. While on the surface, Singh Sr. has always appeared devout, internally he struggles with religion and its place in his life, especially as he's gotten older. "I have never been irreverent," he told me, "but to this day I don't know if I am a theist or an atheist. Harbail prayed, and sleep came easily to him."

There were four teams at Khalsa College, and competition was fierce. The school had produced some national athletes, and in Amritsar, the best of the best from all over the Punjab region competed for a chance to travel India and play against other universities. Many players ran out their four years at the college without ever suiting up for the coveted 'A' squad, but Singh Sr. played his way onto the team almost immediately.

Of course, like any great university, Khalsa had its rival: Government College University, which today is part of Pakistan. Government College was comprised mostly of Muslims, while Khalsa was predominately Sikh. Their games were the first example, Singh Sr. said, of a time when playing field hockey took on a different tone—a religious one. However this was pre-Partition, and both areas were still under British rule. The divide between the religious sects in the country had yet to be fully demarcated, and racial tensions had not yet been set afire. Hindus and Muslims—like the members of all India's many religious groups—were more concerned with getting the British out of India than with each other. And many Muslims knew little about the potential plan for a nation of their own in the land that would become Pakistan—its name an acronym for the five northern regions of the area: Punjab, Afghania, Kashmir, Sindh and Baluchistan.[60]

Still, the games with Government College were some of the roughest Singh Sr. has ever played. Being on a team of mostly Sikhs, playing a team mostly of Muslims, amped up the intensity.

Government College was the powerhouse, having won the Punjab University Championship in multiple years, including 1942. In 1943, however, there was a new kid on the block. Singh Sr. helped Khalsa beat Government College twice, back to back in 1943 and 1944. His scoring prowess also landed him on the Punjab University team, a regional all-star squad that travelled to other states and played in various tournaments, including the All India Inter-University Championship.

By 21, Singh Sr. was the captain of the Inter-University squad, and he represented Punjab State at the National Hockey Championships in 1944. He was now traveling the country as a field hockey player, growing accustomed to his celebrity status as an athlete—and the stigma that came along with being part of a visible minority.

By this time in his life, school was a distant second to Singh Sr.'s one and only love: field hockey. Khalsa College was where he laid the proper foundation for what would become a legendary career.

"Had I continued to stay on in Moga, perhaps I would have [become an athlete], had I failed—I would have ended up amongst the 'also rans'," he says.

His long, gruelling days were tailored around practices, rain or shine. Bruises were played through and seen as badges of honour. Singh Sr.'s desire to play was almost maddening, and the centre forward position brought with it a great deal of attention. Every time he got the ball in prime scoring position inside the half circle, defenders descended upon him like a ravenous platoon; whacking, hacking, getting any type of shot they could in with a wooden stick that at the time weighed 18 to 22 ounces.

Singh Sr. shows me one of these traditional sticks, a long, thick-cut slab of timber that could easily knock someone down with a swipe to the shins. Appearing more weapon that tool, over the years it has morphed from a cumbersome piece of equipment to a smaller, graphite version in today's modern game.

Injuries were common, even expected. In one game, Singh Sr. lost part of his tooth to an errant stick on a clearing attempt, though he didn't even notice until the match had finished. Pumped full of adrenaline, he galloped on; nothing could stop his domination. In his autobiography, he mused on his desire to put his body in harm's way, and on the sacrifices field hockey was asking of him:

"Is it the aura of victory so compelling that it goads him on to give of his best in the face of challenging circumstances? Has it something to do with patriotism? Or is all the trouble taken just for the glory of sport, that much-bandied phrase? I have no answer. And I don't want an answer. It is a charm that can't be explained away in a few words."

Singh Sr. was a kind player, too, picking himself up off the dusty field and resuming play no matter what his opponents flung at him. He was known to help combatants up after they'd fallen, or simply smile when he was blatantly fouled. Any premiere athlete knows the pain that accompanies the spotlight—the shadowing, the trash talk—and life for Singh Sr. was no different. But he managed the difficulties with aplomb.

An interesting aspect of field hockey is that, unlike ice hockey, there are only right-handed sticks. Defenders don't have to worry about ambidextrous opponents, as hitting the ball with the curved side of the face is illegal. Martina Navratilova, a famous left-handed tennis player, drew fits from players who were used to facing mostly right-handed opponents; but in field hockey all opposition comes at you with the same stance. Thus a goal scorer must employ a bag of tricks, or like Singh Sr., possess an undying, relentless will to put the ball in the back of the net at all costs.

During one of our whisky sessions in Chandigarh, Singh Sr. shows me unreleased, copyrighted footage from the International Olympic Committee, which he was given when he went to London in 2012. The video showcases Singh Sr. playing in the Olympics, and I immediately get a good sense of his style. His frame is made for field hockey: Singh Sr.'s legs are stocky, his upper body equally built. Most of the time, defenders didn't even have a chance to check him, as he was able to get off shots with lighting speed.

While Chand relied on stick-handling and fancy dangling to get as close to the goal as possible, Singh Sr. was a pure shooter, a power forward, a proverbial beast on the field. He did few extracurricular activities with the ball other than relentlessly pound it on goal. His hard shot could make goalies look spastic; they knew that to stop him, they would have to pay dearly.

Yash Vohra has been the secretary general of the Chandigarh Hockey Association since 1959. He said he's never seen a player as good as Singh Sr., and speaks at length about how, in their respective primes, the Sikh was more accomplished than Chand.

"I tell him sometimes, he is modest to a fault," says Vohra, smiling. Singh Sr. never took credit for his skill, he added, and was a little too inclined to turn the other cheek on the pitch. "He would never retaliate against the other players, even when he had the chance to."

His teammates were another story, especially his fellow Sikh players. Many a scrum started after Singh Sr. was taken down. Amidst what were growing racial divides as the country started to splinter during the lead up to Partition, the penalty took on a new meaning if the offender was Muslim or Hindu.

Luckily, inside the classroom, the teachers at Khalsa College were also paying close attention to their star student. By 1945, Singh Sr. had completed his graduate degree and enrolled in a Master's of English. He had gone from goat to gold, learning multiple languages and mastering his studies, much as he had done with his sport of choosing. The change was surely a relief for his father, who wanted nothing more than for his son to achieve the highest level of education possible.

Harbail, who'd played with the legendary Chand when India toured New Zealand in 1935, knew he had found something special in the young Sikh. But he wanted to make sure he refined Singh Sr.'s talents, and asked him to stay late after practices for additional training. Harbail would bring a sack full of balls, and make passes to Singh Sr. in the slot for ninety minutes or more, so that the young player could fine-tune his shot. The idea was to make sure Singh Sr. could still hit the ball with pinpoint accuracy even after he was fatigued and dripping with sweat. Today, he credits his ability to score late in games to this training; Harbail instilled a mental discipline in him, a conviction that every shot he was taking was going to be his last, so he'd better make it his best.

★★★

In the fall of 1945, Singh Sr. ran up headlong against the full power of the British Raj. The encounter came in the form of a surly, pot-bellied boisterous British man—Sir John Bennett. The Punjab Police chief, known for his cunning and corrupt nature, came looking for Singh Sr. at Khalsa College shortly after he'd graduated. Bennett had one thing on his mind, which he claimed came from all the way up the ranks of British Raj authority.

It was his national duty, Bennett told Singh Sr., to play field hockey for his police squad.

"I did not want to play," Singh Sr. recalls. "He told me I was going to play for his team and I said 'no'. How could a former freedom fighter's only son have any truck with the police, the British Police which only believed in crushing any uprising?"

Singh Sr. was not a fan of the British—to put it mildly. He remembers horrible tales of how Raj police abused and mistreated freedom fighters in prison, subjecting them to unthinkable acts of torture and isolation, starving and beating them relentlessly to try and instil a sense of submissiveness upon release. His father rarely spoke about this time in his life, but it's clear from Singh Sr.'s face that he knew unthinkable thoughts hid behind Dalip's iron eyes. Singh Sr. speaks about this cautiously, his father's legacy floating about him like some inchoate, ominous presence to this day.

Of course, Bennett did not take no for an answer. The British still ruled the country, and there was no questioning Raj authority. Channeling his father's rebellious ways, Singh Sr. snuck onto a bus incognito and fled to Delhi to escape, where he played for the Public Works Department team. In addition to ordering him to play for the police team, Bennett was demanding Singh Sr. become a police officer, too. It was the last career path Singh Sr. ever wanted to take.

In Delhi, he joined a local club team, but his superior play ultimately sealed his fate. His name started floating through the field hockey grapevine, along with a breathless tally of his goals, and Bennett sent officers to track him down. They came to the city, found Singh Sr. living with friends, handcuffed him, and escorted him back to the Jullundur Cantonment by night train. It was a long ride back north, the two silent officers sitting across from him, his hands shackled behind his waist. He watched his freedom rolling away like the disappearing geography.

Up until that moment, the British Raj had been an external complication. Now it had directly affected the young Sikh man, and at last his mind was made up: independence must happen. "The British had to go," he told me.

An angry Bennett confronted Singh Sr. upon arrival. Fearing for his safety, the Sikh agreed to join Bennett's Anglo-Indian run squad, and the police chief was thus appeased.

"He said I would become a police officer and play for him, and that was the end of it. I was scared," says Singh Sr. "They fingerprinted me when they brought me back. So I decided the best thing to do was to play for them."

In retrospect, Singh Sr. adds, his unlawful detainment was a blessing in disguise. Bennett was a powerful policeman with deep pockets fed by the British Empire, which was increasingly desperate to keep its chokehold on the Punjab. Other areas of India had started to rebel, or had already broken from British rule. But the western portion of the country was still under the empire's direct control. It was here that Sikhs, Muslims, and

Hindus were particularly mixed instead of segregated, and the British knew if independence went forward too soon, the area would become a cesspool of destruction.

By this time, the calls by Muhammad Ali Jinnah and the All India Muslim League—the main communal party of Muslims—for their own nation had grown clamorous. The Indian National Congress was leading the independence movement's final push.[61] At first, the INC's goal had been to gain more rights for Indians within a British-run administration. But as its power grew in the twentieth century, and particularly in the wake of the Second World War, the aim shifted to complete sovereignty.

Breaking from Gandhi and Nehru, who sought to unify all Indians within one secular nation, Jinnah, who feared being a minority in a Hindu-dominated state, penned the Lahore Resolution in 1940, in which he argued for a separate country to be known as Pakistan.[62] He would get his wish, though it would come at a grave price, dividing neighbours and friends along religious lines and creating the India-Pakistan conflict, the border of which today is one of the most heavily militarized in the world.

The fires of Partition were ready to be lit; the lurking rage had been stoked and fanned by treatment much like Singh Sr. had experienced at the hands of Bennett. Riots and targeted killings had started to erupt around the country. Lines had been drawn, sides had been taken, and it was only a matter of time before civil war tore deep caverns into the nation.

Having shed the troublemaking habits of his youth, Singh Sr. fell in line and did what he was told. He knew being a police officer brought its own element of power. At a time when it looked as if the nation was ready to detonate, he wondered if being uniformed and equipped with a firearm might end up saving his life.

As a member of Bennett's Punjab Police team, Singh Sr. competed in All Indian tournaments across the nation—in Delhi, Lahore and Mumbai. Not only was he gaining a name for himself, he was garnering comparisons to an army service man, a man with three gold medals on his curriculum vitae.

"Was this kid the next Chand?" they asked inside the sport's circle. As with any rising prodigy, the parallels were drawn. But the Hindus were reluctant to take the crown from one of their own, and thus downplayed Singh Sr.'s play. Chand, they felt, could never be knocked from his perch atop field hockey greatness, especially by someone of minority descent.

Race bled into the pens of the newspapers writers; they inked stories in defence of the Hindu player whose throne Singh Sr. was eyeing. Though a sporting hero might have been a welcome distraction, this was not a time for the country's most famous athlete to be from what many thought could become another splinter ground like the Muslims. To the Hindu–controlled media, the idea of a Sikh being the best field hockey player in the subcontinent's history was an abhorrent thought.

The names of some of India's most prominent newspapers speak volumes about how controlled India's press was, and still is, by Hindu interests: *The Hindu*, which was established in 1878, and *The Hindustan Times,* which was established in 1924. The largest newspaper in India, the *Dainik Bhaskar*, which is published in Hindi, is owned by the Hindu Agarwal family and has its head offices in Gujarat where Prime Minister Modi is from. The World Press Freedom Index, done every year by Reporters Without Borders, still ranks India incredibly low for a democracy, ranking 136th out of 180 countries, lower than South Sudan, Afghanistan and Algeria.[63] There's also the Official Secrets Act of 1923, a holdover of British rule, which the government has used for years to withhold information from the public.[64]

During this time in Singh Sr.'s life, many of the newspapers were still controlled by the British, who oversaw the Hindu journalists closely, and could have wanted to downplay a fierce debate between Hindus and Sikhs during such a tumultuous time.

This was the first time Singh Sr. would face a news body largely united against his stardom. Hindu journalists, who control much of India's media even today, went to extra lengths to downplay his prowess, sometimes erroneously reporting the number of goals he scored or consciously misspelling his name, he says. Singh Sr. had no defence against these slights. His growing legend was being undermined and erased as quickly as he tried to pencil it in. All he could do was keep playing, and keep scoring.

In contrast, police life turned out to be cushy—at first. As Singh Sr. moved from station to station in the Punjab area, local statesman would roll out the red carpet to welcome the British run Indian Imperial Police. Elders would gather around Singh Sr.'s bedside at night to help him remove his dusty boots and tuck him in. Having never experienced such a lavish lifestyle or blatant caste division, Singh Sr. found it unnerving and odd. The lower caste workers tried to offer massages and cold towels, but he refused. Being waited on was not within his emotional vocabulary. Singh Sr. would regularly do his own cleaning and laundry, in part to prevent the locals from fawning over him.

But soon the police work turned jagged, uncomfortable—and then downright unbearable. Singh Sr. might have picked the worst point in history to become part of the British Raj's authoritarian squad of supposed peacekeepers. Before his eyes, the underbelly of the Indian world would turn over and expose itself, revealing a plethora of wormy, unthinkable atrocities to which he would be forced to bear witness. The memories left a permanent scar, which haunts Singh Sr. to this day.

He shares with me just a few of these memories, and only when pressed. It's clear that this idealistic, nationalistic man wants nothing more than to forget Partition ever occurred, and for good reason.

While enrolled at the police training academy fort at Phillaur, word came in that a 21-year-old Army sepoy had raped and killed a six-month-old girl. Singh Sr. arrested the officer and brought him to the police station, where he confessed to the crime. Having returned from the First World War, he exhibited clear signs of what we would today call Post Traumatic Stress Disorder. After a brief interrogation, the sepoy, eyes glassy, his posture void of any sign of remorse, showed Singh Sr. where he'd abandoned the bloodstained body of the baby, wrapped in a dirty cloth and left for dead.

A few days later in Ludhiana, during some of the civil riots that broke out between Muslims and Hindus in the lead-up to Partition, Singh Sr. entered a village hut and discovered a gruesome mass murder. The family had been butchered over a simple land dispute between persons of different creeds. Singh Sr. remembers the bodies of women and children lying on the floor, eyes staring lifelessly back at him, their crusted blood ground into the mud. Women and children, cut up with knives and tools, their bodies hacked and slashed, now covered in feasting flies and maggots.

In another village, he entered a makeshift warehouse for storing grain and found the remnants of a murdered Muslim family. The bodies had been there for weeks; in the hot air, the stale, vomit-inducing stench of rotting flesh was unbearable. Seven bodies, hidden inside the masses of wheat bran, supposedly murdered because of the mere fact of their religious affiliation. The killers would never be found.

While Singh Sr. understood the passionate desire for rebellion against the British, the infighting between various religious sects in India forced him into deep philosophical reflection.

"Man is a strange animal," he says. "He can be good to the extent of being a brute. He can be stupid. He can stoop to any level to conquer some urge that twists and distorts his consciousness into emotions and sentiments that can't be explained. Yet he can be very human."

To survive, Singh Sr. forced himself to become cold and calculating. He went from crime scene to field hockey pitch. There, too, the games took on a measure of political rivalry. The Hindus and Sikhs had found common ground against the separatist Muslims—who threw themselves at Singh Sr., hacking at his body with their sticks long after the play had gone the other way, uttering racial slurs as they shoved and cross checked the Sikh.

"They called me a dog, all sorts of names, basically that I should not play and go die somewhere. It was not the usual talk between competitors."

Singh Sr. somehow found solace in the punishment, using the pain on the field to motivate himself, feeding his play with anger. These games would help build his steely resolve, hone his ability to play amidst stormy conditions, be it blistering heat or an icy chill, and through emotionally sinister elements, too. In the face of chaos and hatred, Singh Sr. did what he did best, the only thing he could do:

He scored goals. Lots of them.

During this time of national strife, it seems odd—or possibly fitting—that Singh Sr. also found the love of his life. Having started his career as a policeman by default, his parents sought to arrange his marriage. Although stories abound in India of horrible forced matrimony, expensive dowries, and inter-family violence and murder, this would not be the case for the Sikh.

During the rainy winter season of 1946, Dalip and Karam asked him to carry a letter from the cantonment just outside of Moga to the tony Model Town of Lahore. Singh Sr., dutiful to his professional duties and—as always—deeply respectful of his parents, set about the daylong journey without question. Even amidst the racial tension, he was adamant about obeying orders and making the trek to the upper crust milieu.

Today, he still remembers the address on the creamy white envelope he carried: "81G Model Town in Lahore." He did not know the cunning purpose of the letter. It was addressed to the parents of Sushil Sandhu, a well-off family in the city. The envelope contained a handwritten letter from Singh Sr.'s parents, asking them to inspect this messenger as a possible suitor for their daughter.

Amusing in retrospect: Singh Sr. was comically, and completely unwittingly, carrying his own marriage proposal.

Sushil's father was a civil engineer who had studied abroad in Scotland and England before returning home to a high-ranking government position, and had passed away, however his legacy was still extremely intimidating. Singh Sr. was incredibly nervous to deliver the letter to such a prestigious household.

Much to his surprise, a lovely young lady answered the door. Singh Sr. had arrived in uniform, a rather goofy look on his face. Sushil's mother came down, took a considering glance at the young man, dressed in regalia, presenting the letter like a sacred stone. Then she opened it, read its contents, and shot a perplexed expression at the police officer in front of her.

Content to carry out his mission, Singh Sr. says he took small notice of Sushil, now standing behind the doorway, peering around a corner to eye the young officer. It was not love at first sight, he says, but he definitely noticed that she was stunning.

"All I remember," he tells me, "is she was very beautiful. But I was so worried about delivering the letter properly I did not notice her nearly enough, I fear."

He made brief eye contact and then stood at attention, ever the professional, waiting for further orders.

When Singh Sr. returned to Moga to visit his family, they quizzed him about the Sandhu daughter. He could only shake his head in response. Field hockey star, yes; romantic at heart, definitely not.

Tej Dhesi, Darshan's daughter-in-law, came to the Bhomia house in Chandigarh to give me a female perspective on the woman who would become Singh Sr.'s life-long partner. Tej knew Sushil since she was young; while Balbir repeatedly describes his wife as the love of his life, others are a bit more expansively eloquent in recounting her demeanour.

"She was very affectionate," says Tej. "A loving, caring person. She was so full of life, and she never complained, even though her husband was always talking about hockey."

Indu Sandhu, the older sister of Dhesi, says this is true, and then some. "She used to tell me that's why she married [Singh Sr.]," she says with a chuckle. "She was his biggest fan."

It was true; apparently the young lady had heard all about the humble Sikh sports prodigy. And Singh Sr., rather playfully, had been duped into falling in love, although he wasn't necessarily complaining.

Sushil was an athlete in her own right, a very good college badminton player. Singh Sr. tells me proudly that during their courtship she would regularly beat him in matches on the lawn, showing little mercy for her soon-to-be husband. She was his perfect counterpart, encouraging his athleticism and physical fitness outside of the game. Instead of love at first sight, it was love at first match.

However, not everyone welcomed the blossoming romance. Sushil's brother Hardev, a freedom fighter forced underground by the British, heavily disapproved of his sister marrying a British

Raj policeman. Partition actually ended up helping the young couple; those against their wedding were underground or focused on breaking free of British rule. The potentially controversial couple slipped under the radar during a time of all-consuming national strife. Amidst the chaos of Partition, Singh Sr. remembers quiet evenings spent with Sushil. Their love was tested early, and they found solace in each other's company during the country's most brutal period.

Heading outside, in uniform or not, or as a woman, wasn't safe. So Singh Sr. and Sushil housed up together in private, enjoying evenings talking, making meals and playing games. He said this was the time he fell in love with her, able to see her personality on full display as the two of them hid from the outside world's madness.

Balbir Singh Sr. and Sushil Sadhu were married in an elaborate ceremony on November 27, 1946 in Model Town Lahore. Friends and family came from all over India, and no expense was sparred. Though he is a man who's won many prestigious awards in his life, Singh Sr. ranks this as the happiest day of his life.

Amidst it all, Singh Sr. was playing field hockey for various teams, including his police club and the Punjabi state team. Married life did nothing to quell his libido, a topic he touches on in his autobiography, speaking rather honestly about one of the longstanding taboo subjects for athletes in sport: ". . . and those who say sex is a handicap to sportsmen know nothing about the human mechanism. Regulated sex can do no harm to any player or young man in pursuit of higher goals."

I ask him to elaborate on this point in person, and ever the gentlemen, he simply smiles.

The spoils of married life would have to wait. India's racial froth was bubbling over with the poisonous liquid of hate. It was 1947. The final days of the British Raj were upon the subcontinent, and the events that unspooled next would end up defining a nation's existence—much to the dismay of its leaders and civilians.

Months before Partition, Singh Sr. was selected for an Indian all-star team handpicked by the Indian Hockey Federation. The team had four Sikhs from the Punjab region and played a slew of matches around the country: Bombay, Bangalore, Hyderabad and Madras. It would be the first time Singh Sr. had visited many of these cities, but he largely kept to himself, fearing for his safety as a minority in a country embroiled in political and religious turmoil. The squad was one of the initial development teams towards a probable "Indian" team in the next Olympics. Singh Sr. was at the top of his form, cementing himself as the number one centre forward in the country, and leading the all-star squad in goals. If the Olympic squad had been selected solely on statistics, he would have been the first draft pick.

But then Partition came, and ground the country to a deadly, screeching halt.

In the summer of 1947, Singh Sr. was posted in Ludhiana at the police station's rural detachment. He was now a sub-inspector, having been promoted largely because of his invaluableness on the field hockey pitch. The madness and bloodshed convulsing India had reached fever pitch. Although the country would gain the independence it had so desperately sought, that freedom would come at a hefty price.

On all sides, the shaky British Raj regime was crumbling; war in Europe had sucked the energy out of the Empire, and directed Britain's attention back home. The British were broke, the Second World War had cost them dearly, and holding their controlling interests in India were no longer financially viable. The partition of the Punjab area in mid-August 1947 took place as part of a negotiated settlement, brokered by the British, between the Indian National Congress and the All-India Muslim League. It was part of the larger effort to divide India and transfer power to India and Pakistan.

The principle on which India and the Punjab area in particular were divided dictated that Muslim-majority strongholds be separated from the rest of India and given to Pakistan. The demand for this form of partition was made by the All-India Muslim League, which insisted that Indian Muslims were not a minority (at the time, they represented some 16 percent of India's population), but a separate nation by virtue of their Islamic faith and culture.

On August 15, 1947, the Indian Independence Act led to the creation of two separate nations in the blink of an eye, or more specifically, the span of about 24 hours. Every year, the Islamic Republic of Pakistan celebrates its Independence Day on August 14th, and India the day after.

Tension due to displacement ignited full civil war in the form of race riots, looting, and hate crimes of all varieties. The subsequent political strife forced millions from their homes as Muslims headed to Pakistan and Bangladesh, and Hindus left these areas for India. Caught in the middle were the Sikhs and various other religious minorities. No one was safe.

It was a horrible time, says Singh Sr. He talks of the period in an icy and calculating manner that stands out from his otherwise warm and heartfelt demeanour. As a policeman trying to keep the peace in the turbulent Punjab area, he was thrust into the middle of the violence. Dispossessed families left behind all they had known to make dangerous, cross-country moves; simultaneously, separatists seized the opportunity to murder those that did not follow their faith or political ideals.

"It was very tragic," Singh Sr. says, his words slowing. "Blood everywhere, blood on buses, blood on trains, blood on canal waters."

In the book *Midnight's Furies: The Deadly Legacy of India's Partition*, author Nisid Hajari outlined the sheer magnitude of it all:

"Nearly seventy years later, Partition has become a byword for horror. Instead of joining hands at their twinned births, India and Pakistan would be engulfed by some of the worst sectarian massacres the modern world has ever seen. Non-Muslims on one side of the new border in the Punjab and Muslims on the other side descended with sword and spear and torch on the minorities who lived among them. An appalling slaughter ensued.

"Gangs of killers set whole villages aflame, hacking to death men and children and the aged while carrying off young women to be raped. British soldiers and journalists who had witnessed the Nazi death camps claimed Partition's brutalities were worse: pregnant women had their breasts cut off and babies hacked out of their bellies; infants were found literally roasted on spits. Foot caravans of destitute refugees fleeing the violence stretched for 50 miles and more. As the peasants trudged along wearily, mounted guerrillas charged out of the tall crops that lined the road and culled them like sheep. Special refugee trains, filled to bursting when they set out, suffered repeated ambushes along the way. All too often they crossed the border in funeral silence, blood seeping from under their carriage doors.

"Across the Punjab, the limbs of thousands of corpses poked from shallow graves like twigs, gnawed on by wild dogs. Estimates of the dead range widely yet are universally shocking. Not long afterward, one British official, working off casualty reports and his own inquiries, put the number at 200,000. Others, claiming to factor in those who had died of disease and hunger and exposure, insist that more than a million perished. At least 14 million refugees were uprooted in what remains the biggest forced migration in history. Western Pakistan was virtually emptied of Hindus and Sikhs; the Indian half of the Punjab lost almost all of its Muslims. The conflagration stands as one of the deadliest and most brutal civil conflicts of the twentieth century, unrivalled in scale until the 1994 massacres in Rwanda."

Neha Saleem, the granddaughter of Mohammed Azam—a family friend—who was Muslim and left for Pakistan during Partition, recently connected with Sushbir via Facebook. The two have met and shared stories, rekindling a family bond violently severed by the bloody convulsions of politics.

In looking back on Partition, Singh Sr. says the long, chaotic months of violence are something he's spent years trying to make sense of. A Sikh by birth, and a nationalist by choice, he wanted nothing more than for India to remain an undivided nation. Alas, cooler heads did not prevail, even with Gandhi on a hunger strike, his body withering away in a futile attempt to stop the killings.

"It was hard to look at the dead bodies lying in the fields and in the canals," says Singh Sr. "Many people I knew died."

He trails off, eyes to the ground. In this instant, he's a million miles away, faced with the remembrance of something that happened more than sixty years ago.

His family suffered. His father Dalip, still in Moga, sheltered a Muslim friend in the school's storeroom for more than ten days while angry Sikh mobs turned the town upside down looking for him. Dalip tried to convince the friend to don a *kachha*, the Sikh-styled underwear, and a turban so he could flee west. The man refused, and accused Dalip of trying to recruit him to Sikhism. He fled, only to be brutally run down and murdered a few hundred feet from the school.

The randomness of the violence left much to simple chance. As the mass exodus of Muslims began the trek to Lahore, Singh Sr. found himself working around the clock in Ludhiana, trying to keep the peace. Looting, fires, killings and abductions were destroying large parts of the area. One of the more terrible moments for Singh Sr. came when he and his fellow officers arrived at a bus stop some seven miles from Ludhiana, on Jagraon Road. A woman was there with her two sons, ages ten and six. Their father had been murdered in the riots, dying in front of them as the Sikh family fled Lyallpur, which is now Faisalabad. They got off the bus, and she sought refuge under a tree to feed her sons breadcrumbs, the only food they had left.

Before they could even react, an out-of-control car skidded off the road and smashed into the tree, killing all three instantly.

The following day Singh Sr. headed to a remote village on the outskirts of town. When he arrived, he found the predominately Sikh community had been burned to the ground. He remembers the smell of burning flesh, the screams of the dying inside the huts and homes as he stood by helpless, unable to do anything. Later, the police officers learned that Muslim extremists had taken the young women from the village, raped and murdered them, then lit the rest of the homes on fire with the families still huddled inside.

After the village massacre, Singh Sr. and his fellow policemen drove home. It was night; they were mentally exhausted, at a loss for words. They were safe now, and were told to unload their rifles. However, Singh Sr. noticed another officer, Kartar Singh, had forgotten to unload his. When Singh Sr. questioned him, Kartar, angry and stressed, started to repeatedly cock his rifle's hammer back to show there was no bullet—which is when the gun went off, sending a slug through Singh Sr.'s turban and narrowly missing his skull.

The bombastic noise echoed through the vehicle's interior, shattering the windows. Singh Sr. burst out into the night as the van came to a screeching halt, nervously checking himself for wounds. Unwrapping his turban, he saw a burnt hole where the slug had passed through, inches from his brain.

Kartar, broken and despondent, fell to his feet, crying and apologizing profusely. Singh Sr. helped him up, consoling the man who'd almost blown his head off.

"It was a miracle I was alive," he says now.

He'd managed to get his wife out of Lahore just in time, securing her safely in the Ludhiana Sadar Police Station. But Sushil's mother stubbornly refused to leave her home. Luckily a few of her Muslim neighbours in the city offered her asylum (she ended up staying for close to six months), but she would ultimately have to abandon her family's house and its prized gardens, forsaking most of the wealth they'd gained. In the aftermath of Partition, Sushil's mother was forced to live in a shared room with a hand pump for running water, a far cry from the tony neighbourhood to which she'd grown accustomed.

Partition hit Sushil's mother especially hard; her husband, a retired engineer, had passed away, and she was alone. Sushbir said she was a strong and proud woman who ventured on amidst the grave circumstances.

"She had to begin her life from scratch all over again with nothing to fall back on," says Sushbir, shaking her head sadly. "That is the cruel effect that destiny had on so many like her."

Sushil's brothers, all university educated, were forced to get jobs as mechanics and guards for the railways. Singh Sr.'s wife's family had been cleaned out, and had to restart their lives with literally nothing to show for it.

Many nations paid a heavy price for separating from British rule, but it could be argued that none paid as much as India. Singh Sr. talks of his close Muslim friends, now gone, taken unapologetically away by the gusting winds of independence.

"Azam, Maqbool, Shahrukh, Mekhmood, Aziz, Khurram," he says, listing off Muslim friends and teammates he would never hear from again. "I still do not know if most of them lived or not."

The violence of Partition ended slowly. Many paid the ultimate price for their country's independence, including one of its leaders. On January 30th, 1948, Nathuram Godse, a Hindu distraught over the separation caused by Partition, sought out Gandhi after he'd finished prayer and pumped three bullets into his chest at close range.

The death of Gandhi brought the country to a standstill, but it only further ignited a new wave of violence, as if the killings might cause the entire nation to self-implode.

In Moga, Singh Sr. and Sushil's families found themselves all in the same city, trying to stay alive and wait for any sign of safety. Singh Sr. was soon transferred to the Ferozepur Cantonment, the station that covered the military, army, and civilian areas mere miles from the new India–Pakistan border. As the violence slowly died down and the barbed wire fences went up, the border became a dead zone with heavy military presence on both sides.

The police tried to investigate as many cases of murder, rape, abduction of women and theft as they could, but it was futile. Witnesses refused to talk, evidence was hard to come by, and many were so distraught from what had happened that they were willing to point the finger at anyone they could, regardless of whether or not they could substantiate their claim. As many as half a million people had perished in the various stages of the genocide,[65] but with no definitive villain, convictions for such heinous crimes mostly got lost in the shuffle.[66]

★★★

The relocation to Ferozepur for Singh Sr., though dangerous, granted him the chance of a lifetime, an odd chance that appears today as prophetic. India had now taken over running the police force, and Sir John Bennett had disappeared in the fiery smoke of civil war. But the job remained the same, just now Singh Sr. was doing it as a free, independent Indian.

Every month, the police force and the army station at the Ferozepur Cantonment hosted a lavish, star-studded ceremonial hockey match. Singh Sr. was competing in multiple tournaments for the Punjab Police—the National Championship for Punjab State, and club tournaments across the nation, such as the Agha Khan Gold Cup and the Gold Cup in Bombay. He was coming into his absolute prime as a field hockey player, the perfect mix of youth and experience. Singh Sr. remembers a stretch in which he was averaging three or four goals a game, beating teams literally single-handedly as times. While field hockey games are usually higher scoring than soccer, for a player to consistently notch hat tricks and beyond was uncommon.

"I felt great, I was playing great. I was happy to play and be done with everything."

But it was the ceremonial match back at the cantonment that left the biggest impression on the young star. Before the game, Singh Sr., team captain for the police squad, engaged in a ceremonial pre-game ritual with the captain of the army squad, none other than Major Dhyan Chand.

"It was an honour to meet him," Singh Sr. says. "He was a very simple man, very polite. Before every match we would shake hands."

But Chand was no longer the man Singh Sr. had seen in that iconic newsreel. Now in his 40s, Chand was well past his prime playing days. The Second World War had stolen his chance to win four, possibly five gold medals for the British Raj. The games in Tokyo and then Helsinki had been canceled during the fight against the Nazi regime and imperial Japan. Now India was a new nation, birthed out of the horrible violence of Partition, independent and clamouring for its own identity after nearly two hundred years of deforming British rule. Chand seemed dated, part of an old world now cast aside both at home and abroad.

Something had happened to the Hindu superstar. He was no longer the man he was in the press; the humble, iconic luminary who was a consummate gentleman and professional. Or maybe he never was to begin with. Singh Sr. says he saw something in his eyes, something missing, or something that had been taken from him. He was simply a man, and everyone was counting on him to remain a superhero.

Chand died of liver cancer on December 3, 1979 in Delhi. According to Cancer Research UK, the most common causes of liver cancer are cirrhosis of the liver, which itself is commonly caused by three things: heavy alcohol consumption over a long period of time, Hepatitis B or C, or inherited diseases including hemochromatosis.[67]

Despite Chand's fading star, Singh Sr. relished the chance to play against the "wizard."

"He was still a good player," he recalls. "His passes were very sharp, his ball control was good."

It was an almost perfectly planned passing of the guard. Gone into history was the storybook hero of the British Raj's field hockey squad. Hindu star Dhyan Chand had met his soon-to-be-replacement, a five-foot-ten Sikh with a full head of jet black hair wrapped neatly in a bun—and a healthy moustache to boot. Compact, fast, and tough on the ball, Singh Sr. was an unstoppable force, a new type of player who combined tough-ness with finesse. Singh Sr. had been forged in a new game, where creed divided teams and allegiances and grudges were more than simple sporting rivalries. The police team never lost to the army squad, and Singh Sr.'s team had emerged as one of the premier club outfits in the country. It was a symbolic meet-ing, the youngster who emulated his hero growing up was now etching his own place in local folklore. Singh Sr. was becoming the next Dhyan Chand.

The Second World War was over. Partition had died down, and London was calling. The Games of the XIV Olympiad drew near, ready to usher in a new era of peace, prosperity and freedom.

Field hockey looked to be the premiere sport to watch. Before the Second World War, the game was largely a British Raj spectacle. While Chand's medals were impressive, he was a tough sell as an international sporting icon given his team was winning matches 24-1 and 11-1 in a 1932 Olympic tournament in Los Angeles that was only held after British Raj lobbied the IOC.

Now the British Empire had left the sub-continent, and two new nations emerged from the chrysalides, both of them field hockey-mad: India and Pakistan. Britain, meanwhile, was entering a field hockey team not entirely dependent on its colonial subjects for the first time in its history. As the ash settled on the Second World War, three powerhouses stood poised, ready to do battle in the lion's den of Wembley Stadium. One would emerge victorious, bringing international glory to its team and country. The English, the Indians and the Pakistanis all had much to prove in this new age of field hockey. The best team in the world had been split into three, and they all frothed at that first medal of the new age.

The burning question was whether or not the world's best field hockey player would even be invited to try out for his country's team. Race had become a sore point in India, and a Hindu-led Indian Hockey Federation was extremely hesitant to let a Sikh player be their iconic poster boy in India's first tournament as an independent nation.

The civil war may have ostensibly ended, but Singh Sr.'s long, arduous climb to the top was just beginning.

CRUSTACEANS OF INDIAN DESCENT

"On reaching the building lobby Didi pressed the elevator button and spoke. 'You must have heard the saying that there's no modernism without barbarism. That's what Shimla is going through. Strip away the young man's face and you'll find an old man's mind.'"

~ Meghna Pant, *One & a Half Wife*

Breakfast is Corn Flakes and buttered toast with a three-time Olympic gold medalist. He likes his milk warmed in the microwave, I'm okay with having mine cold.

My body hates me. I punished it with 22 gruelling hours of travel across the Atlantic ocean, zipping across the Prime Meridian to a London layover on little sleep and even less mental preparation. To help my cold, Sushbir hands me a care package of Indian cetirizine and paracetamol with my morning tea. I'm disastrously failing to fight off the flu I picked up somewhere between YVR and Indira Gandhi Airport, an illness that's been Hulkified by the Delhi smog. The foreign medication appears to be doing the trick, allowing me to function at a somewhat respectable level. I only have two weeks to unravel this mystery, which means exhausting a few days trying to sleep off a viral infection is out of the question.

A hazy smoke blankets the city, lingering overhead as hanging fog, sweat sticking to my forehead like drying glue. A dusty, dry mug of fever, steaming endlessly on an oven coil. The heat robust with dense, grimy pollution, airways forever clogged, jammed with oily, soggy carbon dioxide exhaust. Chandigarh cooks within the humidity, the glare of cracked asphalt, little shade other than rows of blooming yellow trees that line the road. The dial that is India has been turned down here, but it still pushes the senses to the edge every chance it gets.

I have my own bathroom, however there are eight unmarked knobs to turn in the exact order to receive lukewarm water after about fifteen minutes. Tiny ants have taken over the sink, feasting as packs of moving specs on slimy green snot from my nostrils. This is day two of a fortnight inside the rooster coop, and I'm already pining for the soft, warm hug of first world comforts.

The evening before we sat in the living room, stacked full of countless shiny, glittering trophies and started the process of recording Singh Sr.'s life. His family wants his historic existence on record at least, almost as if when he passes, his amazing story might drift off into the unfathomable, unending noise that dominates this country's existence.

We downed warm whisky with ice and started from birth, slowly transcribing, unpacking every historical detail we could, recalling each emotion and feeling this man had in his head, gut or heart. We started overturning stones, and I started unraveling this man's life, story by story, year by year.

Singh Sr. opens up quickly, he's more than inclined to chat about his extraordinary timeline. Literally crawling from a brick and mud hut to the top of the sporting world, he is something of a storyteller's dream—a man from nothing, who gave everything to his country, and got next to nothing in return. I am in the presence of greatness, and Singh Sr. remains the most humble and polite person I've ever met. The sensory confusion is mind-boggling. Here I am, so many worlds away, sharing a nightcap, then breakfast with a legitimate hero and all he wants to do is make sure I have sufficient butter for my toast and that my accommodation is adequate and comfortable.

There is no PR team, no fancy photo shoots, no agent and no endorsement deals. We are rooming in the same house, sharing meals and quiet conversations. At night he puts on his pyjamas and wishes me a good sleep like a regular houseguest, heading to bunk in a room where he has three gold medals hidden somewhere in the shelves.

No country is immune to social ills; but the seedy corruption, terrible nepotism and rampant personal vendettas here are truly flabbergasting. Somehow Singh Sr. appears almost caricature, completely void of selfishness, absent of vitriol, bile or anything other than humbleness. He admits to a few grudges, but after spending some time in his presence, it's clear he lacks a single bone with any sort of vindictiveness.

After breakfast in the Bhomia residence we watch NDTV.[68] The Indian 24-hour news station is like CNN jacked on crack cocaine. Banners flash-flicker with incendiary headlines that read like distress signals, a symbol of how frenetically spastic the national media is, even in comparison to our unapologetically alarmist North American culture:

ATTEMPT TO BRIBE MEDIA?
ANGRY PEOPLE RUNNING INDIA
CLEANING INDIA OR DIVIDING INDIA?

Chockfull of talking heads: local politicians, one-sided journalists, activists screaming at the top of their lungs who rant-dance between Hindi and English. They spew, they ramble, they yell, they wave their hands at the screen when they can't get a word in; and then they yell some more. Even the host yells, and most of the time he's yelling the loudest.

Today's breaking story is the arrest of a surgeon on charges of negligence and attempted culpable homicide in the death of a dozen women who underwent sterilization operations at a mobile clinic in Chhattisgarh—one of India's poorest states in the central part of the country. A doctor operated on 83 women over a period of six hours, which averages out to about one every four minutes.[69] He claims the women died due to medications distributed in a nearby village rather than the speedy operations themselves. The whole thing is part of a campaign to curb population growth in India, a nation of 1.252 billion and counting—fast.[70] Women get paid about 1,500 rupees ($23 US) to have the operation and doctors are given financial incentives to do as many of them, as fast as they can, with little regard for proper procedure.

Next is a debate around India's "godman" which Kabir equates to "if your car salesman told everyone in the neighbourhood he was Jesus." Problem is, in India, where lack of education is rampant, many fall victim to these manipulative creatures.[71] They claim to be Hindu gods, and trick locals into following their every word, sometimes to the death.[72] While in most countries, those who claim to be sent by a higher power are relegated to street corners and homemade soapboxes; in India they lay substantial havoc to an unsuspecting and highly uneducated populous.

After a half hour or so, the TV is too much, and I retreat to my room to prepare for our first event of the day. Singh Sr., Kabir and myself are headed to the nearby Tagore theatre where they're honouring recent medal winners from the Punjab state who represented India at the 2014 Commonwealth and Asian Games.

Located in Sector 18, the building has the wooden frame features of an outdated high school theatre. The auditorium is packed, close to 2,000 people—literally all of them young Sikh men. In India, as in many foreign countries, guys roam the streets in packs. It's unclear if they have jobs, or where they've found the time to attend a ceremonial event on a Tuesday morning. Kabir says many of them do not work, and have nothing better to do.

"They kind of go where they're told in this weird sort of way," he adds.

The event starts with a political speech, and then another political speech, and then another, and then another, and then finally one more. In total, there ends up being well over an hour and a half of mostly unrelated political speeches, mostly in Punjabi, and mostly not about sports at all. As the speeches roll on, I watch the crowd lull itself into a trance-like state of acceptance amongst the noxious lullaby of hot air political promises. The local newspaper *The Tribune* lays out the scene in an article the next day:[73]

"Politicians hijack event to honour sports medalists . . . In the remaining half-an-hour, the champion athletes, 28 of them, scampered to the stage as their names were rapidly announced, rushed across it to collect their cheques, and then hurried back to their seats. If anyone in the almost-packed hall had come to the function hoping to hear the athletes talk about their struggle, experiences, or some interesting and inspiring anecdotes from their lives, they went home disappointed."

At the centre of this political storm—and the centrifugal figure in Sikh politics—is Sukhbir Singh Badal, the deputy chief minister of the Punjab State.[74] Badal is also the sports minister, hence his appearance at this event. He commands attention with every move he makes, moving with an robust entourage and security team packing Uzis, stopping frequently to shake hands and engage in back-patting chats with other Sikh men he deems worthy of conversation.

Badal is a portly man with a turban that matches his tie. He struts into the auditorium tardy with an unchallenged confidence. He's quickly ushered to the front row, as other guests are booted from their seats, and he mingles with the special VIP delegates. Kabir is keeping a close eye on his grandfather from a couple seats back with me, as the crush of people in the theatre at times creates dangerous choke points where photographers and cameraman are literally climbing over each other for the best photo op.

Badal's father is Parkash Singh Badal, who's been the chief minister of Punjab since 2007.[75] Parkash is an elder statesman in the Indian political game, kind of like that flyover state US Congressman who keeps getting elected through acclamation. A career politician, he's held the seat of chief minister multiple times as far back as the 1970s.

Parkash and Singh Sr. have history. It was Parkash who recommended Singh Sr. for the Bharat Ratna,[76] India's highest civilian honour, handed down straight from the Prime Minister. Everyone who is anyone has one: Indira Gandhi, Mother Teresa, Hindustani classical Sitar player Ravi Shankar. In 2011, for the first time in the award's history, athletes became eligible. This decision set off a firestorm of debate, and is one of the main reasons I'm here. While Singh Sr.'s accomplishments warrant discussion of his potential receiving of the country's highest honour, he is not even being mentioned on state TV or in any mainstream media outlets as a potential candidate. Meanwhile, Dhyan Chand had close to a hundred members of the Indian Parliament write to Modi himself, hoping to get the Hindu the prestigious award.[77]

The funny thing about the Bharat Ratna is anytime anyone receives one, controversy is abound. There's controversy over whom to nominate, controversy about the nomination itself, and controversy around the nomination process as a whole. Each camp surrounding a particular nominee has a dedicated team promoting their potential selectee while working to downplay the other potential candidate's accolades. The award has become political fodder, morphing into a weird popularity contest for various special interest groups.

Before getting to the heart of the debate, however, it's crucial to point out that India has a complicated relationship with its heroes and legends. The recent treatment of India's first Prime Minister makes this evident. Jawaharlal Nehru[78] was one of the founding members of India's push for independence, Gandhi's closest confidant and right-hand man, and father of subsequent Prime Minister Indira Gandhi (no relation to Mahatma). Nehru was one of the founders of the Indian National Congress—which after decades in power got steamrolled by Modi and his BJP (Bharatiya Janata Party). The BJP are Hindu nationalists,[79] and in 2014 they rode a wave of popularity and festering dissent for Congress while promising a "new India".[80,81] The BJP is backed by the RSS (Rashtriya Swayamsevak Sangh), a conservative Hindu nationalist organization hell bent on creating Hindustan where the religious group controls the country's culture outright.[82,83] The RSS does a lot of Modi's dirty work, allowing him to push a hardline agenda while keeping his populous image squeaky clean.

In his book *Midnight's Furies: The Deadly Legacy of Partition*, writer Nisid Hajari outlined how the RSS originally took inspiration from Hitler's Brown Shirts, as the militant group secretly trained in the use of swords, rifles and crude bombs during wartime; the British had banned any such private armies or militia groups during this time. Now they operate almost as cultural militia, upholding strict conservative Hindu norms through various things like intimidation, bribery, corruption and terrorism.[84] Imagine the Tea Party if they were allowed to run amok through America, pushing their values on the population at will, with little fear of oversight or repercussion, and a boatload of secret funding.[85]

Modi's movement has picked up steam as of late, with Hindu hardliners even beating and killing Muslims in India for allegedly stealing a cow, a sacred animal in the Hindu faith.[86] There have also been reports of murder and abuse towards Muslims for eating beef (note: Muslims are forbidden from consuming pork according to the Qur'an), or participating in the sale or smuggling of it for culinary purposes.[87] This is just the latest wave in what

has been a reclamation project of conservative Hindu values per-
petuated by the RSS and backed by the BJP. [88]

When it comes to Nehru, India's founding father after
Gandhi's death, he is just the latest in a long line of historical figures shoved into modern political debates. After the BJP ousted
Congress, which could only manage a measly 44 seats in the 543-
member house, Modi did mark the 125th anniversary of Nehru's
birthday with a celebration. But his detractors, mostly die-hard
Congress lovers, say he's been appropriating Nehru's legacy,[89] partially because Nehru was a staunch supporter of secularism. Modi
is not. He is a proud Hindu who personally aligns with the RSS
and its notion of a unified Hindustan.[90] A *Guardian* writer recently called him "the divisive manipulator who charmed the world."[91]

Luckily, Nehru was smart enough to award himself the
Bharat Ratna while he was India's Prime Minister in 1955,[92]
something one might find odd for a sitting leader to do in a dem-
ocratic country, but at least he handed himself the award before
anyone could create controversy around it.

This complicated, sometimes skewed history lesson where
historic figures are thrown into modern-day political debates is
nothing new around the world, but I get the sense this is far
beyond average political showmanship and campaign rhetoric.

As Kabir and I both start to fall victim to the noxious lullaby of Punjabi speeches, Kabir whispers in my ear, "Nehru isn't
rolling in his grave . . . he's spinning endlessly."

Kabir continues to explain to me that when it comes to
notable sporting figures, India has a wealth of athletes, but in its
two biggest sports—field hockey and cricket—two names dominate the debate. The first is Hindu cricketer Sachin Tendulkar,[93]
India's greatest, and possibly one of the world's best in his sport.
Tendulkar, alongside a laundry list of professional accomplishments much like any Tiger Woods or Billie Jean King, was part of
India's gold medal winning team at the 2011 World Cup, co-host-
ed by India, Sri Lanka and Bangladesh.[94] In 2013, he became
India's first athlete to receive the Bharat Ratna. However in India,
nothing is ever that simple. Tendulkar had retired from cricket
mere hours before receiving the country's highest honour, which

lit the national press into a bonfire of chatter, finger pointing and accusations of political favouritism for professional gain.[95]

Tendulkar is known as "The God of Cricket", and is treated as such. He has multiple million dollar endorsement deals and lives the life a celebrated, retired national athlete should. Based in Mumbai, he cannot go anywhere without drawing a boy-band crowd of adoring fans. People camp outside his house, sleeping by the gates for months on end for a glimpse of him, and some have taken their love to extremes, one even hanging himself after the batsman failed to reach his 100th century in a pivotal match.[96]

Before cricket became India's sport of choice and Tendulkar became the country's most iconic sporting figure, debuting for the national team in 1989, the country was field hockey mad. India had already declared its proverbial Tendulkar—Chand.

The most compelling evidence as to how well-loved Chand is that August 29th, National Sports Day in India,[97] also happens to be his birthday. Of course this is no coincidence as Modi himself paid tribute to Chand just before I got there with a series of tweets:[98]

"Our tributes to the legendary Major Dhyan Chand on National Sports Day. His determination & dedication towards sports continues to inspire."

What this has inevitably created is a rift between the Tendulkar and Chand camp, who were furious the much younger Tendulkar got the Bharat Ratna first. The Chand camp called foul, citing things like chronology and honouring elders much like most Hall of Fames do with a requisite waiting period after retirement.

The truly puzzling thing is Singh Sr. is nowhere even remotely near to this debate: something I'm still struggling to wrap my head around. While no one is denying Tendulkar is one of the greatest cricketers and Indian athletes of all time, skipping over both Chand and Singh Sr. for a historical honour seems odd.

One night Kabir shows me a recorded clip from *The Times of India*'s 24-hour news station. The yelling heads were debating the next athlete to receive the Bharat Ratna, and all the talk was around Chand and how he'd been robbed by Tendulkar.

Kabir, ever the cunning enthusiast for his grandfather, actually called into the show as Kabir Bhomia, a banker, with no affiliation to Singh Sr. He started to talk about his grandfather, comparing him to Chand, and stating facts that further elevated his grandfather above Chand. His phone line literally cut off mid-sentence.

After the political peacocking has exhausted itself at the Tagore theatre and the athletes are rushed their oversized novelty cheques, Kabir, Singh Sr. and I head outside for a lunchtime function. Singh Sr. doesn't stay long, as being 91 only allows him so much time out in the exhausting crush of people. Kabir has been trying to increase his grandfather's public presence through more functions, however Singh Sr. is an elderly man and tires easily if he's constantly moving in and out of cars and buildings. India is not built for seniors, much less anyone who isn't used to elbow room only crowds that move like sea tides.

Singh Sr.'s modesty is also his biggest fault. While Kabir gently pushes his grandfather into the spotlight, the three-time gold medalist finds every opportunity to retreat from it. We are seated underneath a cascading tent and served pastries, but Singh Sr. offers his seat to me and appears uncomfortable sitting with the "haves" of Indian social life. Further, we pass an actual poster of the event on our way out, which features him, but he gives no speech, nor does much of any shaking of hands. In India's bustling rooster coop where every 'somebody' is jostling for attention, Singh Sr. might as well be dumping a bag of feed on his head and lying on the floor.

This theory that Singh Sr.'s anonymity is solely because of his high level of humbleness is easily disproven by the fact that numerous articles state Dhyan Chand himself was never one for the spotlight, and the fact that the reason Chand himself is getting one-upped by Tendulkar because of modern media's short attention span also falls victim to illogical thinking.[99] If that were true, Singh Sr. and Chand would find themselves in equal boats in comparison to Tendulkar.

On our way to the car we meet Indian archer Trisha Deb,[100] a young athlete who looks as out of place in the spotlight as Singh

Sr., and more than happy to grab her cheque and run amidst the madness. It's pretty clear Deb lets her bow do the talking, as she won two bronze medals (one in individual event and the other in a team event) at the 2014 Asian games in Incheon, South Korea. And while many athletes who also claimed multiple medals were given multiple cash prizes, Deb was not, this small pittance her only reward.

"She's *female*," whispers Kabir to me in the car after we leave.

Deb's coach Harpal Singh Teja is furious with this, and points this out to Singh Sr., who appears to be the only notable-like dignitary who will hear him out. Teja chews out the government's sports department alongside Deb's father while the archer stands awkwardly beside us with a cheque almost as big as she is.

Punjab is known for producing world-class athletes, and in Sukhbir's speech that alternated between English and Punjabi, he stated "money would not be the problem." However it's pretty clear money is the problem. Politicians in India have long gained a reputation for sucking up any available funds when it comes to program spending, taking huge chunks for themselves and leaving scraps for those who actually need it. Kabir tells me numerous stories of bribery and corruption, none of which I can verify, but you get the sense this is something rather commonplace in this country.[101] Also, one cannot imagine a person like Deb actively campaigning for more funding. It's pretty clear she just wants to be an archer.

After we get back in the car, Kabir fills me in a bit more about Sukhbir. He calls him "Caesar's son", in reference to his undying lust for power. His father is a respected politician with decades of experience, however Sukhbir is relatively young and much more fame hungry. He's part of the Shiromani Akali Dal party,[102] which holds close to half the seats in the Punjab Legislative Assembly. In 2012, his party combined with BJP to take control of the Punjab state.

Many Sikhs I spoke to called the alliance a "deal with the devil" in which Sikhs aligned with the ruling Hindu majority to control the Punjab. Since then, instances of religious intolerance towards Sikhs has continued, and even increased in the Punjab area,[103] much to the dismay of citizens who'd hoped a Punjabi politician would actually fight to help Punjabis.

When it comes to Sukhbir and Singh Sr., it is a relationship sadly of apathy. The Bharat Rhatna nomination nod—nothing more than something Sukhbir's father mentioned in passing in an interview—has been the only real gesture between the two camps, when one would think they would've established a rapport long ago. Kabir hopes the more he can get his grandfather out to events, the more he can increase his profile and standing within the ruling government of Punjab, however he's realistic in terms of his expectations when it comes to the grand scheme of things.

"To put it frankly," says Kabir, "they really don't care about him at all."

When we arrive back home the cold medication I've taken won't let me sleep, so I sit down at my laptop and try to digest as much about this story as my brain will allow.

Everything appears to start with an undated article posted online by London's *The Telegraph* newspaper,[104] a ranking that appears atop Google search whenever you raise the subject of international field hockey greatness. *The Telegraph*, with multiple writers covering the sport, is a powerhouse when it comes to international field hockey journalism:

"*Telegraph Sport* canvassed hockey journalists from Australia, England and Pakistan for their definitive list of the top 10 men and women of all time. The results were totted up and—with the 2014 World Cup in The Hague being a men's and women's event—a combined list was drawn up. It is important to note that some journalists declined to take part on the grounds of fairness in compiling such a list, while others factored in that the game has transgressed hugely from an amateur one to the highly professional model today."

Atop the list is none other than Dhyan Chand:

"1. Dhyan Chand—India

"Almost universally regarded as the greatest of all time. Slightly built, with a crouching style, he possessed an extraordinary grasp over every facet of the game. The 'Wizard' could go through a host of defenders and had an uncanny comprehension of when and where to pass. Pictured far left, Chand's 40 goals in three Olympic gold medal campaigns is still the record for the highest individual Games' tally. Residents of Vienna honoured him by setting up a statue of him with four hands and four sticks, replicating his control and mastery over the ball."

First off, there is no statue in Vienna.[105] There's a reference to it on the Government of India's website[106] and on the BBC,[107] but there is no actual statue. The fact that this myth of a statue is the lynchpin of *The Telegraph*'s piece is the first clue in a long and perplexing mystery that plays out like an elaborate, tragic theatre piece.

This debate is *not*, however, about whether or not Chand was a legendary player. He captured three consecutive Olympic gold medals from 1928 in Amsterdam to 1936 in Berlin, and is no doubt one of the better field hockey players of all time. What this debate *is* about is the fact that Singh Sr. isn't even on *The Telegraph*'s list, though when you break it down, his career was better than Chand's in the face of much greater odds. In a world where we rank athletes on merit, championships, and statistics (Google any sport with "greatest of all time"), when it comes to field hockey, the rules have been thrown out the window.

The number two player of all time, according to this list, is Australian Ric Charlesworth, who won Olympic silver and one World Cup gold. Charlesworth went on to a decorated career as a coach, and captained multiple Australian teams at various Olympic games while playing, but never scored a lot of goals (four in 31 Olympic matches). If each sport has its golden statistic, which it definitely does (touchdowns, goals, home runs, strikeouts, baskets) then Singh Sr. should be far above Charlesworth, having scored 22 goals over three Olympics.

In addition, Singh Sr. won three golds, just like Chand; however his were all after India broke from British rule.[108] Atop the sham of a tournament in Los Angeles, Chand and British Raj literally never faced any type of real competition for their three golds. The closest anyone got to beating them was the Netherlands in 1928, who lost 3-0 to them in the finals. That iconic, gritty match against Nazi Germany in 1936 was actually a steamrolling; British Raj slaughtered the Germans 8-1 in the final.

After India's independence in 1947—and the suspension of two Olympics due to the war, the field hockey world underwent a massive tectonic shift. The British Raj squad, made up of Anglo-Indians, Hindus, Sikhs and Muslims, splintered along three political/religious lines due to Partition. When the games resumed in London in 1948, there would be three field hockey powerhouses instead of one: India, Great Britain, and Pakistan with the Netherlands quickly developing their own program.

Singh Sr.'s first gold medal came in London. Forced to scratch and claw his way onto the roster even though he was lighting up opposing teams across the country for various club and all-star teams back home, he still notched eight goals in the two games he did play (scoring six in one contest, however not starting the next match).

In the 1952 Olympics in Helsinki, 12 nations competed in the field hockey tournament including India, Great Britain, the Netherlands and Pakistan. Singh Sr. was vice-captain of the team and was India's flag bearer in the opening ceremony. He scored three goals against Britain in the semifinal, which India won 3–1. He scored five goals in India's 6–1 win against the Netherlands, setting an Olympic/Guinness record.[109] In total, Singh Sr. scored nine of India's 13 goals at the Helsinki Olympics, an astonishing 69 percent of the team's goals.

In the 1956 Melbourne Olympics, Singh Sr.—then captain of the team and once again India's flag bearer—scored five goals in the opening match against Afghanistan, but was subsequently injured by an errant ball that broke one of his fingers. He had to skip the group matches, but played in the semifinal and final. India won the gold against Pakistan 1–0.

Subsequently, he was left off the roster for the 1960 Olympics in Rome, Italy due to favouritism when he was more than capable of playing and leading the team as a veteran.

While Chand scored 40 goals at the Olympics, it's tough to want to acknowledge the 12 he scored in Los Angeles; and its also interesting to note that of the 12 Olympic games he played, his team shut out their opponents in nine of them, and only allowed one goal in each of the other three. In total, British Raj scored 102 goals, and let in three.

Of further note, during the Berlin Olympics, his younger brother Roop Singh scored nine goals to his 13 from inside-left, a less prolific position to net points from. Many also credit Roop as being an excellent playmaker, much like Magic Johnson was to Kareem Abdul-Jabbar, or John Stockton was to Karl Malone. While all great athletes in their own regard, it's tough to picture them reaching such great heights without their partner by their side. The fact that these two Hindus were brothers probably gave their partnership a genetic leg-up as well; think Daniel or Henrik Sedin, twin hockey players, without the other one by his side.

Chand and Singh Sr. are two of a handful of Indian players who have won three Olympic gold medals in field hockey. These players are the only men or women in history to win three Olympic medals in the sport. So what is so extraordinarily perplexing is while *The Telegraph* called Chand the "greatest field hockey player of all time", Singh Sr. is nowhere to be seen on a list compiled by renowned field hockey journalists all over the world.

Why was someone who had such a statistically similar career on the surface to Chand left off? Their playing accolades are eerily parallel: three consecutive gold medals, and tons of goals to boot.

Furthermore, if you Google "best field hockey players of all time" you get a list of fifteen men and woman, and the first picture is Chand's. Singh Sr. is once again nowhere to be found. In fact, I scoured the web, combing through every "best field hockey players of all time" list I could find, from reputable outlets to personal blogs, and there was not a single list that includes Singh Sr. in its top players (note: Chand is pretty much atop every list).

Singh Sr. has been forgotten from the record books, or to put it more cynically, never included in the first place, and the internet has done nothing but perpetuate this myth through the republishing of Chand's accomplishments without ever questioning them in the first place.

In an interesting article by the *Wall Street Journal*, posted in 2010,[110] the writer looks to summon Chand from the grave to come save Indian field hockey from its slide down the international rankings due to the installation of synthetic turf in the mid 1980s. The article delves into the history of Indian field hockey, but never once mentions Singh Sr., or the fact that the guy is actually still alive and could probably help out with this predicament a bit.

When you Google "Dhyan Chand" and a variation of words like "greatness", "greatest" or "best of all time", the search results are endless. The first and most prominent is Chand's *Encyclopedia Britannica* profile is which he's "considered to be one of the greatest players of all time."[111] However when that article is referenced on his Wikipedia page, the wording is tweaked to "considered as the greatest field hockey player of all time."[112] A massive shift in tone.

Then there's Chand's *Sports Reference* Olympic biography that is even more slanted, stating Chand is "considered the greatest hockey player ever. He learned the game from British army officers . . .".[113] While the numbers and statistics on the website are accurate when checked against official Olympic records, the biography is anything but unbiased.

When it comes to the Indian press, Chand's stature is elevated in numerous articles and references. *India Today* calling him "the greatest hockey player of all time."[114] And *The Times of India* stating the following on the 109th anniversary of his birthday, ". . . regarded as the greatest player of hockey the world has seen to date."[115] Then there's NDTV, in which Chand is "India's greatest hockey player who scored over 1,000 goals between 1926 and 1948. He helped India win three Olympic gold medals."[116]

Concerning Singh Sr.'s *Sports Reference* Olympic profile, it says "one of the legends of Indian hockey, winning three gold medals at the 1948, 1952, and 1956 Olympic Games." Chand's on the other hand says he's the "greatest hockey player ever" while his *Sports Reference* biography cites him as a "centre-forward" and also notes his three Olympic gold medals amongst his greatest achievements.

Now this would not be unusual if Chand were alone in terms of the resume he garnered, or if for some reason his three Olympic gold medals were won under much more strenuous circumstances than Singh Sr. Yet the opposite is true. The British Raj squad slaughtered teams because field hockey as a sport hadn't really developed outside of England or its colonies at that time. Case in point: to win the 1932 Olympics in Los Angeles, the Raj players absolutely annihilated the United States 24-1. This was not an Olympic calibre event; merely a tournament thrown together by the US to appease political interests with the British at the time.

Of course this is not to discredit Chand as a player. He was the top goal scorer on the Raj team. But when the competition is just not up to snuff, it's tough to validate Chand as the best ever. Take judo at the Summer Olympics. Japan has dominated the sport, amassing 72 medals (36 gold), but it should also be noted that Japan invented the sport, which like the British, gave them a leg up at the start as the rest of the world worked to cultivate their own programs.

One man atop the field hockey world rightfully deserves the spotlight. However, given that Chand's and Singh Sr.'s careers are so statistically similar, one would think there would be a raging debate between the two, much like there is in pretty much every other sport that has competing athletes at its mountaintop—think Lionel Messi/Christian Ronaldo/Pelé/Maradona, or Serena Williams/Steffi Graf/Martina Navratilova, or Babe Ruth/Willie Mays/Barry Bonds*, just to name a few.

Only when one athlete rises head and shoulders above the rest statistically does the debate form any type of consensual opinion. One can never verify if Chand was better than Singh Sr. because the question itself is inherently unanswerable and open to personal interpretation and opinion. It is an emotional question asking for an unbiased answer, however consensual opinions via discourse and discussion do bring forth clear frontrunners at times. You can debate Lebron James is a better all-around basketball player than Michael Jordan, but until James wins more championships that Jordan or even Kobe Bryant, you can bet the argument of the "greatest of all time" will continue to fall in Jordan's favour.

However unlike most other sports' statistical, analytical, and incredibly passionate debates, field hockey is not fully formed and missing a key player—much like if you just plucked Messi out of the football debate, or ignored Federer when you were talking about tennis.

Many of these pro sports debates get caught in positional arguments—literally. Football has quarterbacks as their prominent position, but what about wide receiver Jerry Rice? How good could Joe Montana have been without Rice, and vice-versa? Field hockey does not have this proverbial positional problem—both Singh and Chand played the same position, and largely played the same style of play, using expert ball skills to net multiple goals.

In a recent *Times of India* piece on Singh Sr. about the decline of Indian field hockey over the years,[117] Singh Sr. is called a "legendary hockey player and chief coach . . . the iconic centre forward" but never once referenced as "one of", or "the greatest field hockey players of all time."

In a *The Hindu* piece about Singh Sr., Chand is referenced, and the comparison is made, saying Singh Sr. "is rated as the next best to the wizard, the inimitable Dhyan Chand."[118] Now the most important part of that sentence is the religious references seemingly at work behind the scenes here. That same *The Hindu* piece states "Singh takes the credit for carving a vibrant Punjabi ethos to hockey."

While Chand played for British Raj, Singh Sr. played for an independent India. Chand's father Subedar Sameshwar Dutt Singh was in the British Indian Army, and he also played hockey while serving as a soldier. Chand joined the Army at the age of 16, and between 1922 and 1926 he exclusively played army hockey tournaments and regimental games. Chand was ultimately selected for the Army team that toured New Zealand and became the foundation for his road to the British Raj Olympic team. He is, in essence, looked upon as a product of British field hockey permeating Indian culture after the turn of the century before Partition.

Chand, unlike Singh Sr., has had the luxury of an ever-growing mythology behind his legacy over the years. The internet a ripe breeding ground to disperse and republish unverified, and in many instances, inaccurate or incorrect facts.[119]

The 1936 Olympic games in Berlin are a perfect example. They will be largely remembered for one thing: Hitler's tyrannical rule on full display and the Nazi regime's terrifying shadow over the event. Chand and British Raj beat Germany 8-1 in the final—with the centre forward netting a hat trick.

There are multiple myths about these games; that Chand scored six goals in the final; that he met Hitler after the match and he offered Chand a position within the German army and he refused; that Hitler had his stick tested for magnets; that he refused to salute Hitler during the opening ceremonies; that Chand actually spoke to Hitler, or met him.[120,121,122,123,124,125]

Mumbai-based author Laxmi Tendulkar Dhaul's *In the Shadow of Freedom* (published by Zubaan),[126] incorrectly states that Chand scored six goals in the finals, and in *The Olympics: The India Story,* authors Boria Majumdar and Nalin Mehta allege that Chand refused to salute Hitler, just a few examples of what is now widespread mythologizing and outright lies.[127]

There's also a plethora of Youtube videos[128,129] and unverified reports and biographies and other pages that try to corroborate this which include Chand's own son Ashok Kumar.[130,131] Then there's a widely distributed and republished piece that first appeared on the Indo-Asian News Service, written by Qaiser Mohammad Ali.[132] The article is rife with factual errors, including that Hitler offered Chand a post in his army *and* German citizenship; that he lost a tooth in the final against Germany, and that he scored six goals against the Nazi regime to win gold; and of course, that fake statue in Vienna. Qaiser recently received the sports journalists' Madhav Gourav Ratna Award, and the Best of News Agencies prize for the Sports Journalists' Federation of India, in 2006.

In Chand's biography, *Dhyan Chand—The Legend Lives* by Niket Bhushan, Wiley Eastern Ltd., 1992,[133] which was written and published after his death, it states that Chand told friends and family he met Hitler after the finals, and Hitler offered him a position in his army, showed him his private box and the two had a conversation about Chand joining the Nazi regime's army, to which Chand allegedly refused.

After scouring multiple sources and archives about the 1936 Olympics, there is no photo or outside verifiable source to back Chand's claim, other than the countless articles that use Ashok's word as its only source. While it could very well be true, and the meeting might have taken place in secret, it remains an unverified report with no photographic evidence, even though Berlin was the first live televised sporting event in history, broadcast by two separate television stations. Jesse Owens, who made an even bigger splash with his display at the games, didn't meet Hitler, even though many claim the two shook hands.[134] The 1936 games produced countless still images, and Hitler is photographed with many German athletes, but no photos exist of him with Owens, or Chand, or any athlete that wasn't German.

But this is not even anywhere near the most compelling evidence against all these claims. Chand actually published an autobiography in 1952 titled *GOAL!: Autobiography of Hockey Wizard Dhyan Chand* by Sport & Pastime, Chennai. There is a chapter on the 1936 final, however Chand does not mention the following: refusing to salute Hitler (in fact he said the Germans were great hosts, which many athletes from various countries including the US said), meeting Hitler, or having his stick tested for magnets. This is literally all that he says about what happened after the final game:

"After the closing ceremony, a grand banquet was held in the Deutsche Hall, where as far as I remember Herr Hitler was present. We left the banquet early and boarded a train at Pottsdammer station to commence our post-Olympic tour of the Continent."[135]

The only mythology around the 1936 Berlin Olympics that is actually true involves Roop Singh. At the 1936 tournament, according to Chand's own autobiography Roop scored almost as many goals as Chand, and there is now a street named after him in Munich.[136] This may run contrary to all the hoopla around Chand, given the only verifiable piece of evidence concerning the British Raj's magical 1936 win involves Chand's brother and not himself.

There's no denying that the British Raj beating Nazi Germany in the field hockey final was a huge political victory, but somewhere along the line fact turned into myth. It has all the ingredients of a Hollywood movie, and one can see why some would want to further elevate this story into mythology. When it comes to Singh Sr. however, the Hollywood elements are all there too, but there is no blatant mythicizing; even though his story is ripe for the picking when it comes to Indian heroics.

★★★

It had been less than a year since India had suffered through the bloody civil wars of Partition. Singh Sr. led a sovereign Indian country—mere months from creation—into the Olympics against England, without British Indians, or Muslim players as many had broken off to Pakistan—who themselves would quickly become another field hockey powerhouse. Singh Sr.'s gold at the 1948 Olympics in London was impressive in its political undertones, however this time the villain was far more directly related to the country itself.

India won the final against Great Britain 4-0 with Singh Sr. scoring two goals, however there is no folklore or erroneous reports inflating his contributions, even though the victory was a massive statement for an independent India.[137] One might think this is a bit of a sour note for the British when it comes to field hockey history.[138] The British Raj and Great Britain never competed against one another in competition before or after Partition. Moreover, the game originated in the United Kingdom, and was only introduced to India through British colonization. Once again, all the elements of a Hollywood movie are there, however unlike the inflation of Chand around the 1936 Olympics, Singh Sr.'s accomplishments in 1948 are largely forgotten.

In 2012 Balbir Singh Sr. was honoured at the London Olympics as one of 16 iconic Olympians. Before a match between India and South Korea, Singh Sr. was interviewed by a British journalist about his time with the 1948 Indian team that beat Great Britain to win the final. The interviewee references Singh

Sr. as "something of a hockey legend" who won "three gold medals."[139]

One would think back home in India, this story might get substantial play. The headlines almost write themselves: *Indian field hockey legend returns to former ruler's den*. The political undertones are phenomenally splashy. Singh Sr., playing for a newly independent India, beats Great Britain, then decades later, comes back to English soil to be congratulated and honoured for his achievement, by the Brits themselves.

However the only pieces online from back home are two *Times of India* articles. The first, referenced earlier, is called "Hockey is a poor man's game, says Balbir Singh Sr."[140] in which Singh Sr. is asked about the decline of Indian field hockey over the years. The London 2012 reference ends the article, and Singh Sr. is noted in the lead as a "Legendary hockey player and chief coach of India's 1975 World Cup winning team".

The second is a short Q&A article titled: "Balbir Singh Senior: The performance of the Indian hockey team has shocked me".[141] On top of that, the picture that accompanies that article is not actually of Singh Sr., rather some unknown man in a turban.

Luckily Singh Sr. gets to talk about his time in London in 2012, and points out some rather interesting accomplishments:

"I have been selected to be a part of the 16 all-time great sportspersons of the world. I was accorded the rare honour of representing the Olympic story in an exhibition titled *The Olympic Journey: The Story of the Games* at the Royal Opera House in London from July 28 to August 12. I am the only hockey player in the world to be chosen among 15 other iconic sportspersons such as Jesse Owens of America. It is a real privilege and all thanks to my parents, family, coaches, teachers, teammates and well-wishers. I gratefully share this honour with them all."

Now let's not forget that while London hosted the 2012 Olympics, *The Olympic Journey: The Story of the Games* is an International Olympic Committee endeavour—two completely separate entities. Seems odd that *The Telegraph*'s number one player of all-time didn't even make the IOC's list of both living and deceased athletes when a player with an almost identical career made the top 16. One would think, given the circumstances, that some unknown Sikh couldn't possibly outrank the great Chand when it comes to field hockey selection?

The Brits have many reasons to be pro-Chand/British Raj, and there are a few glaring examples of this bias. During the London 2012 Olympics, the country temporarily renamed some of the tube stations to commemorate famous athletes and Olympians.[142] There's Chand, Roop Singh and Leslie Claudius,[143] an Anglo-Indian who played with Singh Sr. from London to Melbourne, and further won silver in Rome, the games that Singh Sr. was left off the roster.

Singh Sr. did not get a tube station, even though hundreds of stops were renamed, including those for a handful of other field hockey players. Of the 16 iconic Olympians chosen, 15 got a tube station, making Singh Sr. a rather perplexing outlier.

The British have an odd remembrance of India and their days of rule. A recent *Guardian* piece outlines some famous fictitious works from the era, most notably Rudyard Kipling's *Kim*—about a white Irish kid who grows up as a street beggar under the Raj, and believes he is Indian—which came out in 1901.[144] The newspaper piece is drenched in a longing, wistful sentimentality, part of an odd British reminiscence where "colonialism" is debated rather than dismissed outright.[145] There's a sense of nostalgia void of the fact that the British were largely unwanted rulers, of storybook days gone past in which the Raj brought order to an unruly area and took a healthy dose of civility and structure with them when they left. As one might say, leaving India to the Indians.

This odd, awkward marriage between the Brits and the Indians is chronicled extensively, first and arguably most famously in E.M. Forster's 1924 novel *A Passage to India*, in which the two cultures clash during the growing independence movement of the 1920s while trying desperately to achieve friendship, cohesion and understanding of each other's customs and religions.

In the subsequent 1984 Academy Award winning movie based on the book, Dr. Aziz, an educated Indian man who is extremely curious and smitten with the Brits, has a conversation with a fellow Indian colleague named Ali, who is himself incredibly skeptical and argumentative towards British Raj.

"Why do we spend so much time discussing the English?" asks Dr. Aziz.

"Because we admire them, doctor," answers Ali.

"That is the trouble."

The Brits love Chand, as he's seen as a pitch-perfect product of British Raj. Chand recently received the Bharat Gaurav Lifetime Achievement Award, which was awarded to him posthumously and accepted by his son Ashok at the House of Commons inside the British Parliament.[146] Even a recent *The Hindu* piece about the 1948 gold medal match, in which Singh Sr. led the team to victory, features a photo of Dhyan Chand[147] as its main art.

It's getting late, and all this information is swarming my head like an angry beehive, so I retreat to the dusty concrete rooftop in the hot Indian night. My vision lined with dense, dark rows of trees and power lines, a dilapidated playground off to the left side of the house, littered with feral dogs searching for scraps of food. Kabir comes up with a drink, and we sit in the black night discussing the perplexing state of his grandfather's legacy.

The conversation slowly moves to Sikhs, and Kabir runs me through the history, leading with a rather inflammatory statement about his people's treatment throughout the years. "This is a negative way of looking at it," he says almost sheepishly, "but the Sikhs have been neutered."

Sikhs have long been subjugated in the South Asian continent; religiously, culturally and historically forgotten throughout the history of the country. It's an apparent oppression well documented, but one that remains below the surface of the country's international image.

When India finally broke from the British Raj in 1947, the bloodshed of Partition was only the start of a festering wound that plagues the country to this day. After almost 70 years, the India–Pakistani border remains a virtual war zone.[148] Daily shelling is ongoing in the northern Kashmir province, mere miles from where I am staying in Chandigarh.

The schism of India's religious groups has been extensively chronicled, with disastrous flare-ups further compounding instead of healing a wound that should've closed as the country gained independence as a secular nation; the one which Gandhi so famously hoped for before his assassination by a Hindu hardliner.

There was the The Emergency[149] which started in 1975 when then Prime Minister Indira Gandhi declared outright rule in a nation crumbling under political and economic hardship. A tough woman in a political sea of men, she had a grey stripe of hair running atop her head, much like the Bride of Frankenstein. But she was no silly caricature, rather a massive political force to be reckoned with during some of the country's most tumultuous times.

Sikhs were one of the most outspoken vocal minorities to The Emergency, reacting against what they saw as fascist tactics from what was supposed to be a democratically elected government.[150] They protested and marched countless times over a two year period, demanding an end to the gag-like provisions Indira brought forth with no proper discourse or oversight.

Then there was Operation Blue Star,[151] an Indian military operation in June of 1984, ordered by Indira in what some believe was a heavy-handed crackdown to curb dissent amongst Sikhs. In his book *India After Gandhi: The History of the World's Largest Democracy*, Ramachandra Guha explained the intent of Indira's government:

"Operation Bluestar . . . was directed at armed rebels, rather than a peaceable gathering—but its consequences were not dissimilar [than the attack on the Golden Temple in 1919 when British troops fired on a ground of unarmed Indians]. It left a collective wound in the psyche of the Sikhs, crystallizing a deep suspicion of the government of India. The Delhi regime was compared to previous oppressors and desecrators, such as the Mughals, and the eighteenth-century Afghan marauder Ahmad Shah Abdali.

". . . As one elderly Sikh put it, 'Our inner self has been bruised. The base of our faith has been attacked, a whole tradition has been demolished.' Now, even those Sikhs who had previously opposed [Jarnail] Bhindranwale Singh [a vocal Sikh opponent of Indira's heavy-handed rule], began to see him in a new light. For, whatever his past errors and crimes, it was he and his men who had died defending the holy shrine from the vandals."

The army took control of the Harmandir Sahib Complex in Amritsar, Punjab, and killed Bhindranwale and his followers. Less than four months later, Indira was assassinated by two of her Sikh bodyguards in what is widely believed to be an act of revenge for the military takeover. Subsequent anti-Sikh rioting took place, killing thousands of Sikhs, many of whom were dragged into the streets and lit afire. Calls for a separate Punjab nation—Khalistan[152]—have long been a political talking point for Sikhs at home and abroad. Militant Sikhs themselves retaliated with the Air India bombings in 1985, however only one man affiliated with the group has ever been prosecuted.[153]

Even Modi is no stranger to the country's religious schism. His involvement in the 2002 Gujarat riots[154] has long been a black smear across his neatly crafted image, an issue I covered locally when he visited Vancouver for three days of economic talks in April of 2015.[155,156] In 2002, approximately 1,000 Muslims were killed in retaliation after a train carrying Hindu pilgrims was burned in the city of Godhra, however the cause of the fire was never proven. Modi, chief minister of the Indian state at the time, was alleged to have provoked some of the retaliation against the Gujarat Muslim community. In 2012, he was cleared by the Supreme Court of India of any wrongdoing regarding the riots.

My first full day in Chandigarh has been nothing short of extraordinary. Kabir and I retreat down the stairs, and before I head to bed, world weary and ready to pass out for a week or two, he tells me a famous Indian fable. Repeated in multiple cultures, it has a particular sense of resonance in his homeland. My eyes bloodshot, veins swimming with influenza, I lean against the door to my muggy room as he rolls out the story:

An Indian fisherman is transporting a ship full of crabs by sea to sell. He does not cover the crates that house the crabs. A new worker, green to the whole process on the boat notices this, and rushes to tell the fisherman.

AUSTERITY GAMES

"I tell them that if they would only read the *Mahabharata* and the *Ramayana*, study the Golden Ages of the Mauryas and the Guptas and even of those Muslim chaps the Mughals, they would realize that India is not an underdeveloped country but a highly developed one in an advanced state of decay."

~ Shashi Tharoor

In 1928, the first National Championship of Indian field hockey took place. Held every two years until 1944, when it became a yearly competition, the nationals started off as a loosely organized gathering of the best of the best. In India, club teams were predominately divided into various companies and government arms—Indian Railways, Indian Airlines, Punjab Police, the Calcutta Port Commissioners, the Nagpur Railway team. But for the National Championships, various club members came together to form multiple star-studded all-star squads.

As one can imagine, pre-Partition, the tournament was far from regimented, or properly organized, but it still managed to bring out the cream of the country's talented field hockey crop. India was a plump breeding ground for field hockey players, like ice hockey in Canada or baseball in the Dominican Republic; woven deep into its self-identity. Every boy growing up wanted to be superstar centre forward Dhyan Chand, combing their hair neatly, carrying wooden sticks and balls through the cramped alleys and dusty streets of Delhi, Bombay and everywhere in between. You couldn't go more than a few blocks without encountering a makeshift game on a flat patch of dirt.

These boys all wanted to lead their new country to international glory, to bask in the glowing fame of superstardom. But only one man in a nation of hundreds of millions, a man still in his early 20s, would get the chance to live out this iconic dream. He would do it despite mounting hurdles at every turn, and despite the snake-like system of backstabbers and jealousy surrounding him, nefarious creatures who either wanted a piece of his fame, or wanted nothing more than for him to fail miserably.

The Indian Hockey Federation did not have an official trophy for the finals of the National Championship—instead using a shield that had been won by an All-Indian team that had traveled to New Zealand sometime in the 1940s. Presented to them by their Maori opponents, the trophy came home and became the de facto symbol of excellence.

The IHF itself had been born out of the British Raj's push to include field hockey at the 1928 Olympics in Amsterdam. But the IHF was marred in endless controversy from the outset, as the two captains chosen for the 1928 British Raj squad were Indians living in England at the time. Jaipal Singh, one of the leaders, upset over backlash from the Anglo-Indians, actually walked off the team during the Olympics due to racially motivated infighting.[157]

Now the Punjab state squad was giving the shield a new home in the north of the country. The multi-ethnic team, led by Singh Sr. captured the trophy in 1946 and 1947, right up until Partition. But here again the bloody civil war destroyed what many Indians had spent so much energy creating. The shield ended up in Lahore at the headquarters of the Punjab Hockey Association, and after Partition the West Punjab Authorities refused to return it across the newly made international line. This led the Indian Hockey Federation to get their own trophy—the Rangaswamy Cup, donated by an editor of *The Hindu* newspaper.

The British departure from India meant Sir John Bennett—the tyrannical ruler of the Punjab Police—was gone. Sant Prakash Singh became Punjab's first Indian Inspector General of Police. Along with Ashwini Kumar, Singh Sr. credits these two for slowly bringing the club team out of the ashes after Partition gutted their roster from the inside out. Ashwini, a tall, slender man who had distinctly Anglo-Saxon features including a long, straight nose and cascading tide of jet black hair, was the perfect administrator. He knew how to glad-hand, strike up a conversation, and pull together various groups when all seemed lost.[158]

The Punjab police team had lost their starting goaltender, left-half, inside-right, inside-left and left extreme as the Muslim players retreated to Pakistan. Now they desperately needed help recruiting fresh blood.

A new Punjab Hockey Association was formed around the same time Singh Sr. was promoted to Sub-Inspector and posted to Ferozepore. Singh Sr. headed to Ambala with the rest of the

Punjab state team—consisting mostly of the Punjab police squad team members—to train and practice for the 1948 National Championships in Bombay. At 24 years old, Singh Sr. was atop his game, leading a ramshackle squad hoping to reclaim past glory.

However they would not fare well at the 1948 National Championships, losing in the early rounds, an embarrassing exit for such a prestigious unit. The loss had a disastrous effect on Singh Sr. personally, as he was dropped from the list of 39 players selected to attend trials before the 1948 London Olympics, now only months away. Two other players on the Punjab team were also left off, leading to a fierce debate between the local and national newspapers, which were divided by religious lines.

"There was a hue and a cry in the press against our omission," says Singh Sr. noting the Sikh newspapers did everything they could to bring the issue to light.

Having won the National Championship the two years previous, and having been chosen by the IHF for a national touring team before the unrest unfolded, Singh Sr. should've still been a shoo-in for the 39, but now different elements were at play. Without the Raj, the country had been left asunder, the ruling government had literally picked up and left unceremoniously. Of course independence was a much-needed change, but Indians now found themselves unprepared to run a sovereign nation.[159]

Devastated by being cut, Singh Sr. headed back to Ferozepore, made sullen by the realization that his Olympic dream of mimicking his hero Dhyan Chand was over. When asked today why he was left off the original 39, Singh Sr. has a tough time answering.

"Well I can't say anything, what was the reason . . . maybe some players had some influence and they . . . I don't know, that's the best answer. It is maybe known to them."

He continued to play for the police team, but something was missing, his soul void of purpose. All those long days on the pitches in Moga, the endless practices at Khalsa College, they could do nothing to change his stature amongst the national governing body. Was this his fate, to play nationally, work as a police officer, and wait for retirement to come knocking? Were all the dreams he'd had as a kid simply wishful thinking?

Then a week later, while playing an intra-squad match at Ferozepore's Hearne Park, Singh Sr. received a telegram. He headed off the pitch, wiped the sweat from his brow and put down his stick, catching his breath in the steamy Indian sun. He opened the letter, from A.C. Chatterjee, the secretary of the IHF.

"I had been invited to camp, and I was so happy," Singh Sr. recalls. He dropped everything and boarded the next train to Bombay. He could barely sit still the whole ride, the Indian landscape rolling by out the window as the train took him closer and closer to his dream.

Richard Johnny Carr, a member of the 1932 British Raj squad who dominated the Los Angeles Olympics, and Habul Mukherjee, who had played with and against Chand, were running the camp. Singh Sr. never inquired why he was added, dropped, then added again; he was just happy to be there competing for a spot on the historic team. This was not British Raj field hockey, this was Indian field hockey, and a chance for a new generation of players to make a name for themselves after Partition and the Second World War.

But elation soon turned to frustration. The camp in Bombay was a vicious affair. At stake were 20 positions on the first ever independent Indian squad. Adding another element, it was rainy season and the fields were slippery—a fine gravel laid below the turf came to the surface when wet—forcing many players to forgo shoes altogether. Drenched and covered in wet dirt, the players duked it out in the worst conditions possible. Winning a spot would not come without pain and strife.

Singh Sr. was forced out of his usual position, moving to inside-left, a spot he'd never played in his life. He also had a target on his back; as one of the late additions, he was seen as a threat to those who'd spent weeks cementing their spot on the team. During one particularly rough scrimmage, Nandi Singh, who Singh Sr. played with at Punjab University, came in full force, smashing his head into Singh Sr.'s rib cage in what he believes was a deliberate attempt to injure him. Nandi would blame the rain, saying he slipped, but looking back on the event now, Singh Sr. says that probably was not the case.

"People thought that was intentional, to put me out of action. Maybe they were trying to take credit away from me."

Singh Sr. tried to play through it, but the pain of multiple cracked ribs was too much. Hospitalized for a number of days, he would not travel with the squad to Sri Lanka, instead forced to stay in Bombay to nurse his injury. It was a lonely few nights at the Bombay hospital, left with nothing but gritted teeth, frustrated thoughts and throbbing ribs.

Doctors suggested he take a few weeks or even a month to rest up, but Singh Sr. was having none of this. He wrapped his mid-section tightly in cloth bandages, walked back out on the field and clenched his jaw to hide the pain.

Broken ribs be damned, he wasted no time in impressing all the coaching staff, and after a while it was basically a formality: he was named as one of the 20 players who would represent a newly independent India at the Summer Olympics.

The death of Gandhi was still fresh on the minds of Indians. They had lost their beloved hero; a global symbol of independence, freedom and non-violent resistance shot three times in the chest by a religious hardliner who blamed him for Hindus' suffering before and during Partition.

Across the sea, London was literally in shambles from the Blitz attacks of the Second World War: a sea of rubble, bricks in piles and shelled buildings. The fight against Hitler and Nazi Germany brought the European continent to its knees; countries reduced to wreckage, families displaced, hundreds of thousands dead. Food was scarce, supplies were hard to come by, and many starved as everyone tried to pick up the pieces.

But war be damned, the Brits were going to host the Olympics, garnering an iconic name in the process—the Austerity Games.[160]

Wembley Stadium, originally built in 1923, was converted to an Olympic venue by putting close to 1,000 tons of cinders over the greyhound track. There was no Olympic village to house the athletes, so they stayed in Royal Air Force camps and public schools around the city.[161] Families also hosted athletes so they could have hot meals, and most of the workers went unpaid. The games were a sign of international resilience, proof that although dark and sinister forces had tried to shake the world to its core, good would persevere and live on.

Jack Braughton, who famously competed in the 5,000 metres after a half day's work and a tube and bus ride to the stadium, typified the working-class attitude of the games.[162] Although the entire country was in economic turmoil, it was a warm summer in the capital city, offering a sunny reprieve from the lack of services for athletes and spectators alike.

While Germany and Japan were banned from participating, the rest of the world cobbled together their best, managing to field 3,714 men and 390 women for 17 sports from 59 competing nations. These Olympics were broadcast on television, meaning the spotlight was fully visualized and ready to produce some post-war heroes.

Before he'd left, Singh Sr.'s father had sent him stern letters on how to conduct himself as a proper gentleman abroad. Meanwhile he and his wife Sushil were expecting their first baby. The family was excited he'd been chosen by the squad, but Singh Sr. did not even have time to return home to celebrate or say goodbye before being whisked onto a plane and off to the world's theatre for all to see.

★★★

The Indian men's field hockey team for the 1948 Olympics was a stacked all-star squad. Donning the baby blue uniforms to represent the blue Ashoka Chakra in the middle of the Indian flag and the white shorts that have become their symbolic colours, they were incredibly skilled and immediately intimidating. At each position was the best player in the country, from right back up to centre forward. Singh Sr.—the only player from Punjab and one of three Sikhs—would join the likes of vice-captain K.D. Singh Babu, a flamboyant, sometimes argumentative leader and right-winger Kishan Lal from the Railways squad, who was quiet and unassuming off the pitch, but incredibly fierce on it. More importantly, Singh Sr. was one of three centre forwards chosen for the line-up.

Two weeks before the games were set to begin on July 29th, the Indian team touched down at Heathrow Airport. Dressed in his police uniform with an epaulette—his father demanded he travel in style—Singh Sr. walked off the plane into a country that had ruled, oppressed and subjugated him, his family and friends, and driven his father to political rebellion. Now he was an independent Indian, a free man in a free country. The thoughts swirled endlessly through his head; of politics, religion and ethnicity. This was more than a sporting tournament, it was a political sign of a new planet, one that had endured a Second World War; trying on peace after hardship had dominated the first half of the twentieth century.

Singh Sr. tried to keep the nightmarish images of Partition out of his psyche. He needed to focus solely on field hockey. Hundreds of white Britons surrounded him; the very people he saw as his oppressors, those who had helped drive his homeland into civil war and bloodshed, now greeting him as a visitor. The complexities almost too much to bear, he tries in vain to explain the situation as he set foot in London:

"War-ravaged England was just beginning to re-emerge. With the grant of freedom to a number of colonies the cliche that the 'sun never sets on the British Empire' was no longer tenable. The Britons were in a phase of reconstruction. Yet they did an excellent job of organizing the London games at such short notice. Those were the days of strict rationing in England. Disciplined as they always are, Britons never took more than what was necessary for each man; yet there was no shortage of food in our Olympic kitchens—this gave us an insight into the British character. It was no wonder that Hitler's mighty forces were never able to overrun Britain in the worst days of the war . . . The Britons had been our rulers for 200 years. But the men we met in London were poles apart from the image of tough rulers that we knew back home. They in fact went all out to befriend us."

While still on the tarmac, not even in the terminal, Singh Sr. was greeted by one of these friendly Brits, a character from his past—Sir John Bennett. The man who had sent two police officers to Delhi to track him down, handcuff him, force him to become a police officer and play for his club team, was now smiling in his face like a long lost friend. In fact, Bennett opened his arms, walked up and hugged Singh Sr., something that caught the quiet Sikh off-guard: it would have never happened under the British Raj.

"One must give full credit to the Britons in this regard," Singh Sr. muses. "They can be the best of friends and the worst of rulers."

Bennett regarded him as a prized possession, he added—a hand-picked player from the chaos that was India pre-Partition, anointed by him and thus destined for greater things.

"He looked at me and said 'Welcome to London. Are you happy to see me?' I was polite, I was in no place or regard to do something other than smile."

Singh Sr. exchanged pleasantries with Bennett, and following his father's wishes, acted as a consummate professional. Bennett on the other hand, paraded Singh Sr. around the airport, telling anyone who would listen that he had chosen this young Sikh boy for Indian field hockey glory.

Yet Bennett proved to be a valuable addition to the team's preparation. He told Singh Sr. the pitches in England were heavily turfed and thus much slower, which meant you could not wait for the ball. This information proved crucial in helping Singh Sr. prepare for the pace of play, knowing he would have to make his own magic rather than wait for long passes down a sparsely seeded turf.

After settling into a school outside the city, Singh Sr. and the team came into London for the opening ceremonies. Singh Sr. said it was almost too much to comprehend, how the Brits were waiting on *them*, helping *them* prepare for the ceremonies, welcoming *them* as stars.

"To go from such a modest village to what was the biggest city in the world. A former ruler—it was so amazing and thrilling for all of us. We were really surprised to see rulers become hosts," he says.

July 29 was a sunny day, perfect to host the Opening Ceremonies. Clear blue skies draped the horizon. Atop Wembley Stadium seating was a quote from Baron de Couberton, the founder of the International Olympic Committee: "The important thing in the Olympic Games is not winning but taking part. The essential thing in life is not conquering but fighting well."

Most of the 80,000 spectators wore white. Boy Scouts lined the grassy portion separating fans from athletes. As per tradition, Greece led the procession of competitors into the arena. India was introduced as the new dominion of India, with Singh Sr. and 78 fellow Indians donning blue blazers and white dress pants. The royal proclamation commenced, and 7,000 pigeons were released signalling that the games had begun, circling the athletes in the centre of the field before lifting off into the London sky as if part of the choreography.

It was here at the fourteenth modern Olympics that Singh Sr. would first see some of his former friends and teammates, now part of the dominion of Pakistan, dressed in green blazers, white dress pants and light green turbans. He noticed the Pakistanis were doing everything in their power to avoid the Indian athletes.[163] Tensions were high, a deep-seated wedge between the two nations as the peaceful ceremonies unfolded. Singh Sr. notes three friends in particular who left during Partition: Ali Iqtidar Shah Dara, Mohammad Niaz Khan and Shazada Muhammad Shahrukh. There would be no reconciliation, or even a chance to catch up. Lines had been drawn.

"I saw them, but they did not look at me. We did not make eye contact."

More recently in history, Sushbir reconnected with Shahrukh's daughter via Facebook. Shahrukh, who has since passed away, made the journey from Pakistan to India where he met up with Singh Sr. in his living room some 50 years after Partition. A photo shows the two embracing, temporarily allowed to toss away the terrible past and deep religious lines that separates their two nations.

After a few practice matches on thick grass fields around the city, the Indian team was ready to go. They were set to play at the Guinness Sports Club in the densely populated suburb of Park Royal.[164] But Singh Sr. would not find his name on the starting 11. Instead, his slot was given to Reginald Rodrigues. The Sikh hid his disappointment; his father had told him it was an honour to be there, and that he was not only representing himself, but his country, and should remain professional at all times.

India would make short work of an organized but outgunned Austrian squad 8-0, however Rodrigues would only notch one of the eight tallies, odd for the centre-forward position.

Between games some of the players were invited into the homes of the British, offered meals by a populace still barely scraping by. Singh Sr. says the people he met were nothing short of remarkable, showing them around the town, giving them food when they themselves had little—this was not the Britain he had known. The stark difference an odd pill to swallow.

Two days later, the Indian squad returned to the Sports Club and suited up against Argentina. Singh Sr. had been keeping a keen eye on Rodrigues all day, as he'd been sniffling and coughing up a storm. Sweaty and disorientated, he looked barely able to stand, much less start as centre forward at the Olympic Games.

This was his chance, Singh Sr. thought. He kept his emotions in check, and after verifying the roster which was in his favour, jogged out onto the pitch, hair wrapped in a white handkerchief, the call echoing through his head much like he'd imagined as a little boy watching a newsreel of Dhyan Chand playing for the British Raj in Germany.

"Now starting at centre forward, Balbir Singh!"

Singh Sr. says he was more than ready to put politics and favouritism aside for the chance to do what he did best: score goals.

"When I got the chance, I proved it. I proved I was a capable player."

While Argentina had a decent field hockey team, they were no match for India, and no match for Singh Sr. in particular. The

Sikh boy from the Punjab had arrived, and he wasted no time in showing the world he belonged on the main stage.

Two hat-tricks. *Six* goals in total, for a 9-1 victory.

After the game, Singh Sr. was the talk of the field hockey scene, with many of his teammates patting him on the back and praising his impressive show of skill. Six goals was impossible to ignore, he thought to himself. He'd surely cemented his spot as the starting centre forward of the team on merit alone, regardless if the man he replaced was sick or not.

Singh Sr. could barely sleep that night in his cot. Each goal played out in his head, the sound of the ball hitting the twine, the fans erupting, the feeling of inner joy. He could barely contain himself, tossing and turning in a twirl of sheets; buzzing with excitement; he knew his entire country was back home listening on every available radio.

Two days later India would head back to the stadium to suit up against Spain. Singh Sr. had a spry bounce to his step, a quiet swagger; he was thirsty, hungry, ravenous for more goals for his homeland. He wanted more tallies, another win and another step towards the once unfathomable dream—an Olympic gold for an independent India.

He checked the roster, saw his name on the starting 11. He slid on his cleats and his shin pads, unwrapped his turban and tied his hair up in a bun. But as he headed out to the field to start warming up on the pitch, captain Kishan La stopped him, looking oddly defeated.

"He was a humble player, and he was almost embarrassed to tell me that I would not be playing," Singh Sr. says.

Starting in Singh Sr.'s position would be Nandi Singh—the same player who'd tried to injure him at the Bombay training camp. Nandi's uncle, a wealthy businessman from Calcutta had pulled some strings and lobbied co-manager Pankaj Gupta to play his nephew. Singh Sr. remained stoic and headed to the bench almost in a daze.

"Nandi?" he thought. "But I am much better than him."

"These incidents could have taken the wind out of any youngster," he wrote in his autobiography. "Exclusion from the team did not bother me much; the brusque manner in which I was virtually pulled out at the last moment irked me."

He watched from the bench, heart rate slowing exponentially. India scored, but then Spain pushed back with a flurry of counterattacks. His teammates were sending pass after pass to Nandi, but he could do little with the offerings. He fumbled the ball, committed turnovers and fired his shots wide. Singh Sr. watched from the bench, gripping his stick tight, thinking of all the good things he could be doing with those beautiful passes.

India would be forced to squeak out a 2-0 win over a squad that was never supposed to challenge them. Nandi looked so out of place at centre forward it was almost an embarrassment to the team.

Singh Sr. kept to himself, not wanting to cause a stir or ruffle feathers about whether or not he should have been playing. Having only suited up for one of the three round robin games, he still led the team in scoring and figured this would play in his favour in the post-game discussions.

India had won their group, which meant playing the wild card seed from the three other groups. Great Britain and Pakistan had also won their tables; the Brits tying the Swiss in a nil-nil draw, the only blemish on either team's record. India's path to gold would now go through the Netherlands, who had won three of their group stage games, but lost to Pakistan 6-1.

Much to his surprise, when he looked at the starting 11 for the semi-final match against Holland, Singh Sr. found his name at centre forward. He headed out to the pitch. But moments before the face-off, when he was already on the field in front of all the fans, Lal came to him again, sheepishly. "He said 'Sorry brother, you won't play, very sorry'," Singh Sr. recalls.

The embarrassment of being taken off the pitch in front of the fans at Wembley Stadium was almost unbearable, but Singh Sr. credits his mental toughness for his ability to not make a scene. With a depressed, sinking feeling—as if he was dropping to the bottom of the ocean—he placed himself on the bench, stick between his legs, and watched his country play a sudden death match for the right to go to the final.

In his place was Gerry Glacken, a player from the Bengal area, a Hindu stronghold in the east of the country. The Netherlands proved to be pesky opponents, and India barely squeaked out another 2-1 victory. An exhausted, exasperated breath left the collective nation; they had won, and would now play for gold. Glacken scored one of the goals, but did little to instil a sense of fear at centre forward. India was a great team, a favourite to win it all, but they were like a chess board missing one queen, the most formidable attacking piece at the tip of their spear.

After the semi-final, unbeknownst to Singh Sr., outside powers were being set in motion to clear some air in The Big Smoke. A handful of Indian medical students studying at Oxford University had had enough. They'd watched the game against the Netherlands and were distraught over the poor line-up. They knew Indian hockey better than any spectator, and they knew one man was the answer.

They'd heard and read stories about the quiet Sikh who was an up-and-coming phenomenon back home. They'd seen what he could do in person: two hat tricks, a defiant slice right through the heart of the opponent's defence. They'd made up their minds. If India was going to beat Great Britain in the finals, they needed this Sikh on the pitch.

The group went to V.K. Krishna Menon, India's first High Commissioner in London, and demanded Singh Sr. start at centre forward. Menon did not take much convincing. He'd watched all the games live, and immediately agreed with the group. He went to IHF management, who could not speak against a noted international dignitary.

Great Britain had defeated Pakistan 2-0 in the other semi-final, showcasing their superior talent against the other nation created via Partition. Would they do the same to their Indian counterparts, winning gold at home and proving that field hockey was still England's sport? That the skill of the British Raj traveled home with them when they handed the country over to the lowly locals? Here were the oppressed, returning to the vast walls of the ruler's den where they would have a chance for sporting revenge.

On the day of the gold medal match, a light drizzle trickled onto the field, wetting the sloppy turf. Two players from the Indian squad would go shoeless in hopes of getting better grip. It would be a slippery affair; a gritty, dirty game where the elements would be playing in no man's favour.

Singh Sr., being pushed and pulled off the field like a yo-yo, was a nervous wreck. Would he play in the gold medal game, or be pulled due to the machinations of outside influence? He remained as mentally intact as possible, offering a quiet prayer to the gods that they would simply grant him the chance to play.

When he looked at the starting line-up, he contained his excitement, quickly pushing it away. Slated to start at centre forward, he knew this did not guarantee anything. He shoulder checked constantly as he walked onto the pitch, almost as if Lal might jump from some random bush to deliver more bad news.

Finally, the first whistle blew. He'd made it. Back to business. In the early days, no substitutions were allowed once the game had begun, meaning he had all of 70 minutes to work his magic.

Princess Elizabeth was in attendance, and the stands were jam-packed with Brits. Singh Sr. descended into his zone; his blood flowed with rivers of victory. '*This* was his time, *his* moment,' he thought. Now was the opportunity to prove his worth, to mimic his hero Dhyan Chand and chisel his name atop the field hockey world. He took a deep breath, then darted towards the Brit's backline with gusto.

Seven minutes in, Singh Sr. shot down the right wing chasing a long pass, and rifled the ball into the top corner over netminder David Brodie, his first touch of the ball. 1-0 India.

He did not celebrate, just turned and jogged back to line up at centre. There would be no celebration, only stoicism mixed with intensity. He was just getting started. He wanted to punish the Brits on the field. The only thing that was going to stop him from scoring would be the final whistle.

It was clear to see India were the better team, as they pressured and pounded towards the Brits in the rain, relentlessly going for goal. Singh Sr. was the tip of the spear, and it wasn't long before the Brits were all over him. But it would not suffice.

Fifteen minutes in, he took a pass from the side of the net and roofed his second goal of the game, leaving Brodie looking frustrated as he tried to stop what was an impossible shot.

He was on pace to score six, or more. A legend was literally being made before the crowd's eyes. Then vice-captain Babu, for whatever reason, rushed up from defence during a stoppage in play.

"He said to me that I needed to come back and help defend. I did not understand but I did what I was told."

Singh Sr. invariably became the team's second centre half, and they would score no more goals before the halftime whistle. He did not ask Babu why he was told to defend instead of lead the attack, but looking back on it now, he believes the decision was rooted in personal jealousy.

"He did not want me to score more, so he forced me to play defence."

The second half started, and now India were a wall. With Singh Sr. now at the holding midfield position, they had no central striker but were dominating the middle of the pitch.

He watched as two of his fellow teammates scored from various outside positions. Gold was so close, they could taste it.

The final whistle blew, 4-0 India over Great Britain.

The applause was formal. The Indians jumped for joy.

When asked what this meant for his country and for every Indian who had tasted the bitter pill that was Partition and Raj rule, Singh Sr. cracks a mischievous smile.

"We had beaten our old masters, so naturally we were very happy."

Right after the match, Menon came running down to the pitch and elbowed his way into the team photo. He told Singh Sr. what had happened, of the lobbying he'd done along with the medical students. Singh Sr. says he is eternally grateful, and forever in debt to a handful of Indians studying abroad.

Pat Rowley, a field hockey historian and writer based out of London, was 13 when the finals were played at Wembley, and actually penned a piece for his local newspaper from a schoolboy's perspective after the match.

"I remember how India walked all over Great Britain on a terrible pitch," says Rowley. "Our guys had never played together before and were used to pristine grass pitches. India probably became great because they learnt the game on rough grassless tracks. Balbir was superb that day."

The *Indian Express* ran a piece titled India Wins Fourth Olympic Hockey Championship.[165] One can acknowledge that journalism in the 1940s was not the best, but this article is interesting for a number of reasons. Written by Alex Valentine, a Reuter's special correspondent, Balbir Singh Sr. is mentioned in the article as G. Singh (apparently Nandi Singh was originally scheduled to play) and is nowhere near the headline, lede or even the first four or five paragraphs. Considering he scored the game winner and half his team's goals, one might think Singh Sr. should've been in the headline.

After the team received their medals, Menon invited the entire squad to a reception at India House in London. Singh Sr. was still in shock, an Olympic gold medal hanging from his neck. Born in a dark mud hut with no power, now he was an Olympic champion and India's leading goal scorer to boot—despite only playing in two of the five matches. He'd notched all the decisive tallies in the first Olympic gold medal final of the new era.

Before the victory could even register mentally, the team were .shipped out on a goodwill tour by train to France, Czechoslovakia and Switzerland to play games against local teams for two weeks. Singh Sr. has only a few memories of the trip, largely because he was still buzzing from the win in London, still trying to wrap his head around what his country had accomplished. Then they returned to England, boarded a ship in Liverpool Harbour, and headed for home.

It would be 26 fidgety days at sea, winding their way around Africa down south to Bombay. Singh Sr. would periodically head to the viewing deck to watch the beet red horizon. Once again dressed in his Olympic blazer, his travel bag now heavier with some metallic hardware. The setting sun dipped below the sea, and inside he knew everything had changed. He had left the country as an unknown, and would now be coming back a national hero.

When the ship finally reached its destination, they had to wait another day as it was low tide. Singh Sr. said he could see the celebrations already starting from the port, the people waiting for them to dock so the party could really begin.

As soon as he left the ship, Singh Sr. and his teammates were hoisted overhead and carried like heroes; chants bouncing off their eardrums as everyone clamoured around to try and touch those who had been blessed by the gods.

"We were swept off our feet and it was here that I realized what victory meant to our nation, starved as it is of world class accomplishments. Hockey was the only sport that gave the country something of a ray of golden hope, something to shout about."

He even partook in a little celebrating himself.

"While I was very shy, I couldn't help myself and danced a little bit in Bombay."

After Bombay, the team was ushered to Delhi where President Rajendra Prasad and Prime Minister Nehru oversaw a ceremonial match at the national stadium. The Indian Olympic team would play an All-India squad—the best of the rest. The crowd was raucous, overflowing the venue, people literally climbing over one another to get a look at the greatest field hockey team in the world.

The final score was 1-0 for the Olympians, with Singh Sr. notching the only tally. After the match, the fans surrounded the team again, lifting them up. In the commotion Singh Sr. ripped his Olympic blazer.

"I was not used to being picked up so much, it was tiresome after a while."

Nehru personally congratulated each player, telling them the next goal was already set: gold in Helsinki in four years. He took a special liking to Singh Sr. and arranged for the police officer to look after two of his grandchildren for a few weeks at Shimla, obviously hoping his skill would rub off on them. As the head of security for the two children, Singh Sr. accompanied them around and showed them some of the tricks of the hockey trade.

One of the children was Sanjay Gandhi, the second son of Indira and Feroze Gandhi. He was widely expected to succeed his mother as Prime Minister of India but died in a plane crash. The other was Rajiv Gandhi, the eldest son of Indira and Feroze Gandhi, who became the seventh Prime Minister of India as a result of Indira's death. Rajiv met his own untimely fate, assassinated by a suicide bomber in 1991.

Finally the Delhi parties died down and Singh Sr. got the green light to return home. He headed to Moga, where his very pregnant wife and father were staying. The entire village held a reception for their hometown hero. The little boy from Dev Samaj, the young vandal who had broken their windows before sprinting away on guilty feet, was now wearing Olympic gold from the world's most prestigious city.

Arches were set up across the street adorned with his name, and people pushed and shoved to touch him, reaching out with their hands, calling out his name like a celebrity.

"Balbir! Balbir! Do you remember me?" he recalls hearing.

At times, Singh Sr. said, the attention became overwhelming. He rode an open van throughout town, people raced up to the vehicle to toss garlands, flower petals and confetti. They shouted in unison for hours on end: "Balbir Ki Jai (victory be)! Balbir Ki Jai! Balbir Ki Jai."

They ended up at the school, and his father escorted him up the podium at the auditorium. There were countless speeches, but Singh Sr. said he had trouble remembering what was said.

"I don't remember what words they used to praise me. I only saw myself as a little boy, suddenly grown big, still touching the feet (a sign of respect in Indian culture) of the grown-ups, seeking their blessings."

Then it was back to Ferozepore Cantonment, and work as a police officer, but he couldn't shake one thought. Back in Moga were two of his chums and fellow players, Azam and Shivdev from Dev Samaj school. Both formidable hockey players in their own regard, they never made it out of Moga, and never found the success he did. When he saw them after his Olympic medal win, he knew they were happy, but he also saw the hidden sorrow, of two similar dreams snuffed out by the hard Indian lifestyle. Singh Sr. knew he was grateful, and knew taking all this for granted would be of great disservice to his two childhood classmates.

The celebrations continued at Ferozepore. Deputy Commissioner G.S. Kahlon and senior superintendent of Police A.K. Kaul threw their star police officer a lavish reception. Singh Sr. hadn't even gotten off the train from Moga before he was showered in more garlands and applause. They also laid down a red carpet and played traditional Indian music. All the attention was embarrassing at times he said, but he hid valiantly behind a smile and an endless wave. He was the king of the Indian sporting world.

The country had puffed up its chest, beaten its former occupiers in a show of personal, national and sovereign might. Sanjiv Dosanjh is the programme executive for All India Radio based out of Chandigarh and a friend of Singh Sr.'s. All India Radio is the country's public broadcaster and largest station, broadcasting to all corners of the country. Looking back on the sporting achievements of the country, Dosanjh says it's tough not to rank the London gold as possibly India's greatest ever, even though it happened within a year of independence.

"I did a radio show a few years back where I said that India's win in 1948 was the greatest Indian sporting achievement of all time, and at that time, was the biggest even to date for the young country."

But of course, in sports, you're only as good as your last win, and everyone was already talking about the next goal: Finland, and a chance to repeat.

***

"Don't rest on your oars," says Dalip Singh, Balbir's father as he holds his grown son's shoulders in front of him. "You must continue what you have started for the good of the nation."

The two men are standing in the living room of Singh Sr.'s home in Ferozepore. Off in another room are the women of the household, a very pregnant Sushil, who was about to give birth at any moment to Balbir's first child.

Dalip is trying to tell his son that one gold medal is nice, but two? Well, that would be something else. He is proud of his son, but can only show his love through stern encouragement.

Singh Sr. nods, still a boy in his own home. While outside of his father's company, he is a decorated Olympian, here he is still a child in need of direction.

Singh Sr.'s father would head back to Moga, and Singh Sr. would start the task of amassing the new Punjab Police team for the season ahead. It was November 1948, and the nation had come down with a case of field hockey hysteria. Now recruitment was more of a filtering out process than a search. Everyone who could hold a stick wanted in to the police squad. Men such as Dharam Singh, Udham Singh and Bakshish Singh, all established players with big aspirations, were already pencilled in for Helsinki. The lineup was crammed with speed, skill and youthful exuberance.

Singh Sr. headed to Delhi with his police force and state teammates for their first tournament of the season. The Punjabi men washed over the competition like a talented wave, winning gold and earning Singh Sr. MVP honours. But there were other things on Singh Sr.'s mind. After the tournament he got another telegram, from the Ferozepore Cantonment. His daughter Sushbir had been born on December 21, 1948.

Ashwini gave Singh Sr. some good news on the job front, the reluctant policeman who had literally been handcuffed into the job had now been promoted to inspector and posted to the Punjab Armed Police headquarters in Jullundur Cantonment, a bigger city farther away from the notorious and newly minted India–Pakistani border.

But his child was his first priority, and Singh Sr. rushed back to Ferozepore. He was a father, and a proud one at that. He held his daughter in his hands, his own little fleshy gold medal. While female births were then seen as tragedies, Singh Sr. was celebrating like he'd just captured another Olympic medal. What more could one man want? Olympic gold, a healthy baby, and a new, high paying, comfortable government job. Life was good.

As 1949 rolled around, the Punjab Police team looked unbeatable. At the Aga Khan Gold Cup, a field hockey tournament in

Bombay that still runs to this day, Singh Sr.'s team ripped through their competitors like a sharp sword. Punjabi men had long gained a reputation as tough opponents. They were boys in men's bodies; big, burly, but mobile and shifty. They pushed and shoved competitors off the ball, 11 power forwards at various positions, heads wrapped in buns and handkerchiefs to cover the top-knot.

Sarpal Singh, who played against Singh Sr. in India many times from 1948 onwards, spoke about the Punjab state squad. The 85-year-old now splits his time between Seattle where his son runs a software company and India, and said he will always remember a goal that Singh Sr. scored against his club team in 1949.

"He was falling to the ground, and he was able to flick his stick to hit the ball, and it went straight into the top corner. He had been pushed, but he still managed to score, while falling down and running at the same time, it was quite an amazing feat."

Sarpal added on top of the highlight reel goal, Singh Sr. was a ferocious opponent, and he got the chance to play with him in a few exhibition matches.

"He had such a strong wrist. It was such a bullish shot."

Now the 1949 Nationals had been set, and Singh Sr. was a lock as captain for the Punjab State team. The only question was whether they would win it all—their first chance at national redemption after their poor showing in 1948.

"Though I was only 25 I was already something of a veteran with five national appearances under my belt," says Singh Sr. "With the cream of the talent and hockey 'brain trust' opting to stay on in Lahore, we had begun from scratch. And at that young age I was entrusted with the task of coaching the boys, all of them almost my age."

Singh Sr. drew on Harbail Singh, who had groomed him personally at Khalsa College, and he had Tarlochan Singh by his side, one of the other three Punjabis to win gold at London. The two were the backbone of the young squad, set to face other provinces such as Bengal, who were boasting as many as nine Olympians on their team.

Singh Sr. would also line up against the man between the pipes for India—Ranganandhan Francis who played for Madras. In the round robin game, the Indian netminder somehow managed to keep Singh Sr. and the entire Punjab state team off the scoresheet. He stood on his head as Singh Sr. pelted balls at him with relentless ferocity. But then the playoffs came and Singh Sr. would not be denied a second time. Punjab toppled the Francis wall and won 7-0, with Singh Sr. netting four goals.

Then it was Bhopal, another formidable opponent, for a berth against Bengal, which boasted four Indian Olympians to Punjab's two.

But the Singh Sr. era had begun. The youthful exuberance of a young, fit Punjab squad would win national gold, and Singh Sr. would capture tournament MVP, almost as a foregone conclusion.

He was the nation's golden boy, whether the nation liked it, or not.

★★★

The Indian Hockey Federation, established in 1928, had suddenly gone from fringe organization to the centre of the nation's sporting world. It had produced a gold medal squad, and it wasn't long before the rampant corruption and graft that plagues the nation to this day bubbled to the surface of the sport's governing body.

The Punjab Hockey Association was raising alarm bells: 70,000 rupees had gone missing under the watch of the IHF's treasurer. The IHF president called an emergency meeting in Bombay, and after an arduous investigation, the funds were reclaimed from the disgraced treasurer. The PHA was also irked about how the IHF was choosing the Indian touring teams for tournaments abroad. A single three man panel had been selected, and the Punjab contingency of field hockey players were getting the short end of the proverbial stick in favour of hometown players in places like Madras, Bombay and Delhi.

While Singh Sr. and the other three Sikh Olympians were inevitable conclusions, the PHA was crying foul that other promising young Punjabis were being left off the roster. The IHF had put together a squad for a tour of Afghanistan and Kenya, and although close to a dozen Sikhs were put forward by the PHA—all players Singh Sr. said deserved serious thought—no Punjab players made the trip. The PHA wrote a scolding letter to the IHF, which turned out to be in vain. The corrupt politics of field hockey had cemented itself as a modus operandi:

"Resolved that a strong protest be lodged with the Indian Hockey Federation against the arbitrary manner in which selections for representatives Indian during 1950 are to be made by small committees nominated by the President. The PHA notes with regret that no proper action was taken on a similar protest made by the Association when the IHF team was sent to Kabul in the summer of 1949. It was further resolved that the IHF should be informed in a categorical manner that if the Punjab protest was not given credence, the panel of names forwarded by the PHA should be considered for selection."

The PHA wanted regular trials to be held all over the country, in which camps would produce the cream of the crop, and the selection committee for Team India would be put to an overall vote. But the IHF was having none of this. Three Punjabi players in particular—Ram Swaroop, Gurcharan Bodhi and Charanjit Singh—were all Olympic calibre but weren't even given a sniff by the IHF, says Singh Sr.

"There was panic in the IHF ranks," he says. "The Punjab protest came as a bombshell to them."

After some negotiating, four Punjab players would ultimately make the next trip to Kabul, a small consolation. With this healthy Sikh contingent, India destroyed all the competition laid out by Afghanistan in 1949.

But the IHF proved to be stubborn, and although they relented for Kabul, they reverted to their central leadership tactics as soon as the team returned home. The PHA was so upset about the selection process that they forced Singh Sr. and the other Punjab players to sit out India's field hockey tour to Kenya. Singh Sr. wanted nothing to do with this "war of words", he just wanted to play. He was in his prime, and any game he missed because of political and religious tension was an itch he could not scratch.

R.D. Bhalla, the Punjab-based secretary of the IHF, became a casualty of the war of words as the PHA revoked his credentials. Ashwini Kumar, the head of the selection committee for the IHF, was trying to keep order, but everyone had started playing favourites, leaving unwitting victims on various sides of personal and religious feuds. Singh Sr. tried his best to stay out of the name calling and backstabbing, keeping his mind on the pitch, and focusing on his work and his family.

The Punjab press were calling him the post-war Dhyan Chand. But outside his home state the media were less congratulatory. The ruling Hindu majority wanted no minority to garner much attention, be it Muslim, Punjabi or any other faction. Goals by Singh Sr. were misreported, his name misspelled or omitted altogether. Knowing it would do him no good, the Sikh had long since stopped reading the newspapers. In terms of archival material, trying to find his name in papers is like looking for a needle in a carton of hay. The fact that most Sikhs use Singh as their surname further compounds this, leaving many of this man's accolades forever lost in the rough draft of history.

It was 1950 and Singh Sr.'s police squad was still managing to amass trophies at an alarming rate—the State Championship in Ludhiana, the Scindia Gold Cup in Gwalior and the All-India Kirpal Singh Trophy in Bareilly. Now the 1950 Nationals were around the corner and the Punjab state squad looked primed to win it all, again.

Held in Bhopal in the central Indian province of Madhya Pradesh, an area with an overwhelming Hindu majority, Singh Sr. and his squad breezed to the finals. It was there that they met the host team, and quickly shot out to a 4-0 lead. But then, Singh Sr. says, the referee started blatantly playing favourites, turning innocuous plays into cards and cautions for his Punjab squad. At one point in the game, three Punjab players had been sent off, which allowed Bhopal to score twice. Furious, Singh Sr. ran over to the referee:

"When we questioned the umpire about it, he said: 'The match was so one sided that it would have been an insult to national hockey championship had Punjab won by a bigger margin. I had to balance the teams.'"

Although they would still win 4–2, Singh Sr. had been blindsided by a corrupt referee, as if he didn't already have enough enemies to begin with.

Back home, the PHA were trying to build a field hockey bridge to Pakistan. While tensions were high, the move ended up paying off and on June 17, 1950 a Pakistani team of Punjabis came over to play a ceremonial match in Jullundur. The game was a political victory, and a huge feather in the cap of the PHA and the IHF. Ashwini Kumar was delighted, however his mood changed quickly when his star player fell ill a few days before the match.

By game day, Singh Sr. was running a fever of 104°, but Ashwini demanded he play in the game. He personally drove Singh Sr. to the hospital for treatment, and Singh Sr., always one to please, suited up, and even scored a goal. However once the match was finished he collapsed on the sidelines and had to be rushed to the hospital, running a terrible flu and in a state of delirium from dehydration.

Singh Sr. lay in bed sick for close to a month, slowly regaining his health. The time gave him a chance to bond with his infant daughter Sushbir. Bouncing her on his knee, listening to her infectious laugh, he found being a father offered a form of escapism from the craziness outside his door. At a historical period of such heated emotional fever, it was a physical cold that allowed the most famous Indian hockey player a chance to catch his metaphorical breath.

When July rolled around Singh Sr. was back in action, and took to a two week training program to regain his fitness. In those days, players would pray to Gods, purchase odd elixirs or carry out elaborate rituals to try and gain an edge on the pitch. Singh Sr. was not much for luck, instead he put on his running shoes and started to jog. Or he would train on the field by himself, as in his days at Khalsa College. He was fashioning his own karma, producing his own edge through a tireless work ethic.

The Indian squad were headed to Afghanistan again, and this time Singh Sr. was named captain. Winning was almost a formality; any team with Singh Sr. was touched by gold, or the hand of God. When the 1951 National Championships rolled around the following year, the Punjab state squad won again, a three-peat at the top level. Singh Sr.'s Punjab squad were now a dynasty, having captured the country's top honour in 1946 and 1947 and from 1949-51.

In August 1951, Singh Sr. and Sushil welcomed their second child, son Kanwalbir (Ken), who would immigrate to Canada in his 20s and become a monumental bridge for Singh Sr. later in his life. After he'd celebrated the birth of his boy, Singh Sr.'s mind became singular. One word, one thought dominated everything. He was eating, sleeping and breathing it. It was the last thought before bed, and the first to enter his mind in the morning. The one tournament he wanted to win so badly it would become his obsession: the 1952 Summer Olympics in Helsinki.

But once again, favouritism would rear its ugly head, as outlined in the 2012 book *Olympics—The India Story* by Boria Majumdar and Nalin Meht:

"Even as the Olympic team was being finalized on 13 June 1952, power-hungry administrators were engaged in mini-battles of intrigue to push their 'favourites' into the team at the last minute. The Uttar Pradesh and West Bengal associations were seeking the inclusion of an additional player and unhealthy parochialism was evident in their choices. As *The Times of India* reported, 'The effort to push Malholtra back into the team, who was originally selected and then dropped in favour of Jaswant and Gurung, smacked of provincialism.' "

Even more worrisome was what followed. Telegrams were sent from Bombay to all the affiliated associations, requesting their consent to the inclusion of Malholtra from Uttar Pradesh as an additional half. The telegram mentioned that Captain Digvijay Singh Babu and coaches Habul Mukherjee and Harbail Singh had stressed the need for Malhotra, especially in the event of a India-Pakistan final.

"The latter portion of the plea struck several associations as very odd," Majumdar and Meht continued. "They failed to understand how a player could be indispensable only for one game and could not be required for others."

With Uttar Pradesh making a case for Malhotra, Bengal wasn't to be left behind. Soon after the first telegram had been sent from Bombay, a second telegram was sent from Calcutta. The contents make fascinating reading: "As there are five halves already in the team the eighteenth player should be a forward and Bengal would be prepared to pay the expenses of C.S. Gurung, if elected." Anticipating criticism, the telegram added that Gurung should be selected not because he was from Bengal but because he had performed well throughout the season.

The Times of India made the following comment on the issue: "The state of affairs is very illuminating and depressing, as these attempts to wrangle in players come just on the eve of the team's departure. It may be mentioned that in 1948 also a similar selection of some Bengal players at a late hour had been allowed on the same condition—expenses borne by the Bengal Association."

As Majumdar/Meht continued in their book: "An interesting feature of Indian hockey at this time, evident from attempts to thrust players into the national team by agreeing to pay for their passage, was the poor financial state of the sport. The financial crisis was aggravated when the government decided to further reduce the subsidy offered to the nation's premier Olympic event. The financial condition of the Indian Olympic Association too was dire and it wasn't sure if it had the funds to send all, or even most, of the selected Indian athletes to Helsinki. This was evident from a circular issued by the IOA to the secretaries of the affiliated national federations in which it declared many athletes to be 'doubtful starters' owing to a lack of funds. The circular also declared that the financial condition was alarming and added that the government of India had reduced its grant-in-aid from Rs 1,000,000 to Rs 70,000. State governments too weren't as forthcoming as in 1948 and some had removed sport from their immediate radar in favour of other, more pressing concerns.

As *The Times of India* reported, "This has resulted in a large gap between expected income and anticipated expenditure." To

put it bluntly, the organizing of all things Indian sports was a
bloody mess.

A few months before Helsinki, a touring team from Japan
came through to test their skills against the Indian field hockey
squad, and Singh Sr. and his fellow Indians made quick work of
them. There would be no ceremonial matches, no smiling faces.
At the international level, it was bloodsport. India's field hockey
team had been born in fire much like the country itself, and laid
waste to any competition that stood in its way. It typified the fight
many of its players had to go through simply to remain on the
team. They were good, although ball-hogging and personal showboating were at an all-time high, says Singh Sr.

The last tournament before the Indian squad was picked for
the Olympics would be the 1952 National Championships in
Calcutta. A sprawling mega city at that time, which is today
known as Kolkata, it was also dominated by an overwhelming
Hindu majority. Once again Singh Sr. and his Punjab Police squad
found themselves in the final, suiting up against Bengal, the home
team.

This time the officiating was so one-sided, so blatantly disrespectful, that after the game Singh Sr. had to physically stop some
of his teammates from going into the umpire's change room to
assault him with their sticks. The Punjab squad lost the game and
the championship, banging their sticks on any available surface
after the match in protest, smashing wood all over the venue in
disgust.

Singh Sr. sat down in the room after everyone had cooled off.
He slowly changed out of his sweaty gear, his body covered in
purple welts from opponent's sticks. He could not remember garnering one caution or penalty, although he felt like he'd spent half
the game picking himself up off the dirt. He'd been tripped,
whacked and hacked for 70 minutes, but it was his opponents
who were garnering virtually all of the spot hits.

He leaned forward, shook his head ever so slightly so no one
would see, embarrassed at what had transpired. Field hockey was
political, lines had been divided by religion, and it was now an
outright nasty affair.

LUCKY NUMBER 13

"India is supposed to be a religious country above everything else, and Hindu and Muslim and Sikh and others take pride in their faiths and testify to their truth by breaking heads. The spectacle of what is called religion, or at any rate organised religion, in India and elsewhere has filled me with horror, and I have frequently condemned it and wished to make a clean sweep of it. Almost always it seems to stand for blind belief and reaction, dogma and bigotry, superstition and exploitation, and the preservation of vested interests."

~ Jawaharlal Nehru

Crisp, thin air flowing through the lungs with ease. Fourteen metres above the ocean, on the shores of the Baltic Sea just a relative stone's throw from the Arctic polar region. The air here heavenly; a coastal saltwater tinged climate zone, it's all brisk winds and icy nights, a far cry from the muggy heat below the equator. Cast by the subnormal waters of the Baltic, the breeze carries freely through this city, which acts as a major transportation hub between Sweden, Norway and Germany. For all intents and purposes, Copenhagen is galaxies away from the Indian subcontinent.

He walks off the hard grass of the field, dew crusted into the blades which gives each ball a zip to its destination. This machine of a man, this physical beast is almost retreating from the punishment he's put on his lungs and head. Dizzy, slightly disorientated, he's playing a game he knows well in circumstances that are decidedly foreign. Drawing deep, staggering breaths, he leans on his field hockey stick by the sidelines, glancing towards the stands. Locals have come to watch the team train and acclimatize here, watch them get used to playing on the other side of the planet, so far they are now a short distance from the North Pole.

For Singh Sr., this air provides a welcome escape. Here in the capital of Denmark, preparing for the games in Helsinki, he can regain focus. The team has been chosen, and all the corrupt scam artists and backroom schemers have been left behind like unwanted luggage. Singh Sr. has one job here: field hockey.

The Sikh phenom slowly regains his breath, heading to the change room for a steamy hot shower and meal of rye bread and sea trout. The locals scamper towards the gate to get a closer look at Team India. Such an odd sight: dark-skinned men from what feels like an alien race. The locals are incredibly curious about this overseas team, the best field hockey group in the world—ones who systematically dismantled Great Britain on home soil four

years ago. A team that made quick work of their European counterparts—Switzerland, the Netherlands and Austria, all teams that
beat their own national squad handily.

Singh Sr. stops before he heads into the underground dugout
of the stadium; a little girl, hair so blonde it's almost as icy white
as snow, pushes up against the guard rail right beside the walkway.
She leans down through the bannister, trying to get Singh Sr.'s
attention.

"Sir," she says, waving her hand toward him. "Sir?!"

Singh Sr. stops, looks over, and walks a few paces forward. He
looks around to see if anyone is watching. He's not scared of this
child, but every sense is heightened here in this northern land.
What feels like a city and nation out of some medieval fairytale
he read about as an imaginative schoolboy in Moga.

"Yes," he says, signalling he speaks English.

The little girl looks nervous, but her curiosity gets the best of
her.

"Sir, I was wondering . . . why do you wear number thirteen,
do you not know it is unlucky?"

Singh Sr. tries to glance around at the back of his match jersey, almost verifying the number he knows full well he's been
wearing for years. The girl giggles; Singh Sr. smiles.

"Thirteen in North Indian languages is pronounced *tera*," says
Singh Sr. "Which is also a form of addressing God."

The little girl locks eyes with him. Singh Sr. wipes sweat from
his forehead, watching the fascination on her face as she analyzes
his response. "Tera?" she says with her accent.

"Te-*ra*," replies Singh Sr.

"Te-ra."

Singh Sr. chuckles and points to the sky. "I dedicate my per-
formances to the One Above."

The little girl looks quizzically at him. He looks back down
to her, cracks a mischievous smile.

"For me . . . thirteen is a lucky number."

★★★

Despite all the political posturing, religious separatism and regional favouritism, India still managed to send a stacked squad to the second games of the new era. Four Punjab players made the roster including Singh Sr. This time Harbail Singh—who'd plucked Singh Sr. from obscurity and started his ascent to greatness through Khalsa College—was the coach. This time, Singh Sr. need not worry about his roster spot, nor being pulled seconds before the start. His boss knew exactly what he needed to do with his star player—play him, and play him *all* the time.

Eighteen players made the long journey by air to Copenhagen to acclimatize before heading by plane to Helsinki. Singh Sr. said the transition was tough, regardless of the natural beauty of their surroundings.

"Finland is the land of the midsummer nights—land where the sun keeps low and hardly ever sets on account of its nearness to the North Pole region," he wrote in his autobiography. "The land, dotted with natural lakes and greenery all around, looks beautiful in different phases of sunlight. But this also means that one has to adjust to the daylight hours. The first night was terrible for us: the glare in the open window would not give us sleep. We adjusted to the odd sight of the sun shining in the night by downing our shutters and darkening our rooms with heavy curtains."

While Singh Sr. had to scratch and claw his way onto the 1948 squad, with Harbail managing the team, he was the unchallenged star. The fame brought by London also meant he would carry the Indian flag in the opening ceremonies, one of the greatest honours of his life.

Singh Sr. remembers riding a train from Bombay to Ferozepore after London on his way home, and the chants that greeted him at each station, something he remembered while carrying the flag around the track in Helsinki:

"Long live India hockey! Long live India hockey!"

Their gold in 1948 had energized an infant nation, one almost suffocating under the weight of its own expectations. The Congress Party and its leader Nehru had won the country's first general election, and the nation had a chance to write its own script, one free of British rule, one where Indians would be sole-ly in charge.

The pressure put on these 18 men to repeat was much greater than the expectations of four years prior. The London Olympics was a feeling out process for everyone. Now the stage had been set, and the first champion of the new era had emerged. Pakistan, Great Britain and an upstart Netherlands team had all drawn blood from each other, but no one had defeated India. They were chomping at the bit to bring the king down from the throne, to take away any chance of a repeat and the construction of anoth-er field hockey dynasty originating from South Asia. Since the 1928 games, only the British Raj and India had won, leaving sil-ver and bronze, veritable scraps for the rest to squabble over.

Held at Olympic Stadium, the opening ceremonies proved to be one of the most nerve-wracking days of Singh Sr.'s life. His father had drilled the idea of professionalism into him, and carry-ing the flag on an international stage was the highest honour any athlete or citizen could achieve. Singh Sr. prayed to anyone who would listen that he did not drop the tricolours of white, orange and green, or trip on his own feet while walking around the 400 metre track.

So committed to his duty, he did not even break rank when a pigeon crapped on his dress shoes after they were ceremonious-ly released to signify the start of the Games of the XV Olympiad.

"I stood still, because the occasion demanded it," he said with a chuckle. "But it gave me an uneasy feeling and I was worried if my Indian blazer had been soiled."

After the ceremonies finished, Singh Sr. was allowed to hand over the flag, and he darted around looking for a towel to clean his attire. In his bumbling search, he bumped into an official with the Helsinki Olympic Organizing Committee.

"Congratulations son," said the official, looking down at Singh Sr.'s shoe. "A pigeon dropping on the left toe is supposed to be the greatest sign in Finland."

Dumbfounded, Singh Sr. looked down at his shoe, covered in a Jackson Pollock array of white bird poo. The official handed him a handkerchief, a huge smile on his face.

"You are going to have your luckiest Olympics."

Twelve teams would vie for gold in Helsinki.[166] The games would be remembered as the first time the USSR participated, heightening Cold War tension between the Soviet Union and the US.[167] But Singh Sr. said he wasn't much for politics. He had come to the games to leave all the divisiveness behind, and said that sometimes at the Olympics, where athletes from around the world would mingle and chat effortlessly, he felt more at home than back in India.

While London had adopted a group stage tournament draw, the 1952 games would follow a single-elimination knockout format. This meant there would be no off games; win and you're through, lose and you're done. Harbail knew he had to field his best line-up every match.

India garnered a bye in the first round as previous champions, but this meant a second round date with Austria, an up-and-coming European squad who had upset the Swiss in their first game, sending a message that anyone could advance in this single elimination format. Having spent time in Copenhagen before the games began, the Indian team had played a few matches against local squads from various European countries. They knew they were better, but somehow, on the grandest of stages, the Indian players let their inflated egos take over at the most inopportune time.

Two quick goals opened up an Indian lead. Then, Singh Sr. says, his teammates let their emotions run amok at the Helsinki Velodrome. "The trouble was that some of our forwards tended to overdo the dribble and played to the gallery. Seldom did we create gaps, which were there for the asking. All our goals came by solo efforts."

Singh Sr. would notch one goal in a 4-0 win, but after the match, Harbail was furious, storming into the dressing room, flinging a chair across the room and telling his joyous boys to shut their yaps immediately. He scolded the players for their blatant showmanship, then let them stew in embarrassed silence.

After they'd returned to the athlete's village, Harbail called the entire team into the lounge area, and chastised them one-by-one for showboating, drilling home the idea of modesty and proper play; this was not a circus show for them to play to the popcorn crowd, this was the Olympic Games, the most prestigious sporting event in the world. Singh Sr. said this strictness followed him throughout his career. He had no time for nonsense.

"Don't think your place is assured in the team," said Harbail, locking eyes with Singh Sr. "If you don't play well, we will pack you off!"

The message stuck, their coach's words had come through crystal clear. India had drawn Great Britain in the semi-final, showboating now might cost them the games. There would be no rubber match of the 1948 final in which a newly minted country took on its longstanding rulers, the two heavyweights would duke it out for the chance to simply play for gold.

While Great Britain were formidable foes, once again after the first whistle sounded it was clear India were the superior team. John Cockett, a half-back for Great Britain, spoke about Team India's prowess:[168] "India were the better side, their stick work was considerably better than ours playing on grass pitches. We had the odd Anglo-Indian, whose stick work was almost as good as theirs, but they were magicians and we had to try and make up in other ways."

Singh Sr. says they came out with swagger, but were efficient in their attack, sans the egocentric style they'd demonstrated in their first match. Team India had a mission: defeat the Brits again for the second time and show the world who was the field hockey boss.

"We moved swiftly and smoothly and scythed their defence with copy-book moves," says Singh Sr.

His first touch of the ball was winning a bully-off (a field hockey face-off that has since been taken out of the game) at centre. He pushed the ball through his opponent's legs—one of his favourite tricks—and darted right up the middle of the field, the play cascading away from him like a parting sea. His opponents knew that unless Singh Sr. was in the slot, he would look to pass. Although he scored goals, he was unselfish out of the half circle, always looking for an open player to head man the ball to. The

Brits marked every Indian they could, leaving him only one option: straight ahead.

Singh Sr. tapped the ball forward, head darting left and right, looking for an open teammate. Nothing. He tapped the ball again, almost inside the half circle. Still nothing. Then his mind went into auto-pilot, going straight for goal, and the central defender dove in to try and stop him. Singh Sr. wound up and shot, but completely miffed the ball. However the goalie, expecting a fierce shot from the Sikh phenom, dove in anticipation to his right, while the ball dribbled slowly into the left corner like a golf putt.

"It was an accident that I got the goal," he says, sheepishly.

But it energized the team, and soon Singh Sr. was wiring shot after shot at the keeper. He would notch two more goals, the second Olympic hat trick of his career. The Brits responded with a tally, leaving the score 3-1 at half-time. Singh Sr. headed into the dressing room, having scored five goals already against Great Britain in a game and a half. He was the United Kingdom assassinator.

When Singh Sr. started the second half, he noticed something he hadn't before at the Olympics. Although at home he was well used to the attention, this was the first time he can remember being double-teamed internationally. Everywhere he went he was shadowed by multiple Brit defenders, who did everything they could to impede his play both on and off the ball. The game would end 3-1, and the Indians would once again stick it to their former rulers, who now looked like the master being passed by the student.

Singh Sr. says he was not like Chand, undeniably gifted with his stick work. But he scored goals at the same efficiency, more with power, and a screaming slapshot. He loved to shoot high, picking corners like a soccer player. Goalies, bogged down in heavy equipment, could only throw minor attempts to stop balls above their waist level. Upstairs is where Singh Sr. did most of his goal scoring damage.

"I may not have produced rabbits from a magician's hat, but I did fetch goals for my country—and that is what matters most in hockey," he says.

On the other side of the semi-finals, Holland had beaten Pakistan 1-0 in a tough match. This meant there would be no iconic pre-Partition symbolism for the finals, just the Indians and the Dutch duking it out for the second field hockey gold medal of the new Olympic era.

Singh Sr. headed to the athlete's village, readying himself for an early night's sleep. He knew upon waking tomorrow, he would be in the best position to bring another glorious medal back to his nation's homeland. He tossed and turned, going over plays in his head, thinking, visualizing potential game situations over and over. Without the politics of London or the favouritism debacle seeping into his mindset, he was clear to focus on the task at hand: goals.

The morning of the gold medal match, Singh Sr. woke with a bounce to his step. He was on, his body felt great, his mind at ease. He was in the zone, and about to show the world who the greatest field hockey player on the planet was.

To say that Singh Sr. dominated the final game that day would be an understatement. The fact that he set a Guinness World Record in the process should give proper insight into how well he played.

Five goals, one shy of two hat-tricks in a six to one shellacking for a second consecutive gold for an independent India. Singh Sr. said every time he touched the ball he felt like he could score. The feeling gave him more confidence, and he sprung into attack more often that usual, as if destiny was pulling him towards the net. Two defenders, five defenders, it didn't matter, he was unstoppable. An athlete at his veritable peak at the grandest of stages, rising to the call.

Dil Bahra is a Sikh field hockey historian who lives in London. It was Bahra who submitted Singh Sr.'s five goals as a potential record before the London 2012 Olympics:[169] "The most goals scored by an individual in an Olympic men's hockey final is 5 by Balbir Singh Sr. (India) in India's 6-1 victory over Holland in the gold medal game of the 1952 Olympic Games. It was the fifth of six consecutive gold medal triumphs by India."

Bahra also outlined via email the significance of the record and how it relates to mythologizing around Chand:

"The fact that Balbir Sr. had scored 5 goals in the Final at the Helsinki 1952 Olympic Games was never in dispute/question but in 2008 during the lead up to the Beijing Olympics, The FIH [International Hockey Federation] had a series of "Did you Know" facts on their website which stated that Dhyan Chand had scored 6 goals at the Berlin 1936 Olympics. I knew from my research on Olympic Hockey that this fact was incorrect and I followed this up with the FIH. The FIH still maintained that their records were correct but it took me some two years to convince the FIH that their record was wrong. This was a long process and I could easily write a whole chapter on this—the President of FIH was also aware of this. Once the FIH had admitted they got the whole thing wrong, the President, I believe, wrote a personal letter to Balbir Sr."

The record stands to this day, and there's a huge commemorative plaque of it at the International Hockey Stadium in Mohali, Punjab. Built in 2013, it's an oddly modern facility already collecting dust and garbage. Kabir and I tour the empty arena one afternoon, bypassing security with a quick chat. No games were scheduled that day on the pitch, even though it was a Saturday mid-season. Beside Singh Sr.'s plaque is a requisite picture of Chand and a quote attributed to Wayne Gretzky, however puck is replaced with ball:

"Do not go where the ball is, go to where the ball is *going to be.*"

Also beside Singh Sr.'s plaque is another plaque written in Punjabi which reads: "Reserved for anyone who can beat Balbir Singh Sr.'s record." Singh Sr. shows me the letter of apology he received from the FIH in response to their error, a piece of paper he cherishes like a trophy.

As a Helsinki Olympic official placed the medal around his neck, Singh Sr. looked out to the crowd, clapping in applause. He felt a deep sense of pride he had trouble acknowledging in London. In 1948, the games were mostly a whirlwind, a blur; and a terror simply trying to get onto the field to play. Now he could feel the moment, taste it, breathe it in deep through the pit of his lungs. He was lapping it up, feasting on the accomplishment. His feat undeniable, he'd put on a clinic at the highest echelon. People rushed to the stands by the tunnel, trying to get a better look at him, calling out his name.

"Balbir! Balbir!"

The closing ceremonies a glorious victory lap. The Indian flag light as a feather in his hands. He made the circle, eyes forever forward, a professional to the end. But inside the little boy from Moga was jumping for joy, bouncing off the walls with stick in hand.

Back home his country was struggling to sort itself out. He'd seen it first hand as a policeman. Paperwork flooding his office, Indians forced to try and continue a British system, many workers became managers with little training, unequipped and inexperienced. Nobody knew how to run a country. People promoted friends and families to positions out of default, and a new, clunky system of government emerged.

In this state of confusion, Singh Sr.'s team's gold helped uplift a nation still stung by the death of its philosophical leader Gandhi, left with the more pragmatic Nehru, who although an incredibly intelligent man, was nowhere near the unifying force his friend and mentor had been. The wound of Partition was still deep, but the escapism of international sporting glory offered a temporary form of morphine that dripped through the country's veins.

After the win, the team played a few consolation matches in Helsinki, then headed back to Copenhagen where they'd spent two weeks prior to the games. Singh Sr. says Harbail came through on a promise he'd made to them before the Olympics begun. While in the Danish capital, some of the players on the team had taken to wandering away from the hotel, and making friends with some of the local ladies. Harbail shot them down, imposed a strict curfew, and forbade his boys from fraternizing in any way, shape or form. But he also showed a glimmer of leniency, something Singh Sr. himself would echo when he got the chance to coach the team later in his life.

"Before Helsinki, in Holland, the boys started going out at night with 'friends'," says Singh Sr. "And our coach promised us not to go out, because he said if you win at Helsinki I'll bring you here again, and he took us there for a few days."

The boys painted the town red. They headed to local bars, downing pints of pale lager and chomping on beer battered cod, however Singh Sr. says from his recollection, they avoided the brothels and excessive alcohol drinking.

"We had evoked a workable code: that far and no further."

Singh Sr. says the whole experience was a bit odd, coming from such a traditional, rigid society where public displays of affection were shunned and even banned. To him, the "permissive West" was a bit of a culture shock: people making out on park benches, sex shops, pornographic magazines and dirty movies. For many Indians, the indulgent lifestyle was too much temptation to resist. He lamented about the peculiar settings and how it related to his homeland in his autobiography.

"How I wish our young men could imitate the western concept of sport and make it part of their life, instead of hankering for a lifestyle that just doesn't go with Indians' standards of decency and privacy in personal matters. Sex is a personal matter and I just can't understand why exhibitionism should come into it."

While the overt sexuality of Europe was something to note, Singh Sr. says he was a married man and rather enjoyed bicycling around Copenhagen instead of partaking in other extra-curricular activities. He marvelled at the level of sporting culture in the country, each crisp green field he passed had a game going on. Sports were plentiful everywhere he went—nine pin bowling, tennis, badminton, football. While most of his teammates were wetting their whistles and partaking in the sexuality of the West, Singh Sr. was watching sports and perusing the town on two wheels. He knew if India ever wanted to cultivate a sporting culture, this is where it would begin, on the playgrounds of the nation.

After Harbail's granted 48 hour "detour", the team quickly regained its rigid self. It was back to business and a couple hard practices in Copenhagen to sweat out the booze and toxins from their debauchery. The team was scheduled to play a number of exhibition matches around Europe before returning home to the celebrations.

They headed by train to Frankfurt where they played a few games, and even visited Berlin. At last, Singh Sr. saw where his hero Chand had defied Nazi Germany in 1936. It was here, thinking about all the goals Chand scored, that Singh Sr. realized he'd scored nine out of 13 of his team's markers in Helsinki—a staggering 64 percent. For a moment he said he allowed his head to swell, but quickly shooed the thought away. Taking extra credit was "blasphemy" he thought to himself.

Flying into Delhi, the celebrations began in earnest. It started with an official function, a lavish ceremony at the Prime Minister's house. Singh Sr. and Nehru were now on a first name basis, the iconic leader seeking him out like a conversational missile, eager for his opinion on how best to prepare India's athletes for the 1954 Asian Games in the Philippines. Nehru had spearheaded the first instalment in Delhi in 1951, desperately hoping international triumph would catch fire and build a strong sporting culture back home; alas the nation was busy squabbling over the country, one left void of many Muslims and Brits who had helped fill the gears of the British Raj machine.

Team India then played a ceremonial match against an All-India squad again in Delhi. As the team moved through the country by train, they were once again mobbed at every stop. Singh Sr. says after a while, they collected the oddest of injuries.

"When we emerged from the train they crushed us with their bear hugs and their show of affection—the back-slapping gave us painful backs and shoulders. We endured it all with a smile. We had to pay that little price for being national heroes."

The four Punjab players, Dharam, Udham, Ragbir and Singh Sr., headed to Jullundur cantonment. They were promptly put in the back of a jeep and paraded through town where thousands of onlookers flooded the streets, throwing flower petals at them and banging pots and pans as loud as they could. They climbed houses and treetops for a better view of the Sikh stars, mobbing the Jeep at times to give them small gifts, baskets of fruits, sweets and garlands.

Singh Sr. finally retreated to his work station, dusting off flower petals from every surface of his body. His desk filled with offerings, he looked around the room to see everyone watching him intently. Every move he made, his colleagues were almost in awe.

Here, in their presence, was Olympic greatness.

★★★

It was 1953, and the Gold Cup Invitational Field Hockey Tournament was one of India's premiere annual sporting competitions. The Punjab Police—the perennial powerhouse team of the nation—were ready to duke it out with the Lusitanians of Bombay.

However, neither team seemed eager to head out onto the field to start the game. The match umpire looked at both squads on the sidelines, Singh Sr. and his boys, and the Bombay squad, standing beside the pitch like it might be infected with termites. The referee blew his whistle, over and over, but it did nothing to budge the teams. Frustrated, he left and stormed into the administrator's office.

Finally a tournament official made his way down towards the pitch with the referee. He looked to his left, and then to his right: two full squads, on the sidelines, not budging one centimetre.

"Why are they not entering the grounds?" asked the official to the ref.

"Both teams think it's bad luck to be the first on the pitch."

The official wiped sweat from his forehead, the fans were getting anxious, they wanted a game. He called both team's captains over.

Singh Sr. interjected before anyone else could even get a word in. For years his Punjab team had been getting thrown around whenever they played outside their home state. Bad draws, questionable calls, favouritism—he'd had enough. This time, he wasn't budging, and he knew his two gold medals carried substantial clout.

"It is customary for the hosts to enter the pitch first," said Singh Sr. to his Goan Christian counterpart and Anglo-Indian referee.

It was true, it had long been an unwritten rule. He had them. His opponent fumed, bubbling over with fury. The Sikh simply stood his ground, standing firm, his field hockey stick by his side.

Tales of superstition amongst South Asian culture are rampant, and this belief system extends right down to the core of field hockey. Singh Sr. remembers another tournament in Bombay where his wife wore a distinct white sari to their first game. The Punjab police squad won handedly, and it was decided this was because of Sushil's white dress. But after two days of wearing the dress to every game, Sushil's attire had a distinct look of *un*cleanliness. Two players offered to take it to the dry-cleaners so she could continue wearing it without embarrassment. She ended up wearing the outfit right through until the final game—a win of course.

Singh Sr. and his Punjab boys won after the Lusitanians players relented and went first, but the man himself says the only superstition he's ever really believed in is his lucky number thirteen.

But as the unequivocal leader of the Punjab state and police squad, Singh Sr. found himself trying to make sure superstition didn't destroy his squad. During another tournament in Bombay, while getting ready for the game, one of his players bumped a mirror in the change room. The glass fell, smashing into millions of pieces, stopping everyone in their tracks. They were about to play a tough opponent, and ever alert, Singh Sr. jumped into action.

"I told them it was lucky, and that when I was away playing for India, the same thing had happened and I ended up scoring many goals in the game."

Of course the team went on to victory, fuelled by the white lie, but not without some nerves. Singh Sr. knew if they'd lost, his teammates would be deathly scared of even changing in a dressing room with a mirror in it.

The players were also against receiving garlands before any match, something Singh Sr. could not remedy. Alas the Punjab players made themselves look like poor sportsmen on a few occasions, denying the offerings in pre-game ceremonies, ducking out of the flower necklaces like they were flu-ridden.

This came to a particular head when an unofficial team from Pakistan with nine Olympic players came over for a

Bombay hosted tournament. Tensions were high with the Pakistanis, and they offered garlands before the match was to begin. Singh Sr. did not bow to pressure, and refused the ceremonial offerings alongside his boys, in what could have been seen as an act of war.

Singh Sr. wanted the focus on proper preparation, not seeking out lucky signs to latch onto; he found most of his teammates' superstitions silly and was always looking for ways to downplay "signs from the Gods".

He remedied the situation with a common prayer table in each dressing room before the match, at which he would incorporate religious symbols from all creeds: Hindu, Muslim, Christian, Buddhist and Sikhism. He would ask his players to participate in silent religious meditation before the first whistle, knowing full well what it was actually doing was calming down a roster of men who could easily act like immature little boys.

At home in Jullundur, Singh Sr. settled into his usual lifestyle, managing both work and the team while raising a young family. These were his prime days as a field hockey player and his gift had afforded him the luxury of a job that never really got in the way. He was the Punjab's golden boy, regardless of how he was viewed across the country in comparison to Chand, still the country's iconic sporting champion.

And he didn't rest on his laurels, but continued to perfect and fine tune his game. Nick Sandhu, a former Canadian national team field hockey player who immigrated from the Punjab area in 1977 to Vancouver at the age of 15, said he heard about one of Singh Sr.'s unique training strategies.

"Back then the balls were made of leather, and they were filled with cork inside. So he would take a bunch of balls after practice and put them in water, so they would end up being much heavier. Then he would practice his shot with the heavier balls, it made his shot just insanely hard and fast. It was things like this that really put him head and shoulder above the rest, he was always working at making his game better."

Post Helsinki, the IHF was now pushing India all over the world, even though sports were hard-pressed to find adequate funding. However, the men's field hockey team was a different matter, thanks to many instances of dubious and illegal backing.

The team was sent to New Zealand and Australia during the winter season, which meant fits of cold that shocked the bones. While the northern Punjab occasionally got snow, many players from Bombay and even Delhi were not used to even inhabiting, much less playing in, single-digit temperatures.

Singh Sr., who never drank recreationally, did defer to local wisdom, which held that a shot of brandy would warm the insides before a particularly chilly match. The team would carry a bottle and mix it with honey or water, helping to keep them heated when they were forced to play in conditions where the icy breath fogged their vision.

The team's tour of New Zealand was difficult. As rugby was their go-to sport, the Kiwis played rough, wearing studded cleats that chewed up the turf. This meant a disastrous game of constant turnovers and errors, with flying bodies and errant sticks to boot. K.D. Singh, a star inside right back with the team, was so furious he refused to play most of the 38 matches on the tour.

The team had been put together by the Delhi Hockey Association, under the guidance of the IHF. Losing a player like K.D. Singh further dented the squad's skill set. Singh Sr., relentless, lifted his team to numerous wins, scoring hat tricks or more in multiple games.

On top of that, at each stop on the tour, dance parties were thrown for the team. Hockey was extremely popular amongst New Zealand girls; hundreds of women would come to see India play and follow the squad to the parties afterwards. Singh Sr. said it was an adjustment to see women moving so freely without male escorts, staying out late unaccompanied and flirting endlessly with his teammates. Singh Sr. says they took an odd liking to the Punjab players.

"Being a Sikh made me conspicuous. All Sikh members in the team were sought out by the most beautiful girls: the turbans, beards and *karras* (iron bands) on our wrists were something new to them. They were most eager to know what sect we belonged to."

Traveling to Melbourne, Singh Sr. would get a first hand look at the Olympic stage for the following year. At that point in his career, still in his late 20s, he felt invincible. His body, void of alcohol, cigarettes, and sweets, was sculpted like that of a carnivorous beast. He was thick but lean, strong but agile, and had three characteristics that few players had: hands, speed and strength. Like Maurice "The Rocket" Richard of the Montreal Canadians, who scored goals in an un-flashy, almost brutish manner (and also came from humble beginnings), Singh Sr. was the sport's first power forward.

During 38 matches in New Zealand and Australia, Singh Sr. scored 141 of his team's 208 goals. This averaged out to about 67 percent of his team's tallies, just shy of four goals a game. He was the Pelé of his sport, the Wayne Gretzky; surrounded by the best players in the world, but still head and shoulders above both his teammates and his fierce opponents.

When he returned home, however, he realized that all the free meals and treats had packed close to 16 pounds onto his frame. Over the span of a few months his body had adapted to a colder climate, adding weight as he moved from town to town— and hearty ceremonial dinner to hearty ceremonial dinner. Aghast, Singh Sr. looked at himself in the mirror, saw his belly protruding out like he was pregnant.

"I knew I needed to drop some weight if I was going to continue playing at such a high level," he says. He quickly set about a strict conditioning regime, allowing the Indian sun to sweat off the unwanted belly fat.

Sushil wasn't a fan of the tour, as upon his return Singh Sr. continuously received letters from female admirers in both New Zealand and Australia. He says he noticed her responding to one girl's letter, letting her know Singh Sr. was married, taken and in love with her.

In July of 1954 Singh Sr.'s celebrity status had him posted to the Bhakra Canal. The government were in the process of building India's largest dam, a signal of the country's technological leap into the future along the waves of hydroelectricity that Nehru was calling the "new temple of resurgent India."[170] Nehru spared no expense, having the Sikh posted as Inspector in Charge of his personal security detail at the Sutlej Sadan, a rest house close by in Nangal.

Singh Sr. saluted Nehru when he arrived, and was quickly summoned inside by India's iconic leader. One of Nehru's staff told him to come back at 3:55PM exactly for a special meeting. Singh Sr., never one to question authority, nodded and headed off back to work. He returned with ample time to get to the rest house, but the Punjab governor, Chief Minister and Punjab Inspector General of Police were also on their way to Nehru's base. Singh Sr. did not want to pass them on the pathway, as it would be seen as a disrespectful gesture, so instead he walked behind, antsy in his silence, checking his watch incessantly.

When he arrived at 3:59PM Nehru emerged from the house, and walked right past the other dignitaries to Singh Sr. "Didn't someone tell you you were to meet me at 3:55?" he asked.

Singh Sr. knew Nehru was a stern man, though the country's leader always had a welcoming look on his face, and was never one to jump to conclusions. Still, the accusation was incredibly intimidating. Singh Sr.'s legs started to shake, and he gulped. He was late to meet the first Prime Minister of India, the man who had pulled the nation from the grip of the Raj and walked the country through the fires of Partition.

"Yes sir," was all he could muster, eyes darting around sheepishly.

Nehru calmly motioned for Singh Sr. to continue.

"...I did not want to come to you ahead of the ranking officers," said Singh Sr.

Nehru looked puzzled, then broke out into boisterous laughter. He put his hand around Singh Sr.'s shoulder, shooing away his other guests as the two walked into the house.

"Tell me, Balbir, are you still playing hockey? Are you well, do you play everyday, are your colleagues happy with their playing conditions?"

Singh Sr. nodded, his shoulders relaxing.

Once they got into the house, Nehru stopped and held Singh Sr.'s arm. He looked right in his eyes. His steely resolve,

Singh Sr. thought, had been created in the oven of the country's birth. In hearing that his confidant and closest friend, Gandhi, had been murdered. In watching a nation squander its only chance at independence. This man's resolve had been tested, and he had emerged battle worn and hardened, much like his Sikh counterpart.

He wanted something from Singh Sr., a promise to keep.

"You will have to win again. We must continue to remain world champions. Tell this to all your friends. Tell them India needs them badly. They are the hopes of this nation."

Singh Sr. nodded, swallowing down the terror trying to escape from his stomach.

The leader of his nation was trying desperately to live up to lofty expectations. Now, so was Singh Sr. He had to win gold again, for Nehru, and for the people, as the nation was counting on him to score goals and lead the team to victory in Melbourne. The country was in dire need of good news, a distraction from the perils of a young land's growing pains.

Singh Sr. left Nehru's house, a gallon of oxygen departed from the belly of his lungs. He had just been tasked with saving the country from its highest official, a country he loved deep in the marrow of his existence. A promise he would do everything right down to his last breath to uphold.

THE BROKEN FINGER

"No, I do not want to live jointly with them. There cannot be any equal share between two nations thrown together, one in an overwhelming majority of three to one. It is unnatural and artificial because to every step in matters of life, we shall profoundly disagree, and a constitution of that kind can never stand. We are not only different and distinct, but antagonistic. Why does Britain want to keep us together? We refuse, and if you want to force us you will need to keep your bayonets."

~ Muhammad Ali Jinnah

Metacarpal bone cracks like an eggshell. Proximal phalanx snaps in two like a twig. Pain sensation mainlines shock-waves straight to the brain, forcing a momentary blackout. The man staggers to his knees on the field, but regains his footing just as quickly. The sensory explosion pushes a wail out of his mouth, a tiger growl of pain and frustration. He knows within seconds: his appendage is broken, shattered, smashed to bits.

The index finger on his right hand, the steering wheel of his stick, the guiding light that helps him turn his weapon over on the ball to go backhand. Without this finger, he is like a driver without a clutch, a pilot without controls, a sailor without a fin. He follows the play back, stops momentarily to inspect the damage. Blood drips onto the grass. Within a minute, the finger has doubled in size, swelling in various shades of beet red, deep blue and purple.

The play circles back to him, adrenaline pumping, his body ringing alarm bells, sending out distress signals to every corner of his body. *You are in pain.* It only takes a moment for the terrible agony to wash over him, a thick wave of despair. He receives a pass, but as soon as he grips his stick the sensation is too much. A defender swipes the ball from him, almost in awe that he's just pick-pocketed the best field hockey player in the world.

The play drifts away like a receding tide. He looks around to see if anyone saw what transpired. It is in this moment he experiences an emotion he's never felt on the pitch, a foreign entity enters his body like a poisonous ghoul: helplessness.

The fierce drive from the Afghani centre-back that hit his hand was on a string, pulled tight right to his finger through the centre of a scope. Standing so close to the ball, so confident in his own body and reaction time, he figured he could trap the spot hit for a turnover. Like a steam-hammer ramming into his fingernail, the ball crippled his entire hand as his body coped with the shock, he tried to move out of the way at the last second; realizing his mistake he flinched, but it only did more damage.

Such a low drive from his competitor. He knows full well what his opponent was trying to do: injure the Indian star. Mission accomplished.

Although he would tell no one until the match was over, he already knew what the x-rays would say. Multiple fractures. Holding a stick was like trying to pick up a hot metal rod. He held his hand out like it had been infected, he tried icing it, bending the finger against its will. It was useless, not an injury he could simply shrug off.

This moment would define the Melbourne games for him.

Five goals. Five goals before his finger snapped. They'd slaughtered Afghanistan 14-0 to win the first game of their group stage on November 26, 1956. At 32 years, ten months and 26 days, number 13 Balbir Singh Sr. had notched a hat trick, then potted two more for good measure. While Great Britain had tied their opening match against an unknown Malaya team (now Singapore and Malaysia), and Pakistan had eked out a victory against Belgium 2-0, India was showing it was still a powerhouse, flexing its muscles in front of the sporting world's mirror.

That night, as Singh Sr. sat in the doctor's office at The Royal Melbourne Hospital, he knew he'd been foolish. The Aussie physician held the x-ray up to the light, showing him where the bones had broken. The seismic crack in his plans.

"I'm sorry mate," said the physician. "I don't think you can play anymore."

Singh Sr. left the hospital despondent, utterly furious at his own actions.

"We were never under pressure and my bravado was needless."

Never one to stroke his ego, all the kerfuffle around Singh Sr. had finally gotten to him. All those Indians telling him he was a god, a hero, a juggernaut, unstoppable. Little kids asking if he could pull carts full of sod down the road with one hand, or score goals while juggling three balls at once. The mythology of Singh Sr., however subjugated throughout the years, cost him dearly at the Games of the XVI Olympiad.

For the first time, the games were to be held outside of Europe and North America, way down in the southern hemisphere. This meant the Olympics would actually take place during the winter months, which sent many athletes for a seasonal loop. Although political infighting initially delayed the construction of the Olympic village, plans eventually went through. Singh Sr. said the grounds were like no other, lined with lush gardens and boutique shops, and the locals were incredibly welcoming, even more so than the Brits or Finlandians, which garnered the event the nickname "The Friendly Games".[171,172]

He had been named team captain, a huge honour, and asked to carry the flag in the opening ceremonies for the second time. But none of that mattered now. Not if this defining moment cost them gold.

Singh Sr. sombrely made his way back to the village where a top level emergency meeting was held. Fellow captain O.P. Mehra, Chief-de-Mission Arjan Singh and IHF vice-president Ashwini Kumar huddled around him, asking to examine his hand.

They quickly decided Singh Sr. would not play in the remaining two group matches against the United States and Singapore. Neither were deemed a serious threat, and India would end up winning the two games, scoring 22 goals and ceding zero. This would allow Singh Sr. almost a full week to rest his hand before the playoffs started against Germany on December 3. They prayed to the gods each night, hoping they would heal his bone, fill the cracks with concrete, allowing their leader to return to his place at the front of their platoon.

Each member of Team India was explicitly told not to speak about Singh Sr.'s harrowing injury, but say that he was being saved for the semi-finals and finals. Singh Sr. wrapped his finger in a small cloth bandage, and kept his hand in his pocket as much as possible. He avoided formal introductions, instead going in for a full-on hug. For a few days, his ailment was the best kept secret of the games.

With Singh Sr. out of the lineup, the team feared, India's aura of invincibility would crack. With a chink in the armour of the heavyweight Goliath, other outfits might smell blood and pounce, go for a win against India rather than spend the entire game trying to stop the bleeding.

Rajdeep Singh Gill, former director general of police for the Punjab and the president of the Basketball Federation of India—outlined India's plan after the broken finger.

"Simply the sight of [Singh Sr.] on the field caused teams to play differently. He needed to be on the field, he would terrify opponents; it came to be known how India won."

On a recent tour to Malaya just before Melbourne, Singh Sr. scored 83 of his team's 121 goals in 16 matches. That's an average of over five a game, almost 70 percent. If he was out of the picture, a team could attack fully, rather than give up two defenders to man-mark, thus impeding their own offensive push. Imagine if suddenly the New York Yankees didn't have Babe Ruth batting in the World Series, or if Mia Hamm wasn't starting at forward for the US National Women's team in the World Cup Final.

All too soon, the team headed to the Melbourne Sports and Entertainment Precinct just east of the city for the playoff game against West Germany—a country also ripped in half, the result of political strife caused by the start of Cold War. Singh Sr. was quickly draped by two German defenders, who got so close he could feel their breath on his shoulder. They knew who he was, and wanted to make sure he had zero time with the ball. Singh Sr. had taken a pain-killing injection of cortisone, wrapping his finger as tightly as possible to cut off circulation. He was not playing for tomorrow; he was sacrificing his body for today, trying to make up for his mistake against Afghanistan a few days prior.

"We had sold them the dummy," says Singh Sr. "But the injury smashed my dream of repeating my Helsinki Olympic form of 1952."

Harbail was worried. Singh Sr. was the tip of his spear, and he was not used to winning tight, low scoring affairs. He scrambled to reformat their game plan, to place the onus on defending and controlling the midfield. India was going to have to scrap its way

to a third gold medal as an independent nation. He'd built numerous plays for Singh Sr., the centrepiece of India's dinner table of
attacks. Now his leader would have to follow, and India would
have to play more as a team than they ever had before.

"I cursed myself," says Singh Sr. "I saw myself as a skipper
abandoning his sinking ship. Though each member of the team
was most sympathetic I could not shake off my despairing
thoughts."

Singh Sr. was the perfect decoy. A fit man, he dragged two
players all over the pitch with him. It turned the game into a
tough, ugly affair. Germany, itself a well-trained squad, was relentless, defending attacks that now came from the outside wings
instead of straight up the middle.

Halftime ended in a scoreless tie. Singh Sr. headed quietly to
the locker room, as if he didn't want to draw any attention. Shame
dripped off him like sweat. He could do nothing more than rope
defenders in; he wanted to hide in the corner. Passing was almost
out of the question.

His longtime friend and fellow Sikh player Udham Singh
came up to him at his stall. As a centre half, Udham was responsible for getting the ball to Singh Sr. in scoring position. Now
he was lost, a treasure map with no X. He walked over to Singh
Sr. and sat down beside his despondent brother-in-arms. Their
eyes met.

"I will score," said Udham. "Just get me the ball and I will
do it."

Harbail tried to whip his boys into a frenzy with a rousing
speech, but it was clear that this was going to be trench warfare
right down to the final whistle. Udham came out in the second
half with fire in his belly, determined to right the ship. He took
the ball at centre, and rather than pass, as he usually did, he deked
through two unsuspecting German players. Suddenly the team's
formation was out of whack; the centre half was encroaching
unguarded on the defence. But the two German centre backs
were torn, reluctant to leave Singh Sr.'s side.

Udham went straight for goal, darting between the defender's line. Singh Sr. took off right beside him, four players

heading towards the German goalkeeper like an unstoppable freight train. Udham took one more tap right outside the crease, but pushed the ball a little too far ahead to regain control. Singh Sr. and Udham both darted for the ball, with defenders right on their heels and the German goalkeeper racing out to cut off the angles.

Right before the imminent collision, in the pack of players, Singh Sr. outstretched his arm, extending his stick ahead of everyone. Although he could not shoot, he managed to tap the ball enough to give it one last gasp of energy, changing its direction, throwing the keeper out of line. Everyone collided in a glorious mess, the ball dribbling across the goal line.

Singh Sr. knew he had touched it last, but hugged Udham in celebration when they got up. He couldn't have cared less, and never raised the point error with an official or even told his teammates. They'd scored, that was all that mattered.

The Germans did not relent, just kept chasing players and balls with a undying fever. They were going to make India work for it, right to the final whistle.

Amidst the last, grinding minutes, India's right winger Charles Stephan darted out to the left after a slow pass from Singh Sr. Going for goal, a German defender had seen enough, and literally threw his body at Stephen, snapping his ankle. Stephen fell to the ground, crying out in pain. A stretcher came out and team manager O.P. Mehra tried to get Stephen onto it, but he refused and tried to stand on the broken bone, only to fall back down to the ground screaming.

Unable to make a substitution as they were not allowed under the rules, India were now down to nine men. Stephen stayed on the sidelines, shouting encouragement to his teammates as the seconds ticked away. India went into lockdown mode, trapping Germany in the midfield with a mass of players. With Singh Sr. injured and Stephen out, they would not be scoring. They would ride the game to the bitter end.

The final whistle sounded and Singh Sr. dropped to his knees, exhausted. He was covered in welts from the German defenders, who'd been hounding him all game. He'd later realize

Nazi Germany's loss to the British Raj in Munich was still very much on the opposing player's minds.

Harbail came to Singh Sr.'s room at the Olympic Village that night. Singh Sr. was depressed, trying to remain stoic in the face of a right hand that would not do as it was told. He ran the play against Afghanistan over and over in his mind, cursing his ego-driven folly. It became a menace inside his skull; he tried to shoo it away, but it was no use. After Harbail went to bed, Singh Sr. took a sleeping tablet, but it did no good. He tossed and turned for hours, finally drifting into a vivid nightmare.

"I was alone on a huge ground. Its undulating surface was strewn with rocks and pebbles. I could see the goal posts. I dribbled away like mad, sweating and panting. The distance seemed enormous. Eventually when I approached the striking circle I was suddenly confronted with a goal boarded up with planks. In front stood a faceless goalkeeper, his hands akimbo, laughing at me, daring me to score. I could do nothing. I tried to lift my hands. They were paralyzed. Panic seized me. I tried to shriek. The effort formed a lump in my throat, it dissolved like dessert sand, dry and tasteless. I got up with a start."

Singh Sr. jerked awake, covered in sweat.

His thoughts moved to his family back home. Sushil, his daughter Sushbir, and infant son, Kanwalbir, entered his mind, offering small respite. He remembered taking them to the Darbar Sahib, the Golden Temple in Amritsar, where the four of them prayed to celebrate his being named captain. The golden walls, the white linoleum flooring on their bare feet, wet from people bathing in the sarovar, which contained *amrita*, holy water from the Ravi River.

Since 1928, India or the British Raj had won gold at the Olympics, five times in a row. A sixth was in reach, but doubt circled Singh Sr.'s thoughts. How would his country receive the team back home if they lost? he wondered. He needed to find the strength to overcome this mental hurdle. He needed God by his side.

Compounding the stress was India's opponent in the gold medal match. Pakistan had beaten Great Britain 3-2 in a thrilling, back and forth game. The political ramifications of the final, to be played on December 6, were lead heavy. The images of Partition overhung the event; each player struggled to shake the horrors they had endured: Muslims watching the slaughter of friends and family by Hindus, and vice versa; Sikhs, witnessing unspeakable atrocities in the name of freedom—rape, murder, assault, homes burnt to the ground with people still inside; Gandhi, starving himself to stop the violence, to stop people who'd shared villages for centuries from killing one another. Hindus and Sikhs forced to head east, and Muslims forced to the west as an independent India sprouted up like a flower bud on a barren battlefield. This was more than a field hockey game. To the souls involved, it was something much more impactful.

Singh Sr. spoke of the pain in his autobiography, both his physical injury and the tormenting memories of the most horrific time in his country's history.

"No two persons mean the same thing when they say: 'I know what pain is,'" he wrote. "They only agree that something hurts. The human race has been suffering and inflicting pain from the time early man looked upon pain as the handmaid of evil spirits, to present times when it has become a test of faith for the religious, a "passion of the soul" for the philosopher and a symptom for the physician. How does a sportsman look at pain? What does it mean to him? How does he live so constantly within its walls? . . .

"Look into any sportsman's dressing room, the little room where the ego thrashes furiously against the "villain of pain," and you will find why the sportsman strives so hard to remain something special, something of a superman that obviously he is not. Loneliness, desperation and frustration, all ordinary emotions, are trebled in dressing rooms. They cannot be seen; they can only be sensed. Sportsmen, especially those in contact sports, confront and suffer pain, yet they continue to play."

Singh Sr. surveyed the eyes of his fellow teammates as they made their way back to the Olympic Village, waking laboriously with limps and various ailments.

During his schooling days, Singh Sr. had read about Marquis de Sade, the French philosopher, and Leopold von Sacher-Masoch, an Austrian writer. Singh Sr. had been puzzled by terms like "sadism" and "masochism", about how some people derived pleasure from pain, and through the pain of others. He remembers the lifeless bodies hung in trees, the smell of cooked flesh and kerosene. The horror man caused in the name of religion.

Unable to sleep, Singh Sr. wandered the Olympic Village grounds. Most of the athletes had gone to bed, but he could hear the laughter from nearby pubs where Australians were enjoying the games at all hours of the night.

He walked slowly under the amber streetlights, not sure of his destination. A figure came up beside him: Ashwini, the vice-president of the IHF and Singh Sr.'s boss in the police force. Kumar was distraught to see Singh Sr. out so late, and calmed him with another sleeping tablet. He walked him to his room and waited by Singh Sr.'s bedside as the Sikh star slowly drifted off into another nightmare in which he'd fail to score a single goal for his country.

***

Game day, the present challenge now screaming in his face. Singh Sr. awakes from a terrible sleep. He sits in his room, looking down at his swollen finger. He could barely make a fist, almost as if his entire right hand was paralyzed. During the semi-final against West Germany, Singh Sr. relied solely on his thumb to hold his stick up; now it too was sore and ached with pain.

He noticed a letter tucked into his travel suitcase. It was from his father. He picked it up, opened it clumsily with his left hand. Written in Urdu, it was typical of his father's letters, all business, no nonsense, as it was republished in his autobiography:

"Dear Balbir,

Sat Siri Akal. (God is the only truth). By now you have fulfilled every desire of yours in hockey. The honour that you have earned in this field is also perhaps your last. I believe you are the only player selected to captain India twice in succession in international matches. Your game has been acclaimed all over the world. Another ambition of yours, to become Deputy

Superintendent of Police, has also been fulfilled. According to "The Tribune" of October 23, 1956, your promotion has been gazzetted. I congratulate your wife, our dear children, your mother-in-law, maternal uncles and your loving mother on this achievement.

As captain of the team you will have to be extremely cautious.

1. You must never be arrogant. Arrogance is a disease. Yes, everybody has the right to a certain amount of pride, but not arrogance.

2. It is likely that some members of the team are jealous of you. But you must treat them with kindness and give them full justice.

3. On account of your brilliance, teams of various countries will be itching to pull you down. You will have to be very careful and guard against injuries. At the same time you will have to out-dribble and out-manoeuvre them.

4. You will have to be friendly with everyone.

5. You will have to keep the honour of the National Flag. I have sacrificed my entire career at the altar of *Bharat Mata* [Mother India]. I have never in my life done anything which would tarnish the image of India. You will have to play not for yourself but for your country. You will have to enhance India's prestige.

6. You must score at the first available opportunity. Hockey is not a game for selfish players. You must never allow a good chance to go abegging.

7. You must always be calm and keep your presence of mind. Needless excitement will only spoil your judgment.

8. Alertness is the need of the hour.

9. You must always respect your well-wishers and be of help to them.

10. Every player must live in an atmosphere of mutual trust and friendship and play for the country. We in Moga are praying that India's hockey team wins another Olympic gold medal.

We are all very happy. You must go to Australia with an easy mind and perform your duty. It appears that Sushil and the children are with you at Ambala to see you off. While departing you must look cheerful and look happy. As soon as you reach Australia send us your postal address and also mail your schedule of matches.

- Your loving Father"

Singh Sr. wishes he'd found the letter at the outset of the games. His father's written words felt like a premonition: he had been neither alert nor careful, and he had not kept his presence of mind. He thought of everything his father had suffered through, the unspeakable horrors of prison camp under the Raj.

The Pakistanis came across as a boisterous squad in the newspapers leading up to the final, said Singh Sr. They would be the nation to dethrone India, they claimed; to chop them down from the perch of greatness and bring them back amongst the masses. Regardless of Singh Sr.'s injury, Team India had yet to give up a goal in Melbourne—much to the credit of Francis' stellar netminding, who had given Singh Sr. and his Punjab Police squad headaches throughout the years at the national club stage. Singh Sr. was glad they had him as their backstop. Their last line of defence would be tested to his limits today. They were going to need everything they could muster from a depleted squad as their opponents came looking for blood.

Pakistan held Germany to a scoreless draw, meaning the teams would be fairly evenly matched. The war was about to begin, and this time there would be no prisoners. It would come down to one game, one overcast afternoon in Melbourne, for eternal bragging rights.

After breakfast and morning rituals, the team loaded onto the bus for the trip to the cluster of stadiums at the Melbourne Sports and Entertainment district. Everyone was on the bus, the driver about to start the engine when M.T. Ansari, then secretary of the Bhopal Hockey Association, let out a monstrous sneeze.

Ashwini stopped everyone in their tracks.

He scolded Ansari, then found Singh Sr., demanded he get up, and took him off the bus. Ashwini took Singh Sr. back to his room and stood in front of him.

"You may dismiss me as a superstitious man," said Ashwini, "but I want you to peel off your tracksuit and shoes and lie in bed for five minutes."

Singh Sr. was perplexed, but was in no mood for arguing. They would be late for the game if he did not do as told. He stripped off all his clothes and got into bed.

"The spell of Ansari's bad omen has to be undone," said Ashwini, sitting uncomfortably on a chair in the room as his star player lay naked between the sheets.

Ashwini then took him back onto the bus and told Ansari if he sneezed again he would be kicked off the bus and not allowed anywhere near the team for the rest of the day. Singh Sr., never much for superstitions, sat, confused, all the way to the stadium.

Harbail spoke to his players before they took the pitch. Regulars down with injuries, players suiting up hurt, the team bandaged and bruised but still ready for war.

"This is no time for despair," said Harbail. "God willing we will win!"

Singh Sr. knew Harbail as a God-fearing man; he kept a picture of Guru Nanak, the founder of Sikhism and the first Sikh guru, with him at all times, and would pray twice a day, concluding it with the same statement: "*Wahe Guru* (God is my teacher). I am not keen on any personal promotions. I have only my country's interest in mind. Bless my team. My only wish is that India win the gold medal once again."

Singh Sr. valiantly headed out onto the pitch. He could see Pakistani players he was once good friends with, comrades with whom he had shared a laugh and bled on the field during the days of the British Raj. Now these Muslim men were enemies, their own families raped and murdered during the same period of national strife. No one was innocent; everyone was to blame. While India and Pakistan had engineered a few goodwill games between the two countries since 1947, nothing held the gravity of this encounter.

"We were in the midst of a crossfire," says Singh Sr. "We had scores of friends who only the other day rubbed shoulders with us on the playground. We were friends, sharing each other's joys and sorrows. Suddenly we were estranged. Provocative speeches and actions from the other side of the fence did not help matters. They only fanned the fire of hatred; it spread and charred human hearts. In the early days of independence we found to our consternation that the men we had played with could not stomach anything India did. The distance grew wider and wider and eventually an India-Pakistan clash came to be considered as something of a showdown."

As soon as the whistle sounded, number 13 for India was bumped and knocked, his stick whacked out of his hands, his knees targeted; any part of his body in striking range was punished. Singh Sr. had gotten used to it, the pain of being shadowed, of hearing slanderous statements whispered into his ears—it was easy to stomach under these circumstances. What really stung was he couldn't retaliate the one way he wanted to—by scoring goals.

All he could do was run, so he did. From the first moments of the match, he dragged two Pakistani defenders all over the field, sprinting long looping routes, heading out to the corner, backtracking, filling holes. Every time the play would stop, he'd look over to them, watching the defenders catch their breath. Then again, relentlessly, off like a wound-up toy. He was literally running them ragged.

The rest of India stepped up to the plate amidst the new game plan: Udham, Gentle, Claudius, Amir Kumar. They knew their valiant leader was a shell of his goal scoring self, so they came together as a team, finding unusual ways to puncture the Pakistani defence. Singh Sr. left gaping holes on the pitch for them to move the ball through. The game had an unorthodox feel, the crowd wondering why the Sikh star was making small passes instead of wiring shots at the keeper.

Right after half, when it looked like the two teams were going to beat each other senseless to a nil-nil draw, left-back R.S. Gentle took advantage of a penalty corner. India had the lead 1-0. Now all they had to do was play even for another 30 minutes, and gold would be the reward.

In the 49th minute, Pakistan sailed a shot just wide of the net, then a few minutes later, almost converted on a penalty corner.

They had gone all in, and were wiring shots at Francis with grow-ing fever. The goalkeeper dived left and right, chucking his body like a human shield. Going down a goal ramped up Pakistan's attack, and now they were taking chances, trying to find a way through the stingy Indian back line.

As the game wore on, Pakistan's frustrations grew. They start-ed to realize that something was wrong with Singh Sr., and left him with a single mark: they had no choice. Singh Sr. was able to fetch balls and run the clock out, taking defenders deep and grinding out time, letting opponents whack him to their heart's content. He took balls to goal, but knowing he couldn't shoot, would lay off a pass and set a pick, taking full stride hits in the process. If he couldn't score his way to victory, he would suffer whatever pain imaginable.

The sound of the final whistle was an angel calling out. A beacon of light at the end of a long tunnel. Singh Sr. looked up to the sky, dropped to his knees and wept. God had tested him, but ultimately rewarded him for his resilience. He'd now won three gold medals for his country, equaling his hero, Dhyan Chand.

Rajdeep, then a young boy back in Moga, lay awake in bed, listening to the game on the radio. His father had sent him upstairs, and he protested, but was quickly overruled. It would be 3AM in the morning when the match was played, much too late for a child to be up. But when the final whistle sounded, Nachatter and his wife started cheering loudly, running around the house in the dark of night. Rajdeep says he'll never forget the shouting from downstairs.

"Balbir has won! Balbir has won! Balbir has won!"

The *Indian Express* ran a large half-page article on the win on Dec. 7, 1956.[173] There's a picture, noting Singh Sr. as captain, and mug shots of 16 other players. The article, which has no byline, rips the team for their decision to play Singh Sr.:

"Never, perhaps during their 28-year reign of hockey cham-pions, had India to struggle so bitterly for victory, and so nearly we paid the price for the stupid blunders in composition of the team. A more innocuous forward line had not taken the field in the name of India. It was the unanimous opinion here, there was no need for Balbir Singh to have played with a bandaged finger and with the aid of three pain-killing injections. He was by no means the dashing centre-forward the Madras public had known him, while Hardyal Singh, in excellent form and fighting fit, was languishing on the sidelines."

Regardless of whether or not the decision to play an injured Singh Sr. was right or not, the fact that they still won gold speaks about how the move obviously didn't influence the outcome of the game in a weighty, negative way.

Singh Sr. had now amassed 22 goals in the Olympics. As he led his team out to the victory rostrum, the pride he'd lost during the games returned. Regardless of his selfish play against Afghanistan, his team was golden, and all would be forgotten—he hoped. His body unfurled slowly from its tense state; exhaustion, relief. Slowly, his stern demeanour cracked an unwavering smile.

He stepped up to the middle box, with the captains of Pakistan and Germany to his side. The crowd roared with applause, and he couldn't help but cry, weeping tears of joy after what was his toughest Olympics ever. "The national anthem sounded sweet and the tricolour, fluttering proudly in the stiff breeze, looked a grand sight," he remembers fondly.

After the celebrations died down, Singh Sr. sought out Ansari and patted him on the back, whispering in his ear so no one else could hear.

"Your sneeze brought us luck."

FRAGRANCE GARDENS

"Everyone underestimates their own life. Funny thing is, in the end, all our stories—your life, my life, old Husain's life, they're the same. In fact, no matter where you go in the world, there is only one important story: of youth, and loss, and yearning for redemption. So we tell the same story, over and over. Just the details are different."

~ Rohinton Mistry, *Family Matters*

The fourth morning in Chandigarh I wake to the news that Hockey India has sacked its high-priced Australian coach Terry Walsh.[174] Hockey India president Narinder Batra allegedly outed Walsh because of apparent "financial misconduct", dating back to when Walsh was the technical director of USA Field Hockey. Although Walsh was never charged, or forced to resign, or implicated, Batra said this was good enough grounds to dismiss him while he was coaching India years later.

Walsh, whose contract was about to expire, was also reported from a different outlet to have resigned before renegotiations could start between himself, Hockey India, and the Sports Authority of India.[175] Walsh and Batra had publicly clashed over a number of issues, some of which seem like nothing more than a personal-professional pissing match.[176] It turns out Hockey India has sacked—or lost—four separate foreign coaches since they took over from the deposed IHF post-scandal in 2009 when the entire organization had to be rebuilt under a new name.[177] This included Walsh's successor Paul van Ass.[178] Walsh further noted in a interview that the exclusion of Sikh player Gurbaj Singh, who was left off the roster of an upcoming European tour for "disciplinary reasons" was puzzling to him.[179]

"It surprises me that issues are again being had with Gurbaj. I found him to be an outstanding component of our team. Without key players like Gurbaj, the task becomes seriously more difficult."

Gurbaj, a talented midfielder who was expected to be a key part of the 2016 Olympic squad that will head to Rio de Janeiro, was suspended for "indulging in groupism and creating disharmony within the team" and given a nine month suspension in August of 2015.[180] Gurbaj seemed quite perplexed at the suspension and its length as he stated in a *First Post* article:

"I don't know why such a report was given against me. I didn't do anything."

Gurbaj does not have a history of acting out, so it makes the suspension even more puzzling.

Kabir and I chow down a quick breakfast and get on the road to Patiala, a couple hours drive southwest of Chandigarh along Highway 64. The drive is tough out of the city, cars bogged down on a tight, two lane strip. Acres of cauliflower and maize crops, freshly harvested for the coming winter roll by on each side, interspersed with decaying clay buildings or garbage-filled ditches. Patiala is much like Chandigarh, a predominately Sikh city close to the Pakistan border. It's smack in the middle of a busy thoroughfare, and getting in and out are transportation victories in their own right.

We're here for an interview with Rajdeep Singh Gill. His father was a friend of Singh Sr.'s at Dev Samaj High School. Gill is retired, living in a large gated community on the outskirts of town. Rajdeep was formerly the director general of police for Punjab, the president of the Indian Basketball Federation and vice-president of the Punjab Olympic Association, so suffice it to say he's well-versed on a variety of topics close to Singh Sr. and Indian sports in general. He sits calmly in his chair as he speaks, servants supplying us with hot tea and cookies. He looks like most Sikh men, portly, a moustache and healthy beard wrapped in a polite yet authoritative tone when recalling past events.

Rajdeep and I have a wide-ranging discussion on a number of subjects, and he speaks about how highly regarded Singh Sr. was in the Punjab state when he was growing up.

"He was a huge influence on Punjab, people loved him, they respected him. People wanted to be like him. I remember a lot of people looking at him trying to make sure their shirt was tied up like him, that their hair was tied like his. He was a major influence."

We talk about field hockey legacies in India, and Rajdeep admits Singh Sr. has been cast aside for some reason. I ask Rajdeep if he thinks Singh Sr. is not as famous or well-known as Chand—despite the fact that his career is arguably more decorated—is due to his religious background.

"I can't say for sure, I am not too sure. I don't think so."

Rajdeep continues, telling me the reason Singh Sr. has been forgotten throughout the years is because of a number of "extra hockey reasons" that don't necessarily add up when put together. One has to do with the introduction of astroturf into the game, another is because of the rise of cable television in the 90s and cricket's ascend to power, the other is Chand's place in history (chronologically speaking); also that Chand has passed away and Singh Sr. hasn't, and that around the time India opened up to globalization in the early 90s was when Singh Sr. was spending more time in Canada. Rajdeep is, however, sure that Singh Sr. has actually been subjugated.

"He has not been given his due by the media, by the state government, by the national government."

After the interview concludes, Kabir and I take a short drive across town to the home base of the National Sports Museum.[181] Stationed inside the former palace building of the Maharaja of Patiala, which along with the palace grounds has been turned into the home of the Netaji Subhas National Institute of Sports.

The NIS is known for producing world-class athletes. Multiple Commonwealth, Asian Games and Olympic Gold medalists have come from this Punjab sports factory. The grounds have a myriad of facilities for various sports—field hockey, cricket, archery, basketball. Rajdeep spoke to me earlier in the day about the history of Sikhs that I end up hearing many times during my trip, one rich in folklore and mythology but somewhat rooted in fact.

The only viable way to get to the South Asian continent before the advent of planes and concrete roads was through the northwestern Punjab area, as the rest was blocked by the mountains to the east and west. This meant, throughout the area's history, the Sikhs became the first line of defence for the region. This bred warriors; tough, strong people who were more than adequate when it came to physical strength.[182] A great Sikh warrior lineage carved through generations of battles which naturally translated into fierce sporting world competitors.

The Sikh empire, which reigned for the first half of the 1800s led by founder Ranjit Singh,[183] was pre-dated by the Mughal

Empire—essentially Persian rule under the religion of Islam. Kabir tells me about a dozen battles and wars that took place over the period, noting I will get a more in-depth look at the history the next day in Amritsar during a public school function.

However Kabir and I are not actually here to peruse the local sports history museum, which is spread out over a dark, dusty hall with sparse lighting chronicling the athletes of the state throughout the ages. We're here for a different reason, one that dates all the way back to 1985.

The Sports Authority of India (the governing body for the National Institute of Sports) asked Singh Sr. to donate some of his memorabilia towards a proposed national sports museum project at the time in Delhi. Singh Sr. had a boatload of medals (36) he could offer up, some historical photos and one special suit jacket—his baby blue captain's blazer from the 1956 Melbourne games.

Singh had already donated some of his memorabilia during the Riot Relief in 1984 when Sikhs were targeted in Delhi after the assassination of Indira Gandhi by two of her Sikh bodyguards,[184] which was in turn retaliation for the storming of Sikhism's holiest shrine, the Golden Temple in Amritsar.[185] Singh Sr. had actually donated his other captain's blazers to the riot relief camps and Sikhs who had been pushed from their homes as they were lit on fire with everything in them.

The riots claimed the life of around 2,700 Sikhs according to the Indian government, although many believe the actual number is much higher. Most of the killings took place in Delhi and are just one of many clashes that encompassed Sikhs and Hindus over the years including the Indian Emergency,[186,187] Operation Blue Star and the push for an independent Khalistan which Kabir outlined for me a few days prior, which were all a regular topic at the Bhomia dinner table.

Sikhism is the world's fifth largest religion, with around 30 million adherents.[188] But many have left India after decades of oppression, and in a region where one religion dominates various countries (Islam—both Sunni and Shia—are the official religion in multiple countries across North Africa, the Middle East and Southeast Asia; and Hinduism in India) the Sikhs struggles are compared to the Tamils—a minority ethnic group in Sri Lanka that has waged a similarly bloody civil war for their own sovereign state.[189] In Ramachandra Guha's book *Indian after Gandhi: The History of the World's Largest Democracy,* he outlines the severity of the struggle:

"Here, as there, wrote the political scientist Paul Wallace in 1981, 'language, religion and regionalism combined into a potentially explosive context which political elites struggle to contain'. Within the next year or two this mixture had been made still more deadly by the addition of a fourth ingredient: armed violence.

"Hindu-Sikh conflict was, in the context of Indian history, unprecedented. While it was manifesting itself, other older and more predictable forms of social conflict were also being played out. Thus the journalist M. J. Akbar, compiling his reports of the 1980s into a single volume, called the book *Riot after Riot*—a title that was melancholy as well as appropriate."

The goal of Khalistan is simple: Sikhs want their own country, a wish born not necessarily from a desire to impose Punjabi rule, but from a hope that their concerns as an ethnic group will be validated in a tough political and economic region. Yet the 1985 Air India bombings,[190] in which militant Sikhs allegedly carried out the murder of 329 people in retaliation for the anti-Sikh riots that followed Indira Gandhi's assassination, is yet another example of how brutal violence and vicious retribution has done nothing to help anyone's cause moving forward. The history between Punjabis and the ruling Hindu majority of India is a perilous relationship, prone to flare-ups at any given moment and defined by the various clashes that have taken place since the lead up to Partition.

For what seemed like a good cause back in the 80s, Singh Sr. was more than happy to donate his iconic Melbourne blazer and medals to the Sports Authority of India. The authority said it was going to help revive sports amongst the country's youth, an aim close to Singh Sr.'s heart. While the museum never materialized, Singh Sr. and his family felt as if the memorabilia, particularly the blazer, were in good hands.

Fast forward to 2012. Singh Sr. is chosen by the International Olympic Committee as one of 16 iconic Olympians to be featured at the IOC's Olympic museum in London.[191] After his selection, the IOC got in touch with Singh Sr., asking for his historic Melbourne blazer. But when he asked the Sports Authority of India if he could borrow it back for the event, the group claimed to have searched high and low and failed to find it.[192] With no prep time remaining, Kabir decided to smuggle Singh Sr.'s three Olympic gold medals in his pockets to London, stuffing them in his pants without the requisite forms.

The case of the missing blazer continued. Once London 2012 was over, the National Hockey Museum in London—Dil Bahra and Pat Rowley are founders; it's part of the Switzerland-based International Hockey Federation—came calling.[193] They wanted Singh Sr.'s Melbourne blazer, for a permanent display that would "showcase Indian field hockey dominance" during an era in which the country capped off six gold medals in a row.

Once again, Kabir asked the Sports Authority of India to locate the blazer. Once again they pleaded ignorance. They'd searched everywhere they said. Nothing.

So now we're sitting in front of S.S. Roy, executive director of the National Institute of Sports. He's a lackadaisical looking fellow. Workers drop off files on his desk throughout our meeting. He's pleading ignorance, too, as Kabir pokes and prods for answers he doesn't seem to inclined to give.

Kabir is asking him if there's anything he can do, other than start rummaging through boxes and closets himself, to locate the precious clothing item, which could be somewhere in the museum's back rooms. Roy seems apathetic about the situation; there had been little media attention on missing memorabilia up until then.

Union Sports Minister Sarbananda Sonowal, in an attempt to quiet Singh Sr. and his family, met with Balbir in 2014 as Kabir kept going to the press about the missing blazer. However during their meet, Sonowal never brought up the blazer, rather simply lauded Singh Sr. to the press in attendance and gave him a plaque.

Kabir has taken on the cause of locating the blazer and Singh Sr.'s other memorabilia as a personal quest to help his grandfather regain incredibly important items dear to his heart and his iconic life story. He's taken legal action in the form of multiple RTI's (Right to Information) requests, and has started a media campaign.[194] Exasperated, he tells me he's thinking of going back in time through a wormhole to tell his grandfather not to donate the blazer in the first place, but cannot locate a working time machine.

None of these plans offer much hope, and the saga is still ongoing. The press coverage has been scattered at best, and yawning in nature. Case in point: A *Deccan Herald* piece which features a picture of some unknown Sikh who is supposed to be Singh Sr. as the article's main photograph.[195]

Kabir and I stop for food before heading back to Chandigarh. I'm itching to talk to Singh Sr., and he agrees to take me on one of his daily walks through the Fragrance Gardens, a four-acre park in the neighbourhood. It's a lovely place, lush grass, well kept trees, hedges and squirrels amidst nominal garbage. Singh Sr. moves fast for a 91-year-old. He holds my hand when we cross a busy street—but I quickly realize it's for my safety, not his.

As we settle into conversation, we broach many subjects: Indian politics, race relations, religious customs and secularism. We talk a lot about hockey. Singh Sr. is one of many Indians who wish the country could somehow regain its clout which has it ranked eighth in the world as of late 2015.[196]

Field hockey was India's go-to for much of the sport's existence, from Chand's reign right up until around the end of Singh Sr.'s career. Only in the past two decades has it ceded the crown to cricket. The IHF made an abrupt switch to astroturf playing fields in the late 70s.[197,198] Unable to have kept up with the times and build adequate pitches back home for a variety of reasons, which included poor funding and bureaucratic red tape at every corner, the Indian team quickly found itself a step behind. Pakistan suffered similarly. While many nations keep a strong hold on their country's sport for decades, remaining perennial contenders (think Brazil/Germany/Italy for soccer; ice hockey for Canada; basketball for the United States), India and Pakistan have lost serious footing.

Since 1984, neither has medaled (aside from a bronze by Pakistan in 1992) and only European countries have won gold with Germany becoming the sport's new perennial powerhouse.

India's resume is still amazing: eight Olympic gold medals and a World Cup title. But since the switch to artificial grass, the team has yet to crack the medal podium. The squad actually failed to qualify for the 2008 Summer Olympics in Beijing. Many believe cricket's ascension was partly due to the loss of Indian field hockey supremacy.

Singh Sr. tells me the sport needs to be instilled in Indians at a young age, something he tried to achieve in his second career after he left policing. The idea came to him during his tours of European countries, which had a glut of playgrounds in the towns he visited.

"You need to start when they are really young," he says. "The talent pool is much higher if the foundation is wider. Today they are just going to certain areas and hand-picking them, they are not watching them from the start."

We talk about the IHF, founded in 1928. In 2008, India's Olympic Association (IOA) took over running the federation amidst alleged bribe-taking by one of its top officials.[199,200] It's the second time they've had to step in over corruption allegations. Secret filming by reporters showed secretary general Kandaswamy Jothikumaran accepting money; he subsequently resigned.

In 2008, the IOA went one step further and ousted Indian hockey chief K.P.S. Gill,[201] former Director General of Police Punjab, who led efforts to crush a separatist revolt in Punjab in the years following the assassination of Indira Gandhi. Essentially, Gill went around wiping out Sikh militant separatists by any means he deemed necessary, including violence, murder and rewards for murder.[202] A number of human rights claims have been made against Gill, and in the late 90s he was convicted of sexually harassing a female co-worker; in India nonetheless, where one would think its chauvinistic society would sweep such a charge under its cultural rug.[203,204]

Hockey India,[205] a new organization currently headed by Narinder Batra, has stepped into the void. Singh Sr. said that, because of Gill's personal affection towards him, Hockey India associates him with Gill. It's an odd tie, as Gill was largely responsible for the death of hundreds of Sikhs. Regardless of the reasons, Hockey India does not like him, Singh Sr. says. He suspects the fact that Dhyan Chand's son, Ashok Kumar, was a part of the initial set-up of the organization could also be a factor; Kumar was integral to Hockey India's first years of existence and still figures prominently in the organization's character. Singh Sr. tells me that Kumar has given him the cold shoulder over the years, even though Singh Sr. made him the lynchpin of the 1975 World Cup team's midfield.

In 2015, after I'd traveled to India, Kumar and Hockey India made a feeble attempt at recognizing Singh Sr. He was completely unexpectedly awarded Hockey India's Dhyan Chand Lifetime Achievement Award, overseen by Kumar himself.[206] The trophy has been given out multiple times every year since 2012, and Singh Sr. was not notified of the award, only told he needed to be at Hockey India's annual awards ceremony, therefore he did not invite any friends or family or even prepare a speech to help mark the occasion. The family has taken this award as a half-hearted, lukewarm gesture given its extenuating circumstances.

I ask Singh Sr. about all the mythologizing that's happened around Chand's appearance at the 1936 Olympics in Berlin,[207,208,209,210] none of which has ever been verified by an outside source.

"I am sure it is not true, but how could someone prove it otherwise now? Everyone is dead."

During the course of our walk in the busy Fragrance Gardens, something odd happens. We pass close to a hundred people, ranging in age from young to old, and nobody recognizes Singh Sr. as an Indian sporting legend. That's when it dawns on me. There are over a billion people living in this country, and only one of them has three Olympic gold medals, and an Olympic Record to his name. I imagine myself walking with Carl Lewis in his home state of Alabama, or taking a stroll with Nadia Comaneci in Bucharest, Romania. I imagine the swarms of adoring fans that would follow us, pestering their heroes for autographs, asking them to pose for selfies and showering them with praise to the point of exhaustion.

But for Singh Sr., there is glaring anonymity. As we near the final bend we come back once again to comparisons between himself and Chand, and why he's been given such a tough road to legendary status while Chand has coasted to mythological heights.[211]

The words come out of his mouth slowly, without malice nor spite. Almost as if this quiet, honest man is stating another fact about himself:

"It is because I am Sikh."

He says it not as if a weight has been lifted from his shoulders, or as if it is some grand revelation. He says it like it's simply something that has been a foregone conclusion for quite some time, albeit largely unverbalized. For a man who's spent his entire life turning the other cheek and playing the game, it's an incredibly candid moment, and the most profound statement I'll hear on my entire trip.

We've reached the end of another long, hot day under the Indian sun. I'm hacking out phlegm and sneezing almost nonstop. My cold has settled in for the long haul, setting up shop inside my body. I fall asleep in my room in Chandigarh, listening to the sounds of street vendors passing by the house banging drums and yelling loudly. Questions about the state of affairs I am currently intertwined in churn through my mind. As the story clears like a passing fog, fact and fiction become blurred amidst the mist, and I'm left wondering how I'll ever make sense of this trip other than declaring it much like India—a series of unanswerable questions.

★★★

The doctor has come to see me. Well, not exactly. Dr. Kalra, who back in 1975 was hand-picked by Dr. P.N. Chuttani[212,213]—one of the founding fathers of the Post Graduate Institute of Medical Education and Research in Chandigarh—for the World Cup, has come to be interviewed. He was the attending physician for Team India in Kuala Lumpur, Malaysia, when Singh Sr. was the manager of the only World Cup team to win gold. Dr. Kalra has known Singh Sr. for over 40 years.

Dr. Kalra has agreed to check on my condition, prescribing another round of medication and telling me to drink lots of fluids. I'll feel 60 percent better in a few days, he promises. After his examination, Dr. Kalra regales Singh Sr. and I with fantastical stories about the World Cup and how, astrologically speaking, India's win was foretold in the stars. Then the conversation turns to Singh Sr.'s legacy. Dr. Kalra is furious, outlining the many facts and accomplishments that place Singh Sr. above Chand and merit him national superstardom.

But why? I ask.

"I am not sure," he says to me. "It is a funny thing."

Dr. Kalra, a Hindu, rolls into another story, obviously content not to expand on his brief answer. Singh Sr. reverts back to the question; possibly regretting his candid moment with me in the garden the day before, he says religion doesn't have anything to do with it. Looking back on my notes, the pages are filled with question marks, like the Riddler came through and left his calling card. With such a disastrous history between the Hindus and Sikhs, one might feel that religion has definitely played a part in this—something I can't get Dr. Kalra to acknowledge. It's a frustrating turn of events given my revealing chat with Singh Sr.

Later I speak to Dr. Sudesh Gupta on the phone from the Bhomia household. Gupta is a family friend and a highly decorated individual, a sports sociologist and social activist who's won the Bharat Jyoti Award. When I speak to him he is out of country, working for an NGO.

"One of the greatest hockey players in the world," says Gutpa. "Our country has not been fair to him. He has created all sorts of records, he should be given the Bharat Ratna, but he is not given his due in the history books."

I ask Gupta, flat out, if this is because Singh Sr. is Sikh and Chand is Hindu.

"No, no, I will not agree. India is a secular country, we are proud of our heritage and culture. I don't think this thing is the reason of the matter in India."

I look over at Kabir, who's been listening to the conversation on speaker. He shrugs, offering me an apathetic smirk.

★★★

Guests are a common occurrence at the Bhomia residence. Sushbir is a great host, bringing out hot tea, delectable sweets and various snacks. I've found it's not polite to refuse too much, so have slid the other way and am gorging like any good Westerner does when food is offered buffet style.

Everyone loves Singh Sr., who's the perfect communal saint: polite, kind, and more than willing to turn the spotlight off himself. His humbleness appears rigid at times. Part of me wants to force him, almost shake him, to take more credit for what he's done, but after a while you realize it's just not his modus operandi: he is humble, to a fault.

The day after our walk in the Gardens, two female athletes come by for a visit. Kabir has been setting up daily interviews in the living room, and I've hit the ground running talking to everyone and anyone about all things Singh Sr.

The first is Satinder Walia, a field hockey player born in the 1950s who played when Singh Sr. was amassing his medals. She both coached and played on the woman's national team, and has been a champion of the sport since her early years. However as one can expect, woman's field hockey is nowhere near the realm of the men's game. In India, female field hockey players struggle for recognition, funding, and exposure, even though they ranked thirteenth in the world as of September 2015.[214]

"It was crazy," says Walia about having Singh Sr. around while they were training and competing. "He was our hero. He was our coach, it was special of course."

It's clear to see Walia is proud of her playing days, showing me photos of herself in her early 20s, training with Singh Sr. We share a chuckle about how happy she was when uniforms changed and the women gave up dresses to wear shorts, just like the men.

Many male athletes in India end up getting cushy jobs, Walia says, working at such places as the Indian Oil Corporation, Indian

Airlines, Air India, Punjab National Bank, Bharat Petroleum and Indian Railways. However when it comes to the women, although the national team is highly ranked, not only do their medals go largely unnoticed, their players get little recognition—Walia's worked her whole life and never once made money playing field hockey.

A big part of Singh Sr.'s playing career was his time with the Punjab Police team. In between Olympics, he needed somewhere to play and keep his skills sharp, and the club team was the perfect fit, given his employment as a police officer. He was surrounded by fellow Olympic caliber athletes, and traveled extensively with the team on someone else's dime, playing quality squads around the country. While Moga was the foundational base of Singh Sr.'s career, the Punjab Police squad, and subsequent state team is where he fine-tuned his skills and became one of the sport's all-time deadliest scorers.

When it comes to women, there is nowhere near the same level of club play. There is a network of teams, and one big tournament, the All-India Inter Railways Women's Hockey Championship. That's about it. Despite this, in a country run by men, India's female squad still thrives, outranking first-world nations like Spain, Italy, Ireland and Scotland. One wonders where they would be if they were given the same treatment as their male counterparts.

The other athlete I meet is Cheetan Preet, who competed in the 2012 Asian Games in the 50-metre shooting category. Preet is in her mid-20s (a guess; I'm told asking a women's age in India is extremely faux-pas), and talks of taking a family trip to the shooting range as a young girl. She ended up outshooting all the boys, much to their chagrin, and the operator of the place offered to coach her on the spot.

Today, her athletic career appears to be winding to a halt. Currently completing schooling for a career in civil services, it seems the pressure to marry and start a family is bearing down on her like an inevitable weight. Preet is articulate, thoughtful and well-educated. She talks to me candidly, though her mother, sitting beside her while we chat, corrects her answers more than once in Punjabi, acting as her politically correct PR handler. You

can tell there's a part of Preet that would love to have a real conversation, but she's bound by her surroundings and culture. I do
get a few veiled gems of insight from India's younger female generation, a group that's sorely underrepresented in a nation of blab-
bering, mansplaining men:

On Singh Sr.'s subjugated legacy, Preet says, "That's a very
ugly and sad side somehow of our Indian mentality here. We tend
to forget our heroes, because we are not made to remember
them. There's a lot of leg pulling and I somehow feel like the
respectable people tend to stay out of that, out of the rat race. So
they end up being out of the limelight."

Walia also offers her perspective during this portion of the
conversation:

"I think it is because he is not in the media all the time, he
is not outspoken. He is humble."

Asked whether Singh Sr.'s religious affiliation is a factor, Preet
says, "We would be blind to think that community does not play
a part in this."

As for India's misrepresentation in popular culture now that
Modi has brought the international spotlight to the country, she
tells me, "Somehow we end up being portrayed as superstitious
and staunchly religious. But we're very open minded and scientific. I think people have this notion that we are a nation of snake-
charmers, which is very far from the truth."

After trying to engage in a number of touchy subjects, I think
both of us realize she can only say so much. She calls a male
friend, who comes over with his younger brother to meet me and
Singh Sr. It's as if she's saying 'well I can't really talk about much
of anything with you, but hopefully this male counterpart I know
will.'

Woman are almost a hermit species in India.[215] In a culture
commanded by men, it's tough to really get to know them. They
seem to be forever in the background. But Preet and Walia are
pitch perfect examples of the countless smart, educated females
across the country.

One of the stories playing out in the press during my trip is
that of woman being banned from the library at one of India's

largest Muslim universities.[216] Zameeruddin Shah, the vice chancellor of the Aligarh Muslim University in Uttar Pradesh, said female students would distract male students and overcrowd the library by attracting too many men. Ironically, he also claimed he's "not sexist". The incident set off a firestorm of debate, with the university trying to spin his remarks as "misinterpreted".

Now, following a petition, India's high court is involved. The whole thing stinks of blatant sexism in so many ways, but that's the norm in India. The end result is women have to research subjects elsewhere so they do not cause wandering eyes.

Oh, and the university also banned dogs from the library too, for good measure.

On our drive from Chandigarh to Delhi, the infamous gang rape came up in conversation with Kabir. The two-year anniversary of the attack was approaching.[217] On December 16, 2012, Jyoti Singh Pandey, a young woman traveling with a male friend, was brutally beaten and raped by six men. She sustained internal injuries from a metal rod that was shoved inside her vagina, destroying her internal organs. After she was raped with a blunt object—her male companion was knocked unconscious at the start of the attack—she was thrown off the bus and the driver tried to run her over. She died thirteen days later in a Singapore hospital.

Pandey had been out that evening watching *Life of Pi*, a film based on a novel in which India is portrayed largely as a culturally vibrant land filled with zoo animals, respectable religious debates, and poetic religious imagery. The fact that after a young woman watched this movie, she was gang raped on a bus with a foreign object and left for dead is an impactful juxtaposition to Martel's flowering depiction.

No amount of words can describe the sickness of what happened that night. The utter lack of humanity and sheer evil only scratches the surface. In *India's Daughter*—a documentary about the event India's high court banned[218]—the bus driver, who took part in the rape, blames the woman for being out too late and acting provocative.[219] In the movie, it's stated that every 20 seconds a woman is raped in India; most of these attacks go unreported. Right now—as you've read this paragraph—a women was raped in India.

After the horrific assault, the international press descended upon Delhi like a pack of wolves. Amidst widespread protests and rioting in favour of the victim, justice for the assailants was fast and swift. The men sobbed openly in court when they were sentenced to death;[220] they have appealed their sentences in the High Court of New Delhi, and are still awaiting a trial date.

Kabir provides some context around the event that many international outlets may have missed during the initial media storm. He talks of how India is largely at war with both public displays of affection and Valentine's Day,[221,222] and tells me the vicious attack may have been a product of that issue gone horribly wrong.

Bollywood is a perfect example of this warped view of love, sex and intimacy as outlined in a *The New York Times* piece that states the first big-name Bollywood kiss took place in 2012; it was banned outright through much of the 1990s.[223] While virtually all these flashy pop culture movies hinge around a love story, intimacy is replaced by choreographed dance, and in a country where a fast-growing population obviously speaks for itself, this form of education on all things related to the heart (and of course, getting pregnant) is far from adequate in modern times.

While supporters say it's part of a Western attack on the country's traditional values (at one point, Richard Gere had a warrant out for his arrest[224]), or the sort of "cultural pollution" that marginalizes their beliefs, Kabir is much more blunt and straightforward. It's jealously, he explains. Staunch Hindu men have targeted singles bars, parties and concerts, shaming and even beating straight couples who display public signs of affection, because, well, they are single, lonely, uneducated and unemployed.

What's baffling about all of this is that when you walk the streets in India, you constantly see straight men holding hands, or wrapping their arms around friends. The history of the country includes the graphic sex scenes depicted in the Kama Sutra,[225] an ancient Hindu text, and the Hindu god of love Kamadeva, who makes couples fall in love by shooting arrows made of flowers from a bow composed of sugarcane. In this light, the whole issue seems downright paradoxical, ass-backwards and completely mind-boggling.

Kabir says single men are deeply scrutinized in India. Compounding atrocious women's rights, which are downright criminal in India, the country has a birth rate that gravely over-produces men. Sex is extremely stigmatized; pre-marital relations are a no-no and so is masturbation, leaving men out to pasture with nothing but angst and time on their hands. While women are openly bombarded with the question of "are you married?" even in public,[226] men are seen as failures unless they've nabbed a wife. In a place like Delhi, single men roam the streets like packs of animals; Kabir says this all plays a large part in both the public shaming of straight couples and the despicable existence of rape culture.

When I bring up gay rights in India, Kabir shakes his head like I'm digging a conversational grave.[227] Homophobia is the widely accepted norm.[228] Being gay is punishable under the law, and the Indian Supreme Court took a step backwards recently, reinstating a ban on gay sex following what looked like a promising four-year period of decriminalization.

After meeting Walia and Preet, two educated, thoughtful female athletes, I'm left to wonder how any woman could possibly thrive in this country. That's the often quoted aspect of oppression: the more you tend to push someone down, the stronger they come back at you. Take the Gulabi Gang,[229] an all-woman vigilante group looking to empower women through weaponry.[230] Known in the press as the "Pink Gang", the group has gained international exposure for equipping woman with sticks and defence tactics to simply retaliate violently against potential attackers. Founded in one of the poorest, most illiterate provinces in the country, the group is an example of how oppression can lead to empowerment. In a wildly robust country with a multitude of chauvinistic systems, it is at least a sliver of light against a very dark backdrop. One hopes this social nightmare playing out in real life will one day be a faded scar, something that is remembered, but placed somehow in the past.

***

The Chandigarh Hockey Association is located in a downtown office about the size of a small bedroom. Inside the dusty space a few floors up, where exposed wiring and boxes flood the pathway, the walls are filled with vintage plaques, various memorabilia and trophies. Inside in front of a small colour TV sits Yash Vohra, who has been the secretary general of the CHA since 1959. Vohra is getting old and hard of hearing, yet, when it comes to field hockey, his love for the sport is gigantic. He will talk endlessly about the game, recalling matches against Pakistan, Great Britain, favourite players, and of course, as with any sport anywhere in the world, the unending discussion of who is the greatest of all time.

"In my opinion, there is no better field hockey player than Balbir Singh," says Vohra, his finger wagging at me as if I've asked an almost sacrilegious question. He lays out Chand and Singh Sr.'s accomplishments side by side, then tells me Singh Sr. comes out head and shoulders above. "It is a sad fact that he has not been given more credit," he adds.

I ask Vohra if this is because Singh Sr. is Sikh, and Chand is Hindu.

"No no no no not at all, there is no difference, not absolutely. Not because he was a Sikh. Let me make it clear, there is no discrimination in the country, between players and the administration, for religion or any of the sort. The team is always chosen on merit. The selection committee also only chooses players on merit."

I ask Vohra why then, and he explains Singh Sr.'s predicament as a personal one.

"I tell him sometimes, he is modest to a fault."

When we return home, I spend the rest of the day battling my cold, transcribing interviews and trying to recuperate both mentally and physically. The next morning, after breakfast, Kabir, Singh Sr. and I make the journey north from Chandigarh to Amritsar by car on National Highway 1 for a public school function (public means private in India; government means public) at which Singh Sr. is a guest.

It's not anywhere near a normal five-hour commute, though that's the practical distance. You don't get much over 60 kilometres at the best of times; the roads are just too crowded, chaotic and spastic. The fly-overs (highway overpasses) keep traffic from picking up, and the various U-turn routes mean you have to keep your eye on the road at all times. Meandering pedestrians, tractor trailers, shoulder hugging scooters, darting wild dogs and children; I'm pointing out obstacles to Kabir at an alarming rate like a navigator in a off-road rally car race.

I've given Kabir and his mother my cold, and apologize profusely. Singh Sr., ever the iron horse, seems to have avoided my Western germs, but he decides to cover his mouth with a cloth in the backseat and save his voice for later tonight.

This gives Kabir and I time to talk. I'm living off his words when we're in private, off his ability to explain India's many cultural sensitivities and social norms. You can tell he's been pulling his hair out trying to help bring his grandfather into the spotlight, it's evident in the way he paces rooms and flies off into lengthy diatribes about what can be done to remedy the situation.

Today, I decide it's best not to dwell on a subject that has become a never-ending sore spot for the entire family. In a perfect, or even realistic world, there would be a Singh Sr. stadium in Delhi. Singh Sr. would be in line to receive the Bharat Ratna, and he would be living in his own home, not rooming in his deceased son-in-law's house living off a meagre civil servant's pension he had to fight to keep. He'd be front and centre with Hockey India, perhaps in an advisory role. He'd oversee youth hockey camps in Delhi, make VIP appearances at national club matches, and hawk field hockey gear and products like every retired superstar athlete does all over the world. In sum, he'd have earned the right to rest on his laurels and enjoy the spoils of a decorated career playing for his country.

But now is not the time to scratch this wound. So I ask Kabir about India's trajectory after globalization—a wide-ranging, sometimes ambiguous term that is the thesis of Adiga's *The White Tiger*. Kabir notes a portion of the introduction of the 2011 book, *SuperFreakonomics: Global Cooling, Patriotic Prostitutes, and Why*

Suicide Bombers Should Buy Life Insurance by Steven D. Levitt and Stephen J. Dubner.

The book paints a bleak picture of India, arguing that if you had the option of being born anywhere in the world, it is probably one of the worst choices. Poor life expectancy, low literacy rates, high pollution and corruption, toilets in only one in every four homes. Being born a female in India is even worse, to little surprise.

What's really interesting about what Levitt and Dubner found while researching India was the massive effect the integration of cable television had on the country's populous. While state run TV had been around for a while, it wasn't until 2001 that approximately 150 million Indians were exposed to cable television in the span of about six years. What this meant was for the first time, Indians peered into the Western world; or more accurately, what the Western world looked like on TV. Happy families sipping ice cold Pepsi, Wheel of Fortune and The Price is Right making everyone rich, CNN and its talking heads, Hollywood's elite, international sporting events. Quite understandably, many of them gorged on this newfound box of entertainment, hypnotized by the bright lights, the big cities and the shiny white people looking like life was some brochure-ready Barbie and Ken dreamland.

As outlined in *SuperFreakonomics*, the staggered integration of cable TV into the world's second most populous nation was perfect fodder for economists Emily Oster and Robert Jensen. They were able to delve into specific villages, pinpointing when and where certain portions of the country got hooked on the tube. The result had a very compelling effect on India's women.

Examining data from the government, the economists found that females who'd gotten cable television were more willing to exercise personal autonomy and much less likely to tolerate a number of social ills, such as wife-beating and male sex selection. While the book remains open about the data's conclusion, it does paint an interesting picture of a traditional society unceremoniously pushed off the cliff into the modern world:

"What caused these changes?" Levitt and Dubner write. "Did rural Indian women become more autonomous after seeing cosmopolitan images on their TV sets—women who dressed as they pleased, handled their own money, and were treated as neither property nor baby-making machines? Or did such programming simply make the rural women feel embarrassed to admit to a government surveyor that they were treated so badly?"

Kabir remembers when cable television invaded his home in the early 90s; he fondly recalls the first time he bought a pair of Bata loafers he saw on TV. He says parallel reform movements, which included the ascension of future Prime Minister Manmohan Singh as Finance Minister while the country suffered through a crippling economic crisis,[231] and the lifting of License Raj, which freed the business community from extensive government red tape,[232] shot India out of a medieval canon into the modern world.

In the 2012 book *Why Nations Fail: The Origins of Power, Prosperity, and Poverty*, writers Daron Acemoglu and James A. Robinson outline how a host of negative effects came together to create India's suffocatingly poor economy.

"In India, institutional drift worked differently and led to the development of a uniquely rigid hereditary caste system that limited the functioning of markets and the allocation of labor across occupations much more severely than the feudal order in medieval Europe. It also underpinned another strong form of absolutism under the Mughal rulers. Most European countries had similar systems in the Middle Ages. Modern Anglo-Saxon surnames such as Baker, Cooper, and Smith are direct descendants of hereditary occupational categories. Bakers baked, coopers made barrels, and smiths forged metals. But these categories were never as rigid as Indian caste distinctions and gradually became meaningless as predictors of a person's occupation. Though Indian merchants did trade through the Indian Ocean, and a major textile industry developed, the caste system and Mughal absolutism were serious impediments to the development of inclusive economic institutions in India. By the nineteenth century, things were even less hospitable for industrialization as India became an extractive colony of the English."

Kabir says for the country's teens, they've become as global-ized as the next third world country due to TV, the internet and the spread of mobile phones.

"Now there's a younger generation growing up that's known nothing but materialism and the accumulation of wealth," Kabir tells me.

This grand push towards economic liberalization to free India's slums from poverty is vastly overblown, and pretty much completely void of truth. In *Behind the Beautiful Forevers: Life, Death and Hope in a Mumbai Undercity*, writer Katherine Boo outlines how a ramshackle community living amidst the garbage of the city's international airport thought economic prosperity had been a long time coming, but in reality it just flew over-head:

"Seventeen years later, almost no one in this slum was con-sidered poor by official Indian benchmarks. Rather, the Annawadians (the name for people living in the "makeshift settle-ment in the shadow of luxury hotels near the Mumbai airport") were among roughly one hundred million Indians freed from poverty since 1991, when, around the same moment as the small slum's founding, the central government embraced economic lib-eralization. The Annawadians were thus part of one of the most stirring success narratives in the modern history of global market capitalism, a narrative still unfolding.

"True, only six of the slum's three thousand residents had permanent jobs. (The rest, like 85 percent of Indian workers, were part of the informal, unorganized economy.) True, a few residents trapped rats and frogs and fried them for dinner. A few ate the scrub grass at the sewage lake's edge. And these individuals, mis-erable souls, thereby made an inestimable contribution to their neighbors. They gave those slumdwellers who didn't fry rats and eat weeds, like Abdul (a young garbage picker) a felt sense of their upward mobility."

The idea that living below a bustling airport where rich peo-ple throw their garbage away will somehow translate into eco-nomic prosperity for the inhabitants of Annawadi outlines the sheer desperation India's poor have for a better life; starving both physically and mentally, grasping for anything that might shine a glimmer of hope on what is a truly devastating existence rotting amongst the vile conditions of the country's countless slums.

Kabir then talks about the predilection for "aping" the West,[233] a term older generations use to accuse India's youth of wishing for Western things. It relates to Boo's book concerning the idea of chasing the American dream, that if you work hard, and put yourself in opportune situations, good things will happen.

Clearly this isn't happening, and it's clear India's younger demographic, which make up a large majority of the country (150 million 18- to 23-year-olds), are also in the last stages of the country's ongoing culture crisis. Many Punjab teen men wear faded jeans, leather shoes and polo shirts. But they still also sport turbans and *kardas*, traditional bracelets. As their parents force them to hold onto the customs of their generation, they pine for Neymar Jr. FC Barcelona jerseys, trips to Baskin Robbins and chai lattes at Café Coffee Day.

When people in India were offered a different world through their televisions, much like the protagonist in Adiga's *The White Tiger*, they could not help but gravitate towards it. The word "America" appears in Adiga's book more than 60 times. Kabir says India's history of wanting to be something other than Indian is longstanding. He mentions the cultural leftovers of Raj rule, the centuries of profound foreign influence that laid the groundwork for many parts of India, from its government structure, constitution, and law and order to, of course, its popular culture.

I mention a bit by Indo-Canadian comedian Russell Peters in which, when the British leave in 1947, the Indians aren't too keen on running their own country.[234] "No no no no no," says Peters in his stereotypical Indian accent. "We're coming with you... You can't just come here and leave. What the hell are you going to eat?"

Kabir chuckles when I show him the video.

"Yep, that hits the nail on the head."

A piece in *The New York Times*, "How English Ruined Indian Literature" by Aatish Taseer, really stuck with me when I returned home and continued researching the subject of outside influences on Indian culture.[235] The article outlines the country's internal conflict over having English, a leftover from the Brits, as its most commonly spoken language. The author delivers a chilling final paragraph:

"This is as deep an entrenchment of class and power as any the world has known; it will take more to change it than a change of government. It will take a dismantling of colonial education, a remaking of the relationship between language and power. The boatman spoke from anger, but I was not out of sympathy with his rage. It was the rage of belonging to a place that, 70 years after the British left, still felt in too many ways like an outpost."

***

One of the common sights on the highways are traffic cops. Dressed in beige brown military style shirts and slacks, they don't have firearms, but do carry legal weight and have the requisite moustaches. Kabir says they're also one of the country's most corrupt professions as low wages, tough working conditions and a longstanding history of bribery make them ripe for negative influence.[236] He says that for every ten traffic cops there are eleven corrupt ones. The government is trying to clean up its culture of off the book dealings, and having some success in major cities. But any form of state-sponsored corruption crackdown seems like a Band-Aid on a bullet wound given its prevalence within Indian society.[237]

Modi is the latest world leader to say he's going to finally eradicate graft.[238] Promising a grand overhaul of the system might seem like a kiss of death, and Kabir says he's not holding his breath, as "corruption is a way of life here."

It's a depressing remark, one Kabir delivers with little emotion. Bribery and "fast money" in which people pay to expedite services, are so embedded within the culture that one starts to feel if you were to wipe it out, you might wipe out India altogether.

We gravitate back towards religion and Sikhism. Kabir is a moderate, though he sported a beard and a turban prior to leaving

India for South Africa. He plans on growing his beard again, and donning the turban. But for now he's chosen the clean-shaven, short-haired look of a Westerner. I ask him why he plans on going back to the traditional mode, and he equates it to a kind of "settling down" into a more middle-aged way of life. I'm not sure I completely understand his explanation, but then again I'm realizing the complexities of India's religious undertones are going over my head at an alarming rate.

When it comes to Sikhs and their long, complex history with the Hindu majority, Kabir is much less forgiving, restating the fact he believes they've been culturally neutered amidst the Hindu mass. He notes that while Manmohan Singh helped bring India out of a deep economic pit as its Prime Minister, he is not seen as a populous hero, rather a technocrat who came to power through the relinquishing of power and coalition governments.

The sheer mass of Hindu authority allows for a subconscious, almost unspoken patronizing attitude, he explains, equating it to the experiences of African Americans, Jews, and Aboriginal people across the world. It's a complicated subject, one void of a clear answer or proper example or comparison. But it's the life he's lived.

We pass through the Nawanshahr district, which literally means "new city". The highways are littered with elaborate marriage palaces, painted with once vibrant, now fading colours. Imagine a Best Western decorated from head to toe with holiday ornaments and satin streamers. We drive on, pass the Bhakra Dam which runs across the Sutlej River, the Lovely Professional University that sits at the entrance of Jalandhar city and a large amount of KFCs. Giant eucalyptus trees tower over the road at one point, leaning in to offer shade from the sun, which beats down on us like a UV rash.

Kabir is a seasoned Indian driver—something that should itself be an Olympic sport. He weaves in and out of various moving objects with varying degrees of speed, alternating between Google maps, the stick shift, checking and answering his cellphone and sipping warm tea from a thermos, all while chewing nicotine gum to remain alert. I'm getting tired just watching him, but his alertness helps us avoid two or three close calls, including a randomly stopped car in the middle of the highway, darting children, and buses traveling on the wrong side of the road.

When we finally get to Amritsar, we're greeted by one of the worst traffic jams I've ever experienced. The one highway leading into the city, usually six lanes, has been squeezed off to each side. In the middle, men are working on some sort of commemorative arch, which stretches over the road. We're forced onto the curb, six lanes of traffic trying to find room within one and a half. It's like squeezing a pack of marathon runners through a crowded, twisting hallway.

We realize we won't even make it to the hotel at this rate, and Kabir pulls a u-turn and we beeline for the event. Singh Sr. is an honoured guest at the 7th Annual Day Celebrations for the International Fateh Academy. The school grounds are housed in a large, temple-like building painted beet red on the outskirts of town. It's a traditional Punjab school for ages ranging from kindergarten to high school, which promotes Khalsa (the teachings of Sikhism). The theme of the event, rolled out through a number of plays and presentations by the students, is a history of the Punjab people.

Singh Sr. was invited last minute by the daughter of Fauja Singh, a marathon runner, however nobody is sure why he's here or where he has to go once we've arrived. It's a small event, but Kabir has talked his grandfather into it, telling him that they "have to start somewhere". Singh Sr. changes into his triple gold medal stitched custom blazer and we head through what feels like a rose garden complete with red light district aesthetics.

We're a tad late, but we manage to catch the better part of an hour long speech from none other than Sukhbir Badal, the deputy chief minister of the Punjab State, decked out in a baby blue turban that matches his tie. He's 45 minutes into another lengthy speech in Punjabi, and the crowd looks blazingly hypnotized. I ask Kabir to translate but he says it's pretty much the same song and dance every time a politician speaks—lots of promises, lots of hot air.

The event is outdoors, like a summer concert in the park with temporary red carpeting laid down in front of the stage. Waiters pace the VIP section with hot portable pot cooked snacks on plates, but by this time, I'm struggling to stay awake and politely refuse.

There's a historical play by the children about the Sikhs' history. The most eye catching and violent portion of the presentation—which features lasers, a smoke machine, blaring videos and elaborate costumes—is the Amritsar massacre, or Jallianwala Bagh Massacre.[239] In April 1919, several hundred nonviolent protesters which included Sikhs and pilgrims were mowed down by heavily armed British Indian Army troops under General Reginald Dyer's command. Dyer had declared martial law to crush a local resistance movement, of which many victims were believed to have no knowledge. The massacre was one of many events that turned the Indians against the British, helping kickstart Gandhi's push for independence.

Badal takes the stage again for another lengthy speech, and finally Singh Sr. speaks, in Punjabi, talking about his Olympic medals. By this time the audience is completely worn out and most people look ready to head home or pass out in their seats.

The temperature drops close to freezing as the sun sets, the smoggy pollution melding with the dust from the road and bathing the headlights with a particle feel, an artistic sight as my weary body is driven to a Holiday Inn.

I've left my passport back in Chandigarh, and it's required for check-in. Luckily, I have pictures of all my documents on my phone and we're able to sneak in a room for the night. Before my head hits the pillow, Kabir and I meet in the hallway to chat.

A thought has dawned on me. Manmohan Singh—a Sikh—was India's Prime Minister for a full decade, appointed to power, then winning re-election through a coalition government. How could Sikhs be subjugated, horribly oppressed if one of them held the most powerful position in the country? Kabir asks me how the Kool-Aid tastes, then snickers. He adjusts his glasses, wiping dust from them.

"Who is the president of the United States of America?"

"Obama," I say.

"And what colour is he?"

"Black."

I start to nod, as if the theory he's rolling out is fast computing in my brain.

"And are blacks subjugated in the United States of America?"

I give a telling nod. The second wave of riots unfolding in Ferguson on the other side of the planet on my hotel TV. Tear gas clogging lungs on the streets, African-Americans upset over their social and economic place in the country. A black man was in the White House, but down on the ground, nothing's changed for his fellow African-Americans. I nod again, then head into my room. I'm asleep within seconds, mind and body tapping out, ready to give in to the many Indian substances—both mental and physical—I've bombarded myself with.

★★★

The Holiday Inn in Amristar has one of the most amazing breakfast buffets you'll ever see. Kabir sleeps in like he usually does, but Singh Sr. and I head down to gorge on scrambled eggs, hot coffee, fresh cereal and artistically cut fruit. The place is packed; it's the weekend, when many Sikhs make regular trips to the Golden Temple, which we plan on visiting in the afternoon.

Even in the holiest of holy cities for the Sikh religion, Singh Sr. is not a god, or even a figure of note. People move around him like any other regular hotel guest. Workers refill our coffee and make small talk, nobody the wiser that the man they're conversing with is decorated to the nines with Olympic gold medals.

I ask one of our servers, a young male who looks close to 30 and speaks relatively clear English, while Singh Sr. is away getting more scrambled eggs, "Do you know who that is?"

He looks at me, puzzled.

"It's Balbir Singh Sr. He won three Olympic gold medals."

He looks over to Singh Sr., then back at me, but his facial expression is not amazement, rather passing amusement that is he speaking with a white person.

"Ah," he says. "Very good sir."

Throughout my time at the hotel, almost as a game to myself, I pose this question numerous times to staff out of curiosity, and get virtually the same response every time.

Getting to the Golden Temple is a nightmare. There is no parking, and the streets are jam-packed. Construction, pedestrians, you name it, everyone is here and there is little order other than the occasional stoplight—which seems like more of a suggestion than law to many of the locals driving. Kabir gets frustrated, drops us off somewhere close to the Temple, then proceeds to retreat ten to fifteen blocks to find a curbside to sandwich his car into.

Singh Sr. and I head into the Temple, a physical marvel which can see up to 100,000 visitors a day.[240] The white linoleum courtyard in front offers an oddly sterile feeling, even though we're surrounded by dust and dirt. We leave our shoes and receive a numbered ticket. We wash our feet on the way in as is religious custom, and I don a head covering out of respect for entering the Gurdwara. Inside it's a stunning panorama, with the actual Golden Temple in the middle of a Sarovar that contains holy water from the Ravi River. Men take off their outerwear to bathe, and women are provided with privacy protectors to do the same.

Singh Sr. has told me many times he is a secularist at heart, but he respects the religion of his people. He walks slowly, holding my hand, pointing out different facets of this holy area. The history is overwhelming at times. There's so much culture, so many people who appear to be sleeping and possibly living here. Singh Sr. stops at the water to reflect and dash himself with it, shooing away some kids pestering the koi fish. He shows me where Operation Blue Star took place, where some of his people were massacred in retaliation for their protest of Indira Gandhi's heavy-handed political rule.

After Kabir catches up with us, we head back to the car. We're followed by homeless people, in particular a women with bloodshot eyes holding a malnourished baby. She follows Singh Sr. and Kabir for blocks, largely ignoring me when I speak English to her. Her pestering reaches a boiling point when Kabir stops and firmly tells her to leave us alone, which doesn't work. She gives up a few blocks later as we break from the main streets.

I'm then followed by a small boy, who looks sick, utterly malnourished. He's trying to sell me some type of postcard, tugging on my sleeve, trying to hold my hand as he gazes up at me. He's speaking Hindi, the same sentence, over and over. Kabir tells me it means, "I'm hungry."

A report from The World Bank noted India has the highest rate of malnutrition in children on the planet, almost twice as high as Sub-Saharan Africa.[241] But no amount of reading or research will prepare you for the moment when a child holds out his hand to you, and you know he's literally starving to death. I pull out all the coins I have in my pocket and hand them to the boy, who disappears into the slums as quickly as he materialized.

We get into the car but get stuck in the parking garage that Kabir found, driving in circles bumper to bumper as we try to get onto the highway overpass.

When we get out of the city I ask Kabir to stop so I can use the restroom. Once again I dry-heave in the restroom, covering my face with my shirt as I try to pee in a literal pile of crap. The kamikaze mosquitos dive-bomb me at the gas station on the way back from the restroom. I retreat quickly to the car, which gets a chuckle from Singh Sr.

"Bigger than back home," he says, smiling.

"Yes," I say, waving my hands around, trying to swat the massive creatures away.

Our traffic luck runs out on the way back. We barely avoid three accidents, thanks to Kabir's alertness on the road. The third is the most Indian of situations: out of nowhere, a cow steps down from the divider in the middle of the highway, forcing Kabir to swerve off the road, and me to brace the side door praying there's nobody on the shoulder and no ditch directly below. Luckily we escape disaster. I am not a journalist in a war zone, but on this highway, everything seems like a battle of will.

Singh Sr. taps me on the shoulder from the backseat, offering a condolence in the form of a pat. I'm having trouble acclimatizing; the culture of this nation shocking me, forcing my heart rate to an elevated level at all times. India is overwhelming, her sights, her sounds, her smells and her people offering me no pardon. My white, first world privilege in full effect; the brash, harsh reality the vast majority of the planet's people are forced to face on a daily basis screaming into my eardrum through a megaphone.

A claustrophobic feeling in an open space is something I've never experienced before. In India, personal space is luxury real estate, the country a multi-lane highway of crisscrossing particles with no discernible direction. This indescribable riddle, the unanswerable question. I am in Adiga's rooster coop, jostling for space, stuffed tightly in this wire mesh cage.

CUT FROM THE TEAM

"We talk about a secular state in India. It is perhaps not very easy to even find a good word in Hindi for "secular". Some people think it means something opposed to religion. That obviously is not correct. . . . It is a state which honours all faiths equally and gives them equal opportunities."

~ Jawaharlal Nehru

Out behind the newly constructed Patiala District Jail—built in 1960—about 50 kilometres southwest of what is now Chandigarh, is a patch of imported sand. A line across the back of the brick building which was filled to remedy a particularly pesky plot of unearthed sod where trees had to be removed. Now inches deep with fine particles from the shores of the breezy Indian ocean, it's laid out behind the structure like a beige landing strip. The jail houses local criminals; thieves, murderers and rapists, some still in prison from the gruesome aftermath of Partition.

There's a camp to the left of the jail, the Patiala Police Lines, in which the deputy superintendent resides. Twice a day without fail, he comes out to this patch of sand, straps 20 kilogram bags over his shoulders and run lines back and forth until he is a dripping, sweaty mess. He runs until his chest heaves like an expanding bubble, until his legs light afire with lactic acid, until his heart races like a galloping horse. The prisoners come to the back fence and watch in silence, as he struggles along in his police boots until his body cries for mercy.

Like clockwork, once in the morning, and once at the end of his shift, he makes his way to the sand and pushes his body to the limit, finding his cardiovascular edge. He's blowing out his lungs, expanding them to the upmost capacity, ramping his VO2 as high as it will go.

Ashwini Kumar walks up. This man finishes his laps, laboriously drops the bags on the sand, and stands before him trying to catch his breath, hands on his hips. Ashwini is not only his superior, the Deputy Inspector General of Police for Punjab at Patiala, but high up in the IHF. He holds serious clout over large portions of this man's life.

"How is training going?" Asks Ashwini in his inspecting manner.

The man nods, wipes a waterfall of sweat from his forehead.

Ashwini looks at the bags, the trails of imprinted sand left from pacing back and forth. The prisoners watch the two men, hands through the bars, silent.

"I heard you played for three hours straight yesterday?" Continues Ashwini.

"Yes," says the man, breath now fully regained.

"With the younger group?"

"Yes."

"And the doctor has been conducting regular medical exams?"

"Yes. He said I'm as fit as a horse. Legs like pistons."

The man slaps his legs to test their durability.

Ashwini crosses his hands, analyzing the physical specimen before him. He knew this man was fit, but what did it mean in the grand scheme of Indian field hockey? While training was part of the regular regime for players, physical fitness was still often overlooked. Most players spent days off lounging around, eating milky sweet gulab jamuns and buttery roti bread, praying to one of Hinduism's 330 million gods and carrying out *puja*—the Hindu word for worship—to bring about luck and good fortune.

This man was trying something new, simulating game situations on his lungs, heart and thighs. His efforts were met with skepticism; many players felt as if the gods had not blessed them with the desire or the physical fortitude, there was little that could be done to rectify the higher power's sentence.

It was 1960 and the Rome Olympics were right around the corner. At 36 years of age, Balbir Singh Sr. was hoping to join 33-year-old Anglo-Indian Leslie Claudius to become the first Indian to win four Olympic gold medals. Chand and company had been stopped at three, the Second World War snuffing out a chance for a British Raj four-peat. Now an independent India was about to take its stab at history—go for an unprecedented tetrad in Italy. The team was still tops in the world, still the perennial favourite ahead of Pakistan and Great Britain.

Ashwini had been checking up on his star striker, making sure the highly decorated veteran was still able to hack it on an international level. He had a lot of questions to answer when he got back to Delhi and spoke to the rest of the IHF brass.

"I will tell them of your training Balbir," he said, uncrossing his hands as if he'd finished his inspection.

The year after India had returned with gold from Melbourne was a disastrous one for Singh Sr. An ankle injury sustained from another errant ball caused a hairline fracture and left him in considerable pain. When he went to Bombay with his police team in 1957 for the Invitation Hockey Tournament, team manager Jimmy Nagarwala, whom Singh Sr. calls a "flamboyant character", was falling over himself in his attempts to make sure his star player was taken care of. He massaged Singh Sr.'s ankle incessantly, even in public, much to the dismay of traditionalists. Ashwini wanted to make sure this injury would not be another Melbourne styled debacle.

The sand, it turned out, was perfect for strengthening the foot muscles. Singh Sr.'s legs were tight with tendons, stretched out like rubber bands; his balance finely tuned, his body quick and agile but as sturdy as an eucalyptus tree.

"How is the ankle?" Ashwini asked, pointing to the inflicted appendage.

"Yes, it is fine."

"Okay. Good then."

Singh Sr. nodded, then placed the bags of sand back over his shoulders. He had a few more sets to go, and was now behind schedule due to this interruption. He was on a plan, a regime that would jettison him towards iconic status, elevate him to Indian folklore with one singular, magical word:

Four.

Ashwini knew they needed experience on the squad, but rumblings had started not only about having a 36-year-old suit up, but having a 36-year-old *Sikh* named Balbir Singh suit up. A year after Melbourne, Singh Sr. had been given the Padma Shri Award, India's fourth highest civilian honor. Now he would get the chance to win more medals than Chand—who was himself part of the IHF's roster selection committee.

This was new ground, new territory, and the conniving whispers and shady backroom dealings were in full swing. A fourth gold medal would put to rest any statistical naysayers in the Chand-Singh Sr. debate, which the Hindu press was fine with underplaying. Still, in the bustling streets and packed cafés of the country it was a rousing discussion.

Ashwini, driven to the camp by jeep and accompanied by an armed constable, walked back towards his vehicle, and couldn't help but look back. One final check, and there he was—Singh Sr. running laps in the unforgiving ground with heavy sacks draped over his frame, kicking up dust behind him.

***

"Step on the scale please Balbir," says the team physician.

He steps onto the platform confidently. It's medical testing day at Bombay's Team India training camp; Rome now less than a month away. The players break from the sun, walking around the grounds, relaxing, getting the requisite shots for travel to Europe. The mood is jovial. Chests puffed up, bravado at full strength, these boys knew they were still the team to beat.

The IHF's physician taps the weight on the scale to the left with his pencil, then a little bit more, then some more. He looks at Singh Sr., shirt off, standing in his shorts, muscles chiseled and lean. The doctor continues to tap the weight to the left, taking kilograms off to balance out the marker. Then he stops, finally, to his own amazement.

"You have lost weight," says the doctor, scribbling on his pad.

Singh Sr. smiles, steps off the scale and puts his shirt back on. Whatever fat remained on this man's physique had melted away under the scorching Indian sun.

Two years previous, Singh Sr. had captained Team India at the 1958 Tokyo Asian Games. The format was a simple round robin, and it brought two squads to the top for the final—Pakistan and India. However, going into the match, Pakistan knew the rules: a scoreless draw would give them gold through goal differential. India did not.

"They were all along playing for the draw to take advantage of the goal average rule, which was deployed for the first, and incidentally, the only time in a major tournament," says Singh Sr.

Ashwini called the game "more akin to wrestling than field hockey" and scolded the officiating team and games officials for not letting India know there would be no sudden death overtime. Ashwini and the IHF were certain Pakistani representatives had "kowtowed" to committee members from the Games organizing body.

India came back from the games furious, and Singh Sr. spoke of the unjust tournament in his autobiography:

"On my several trips abroad, both as player and official, I have observed that competitions at the highest level are a far cry from a laymen's view of sportsmanship. The glorious word "sportsmanship" and that high-sounding phrase "in the glory of sport" look tall in print, but they just do not exist. Coaches play mean and ask their burly defenders to bully the forwards, especially those they fear. The players who exchange bouquets before the start of a game, never fight shy of maiming their counterparts with needless body play and threatening postures . . . The officials in the Committee rooms are forever making and unmaking cliques. It is a vicious circle."

Singh Sr. says the IHF's leadership had run amok with power, and was more interested in maintaining a chokehold on rule then actually helping India put forth the best squad for each tournament. Before Tokyo, the team was oddly made to run long distances over a month-long camp while getting requisite shots and medical check-ups, which left them sore and fatigued heading into the tournament. Many of the players who went to Tokyo were sick and dehydrated. They played while fighting off colds and flus they'd picked up while traveling tired and depleted of electrolytes.

Singh Sr. says the IHF had let the three gold medals go to its head; they believed they could simply jog their players into shape, show up and collect the championship on credit.

"And here I would put the blame on our administrators who lied by constantly referring to our players as 'the greatest', the 'world champions' and 'the invincibles'," wrote Singh Sr. in his

autobiography. "Some of their hollow optimism from an incorri-
gible sense of pride and false prestige."

Regardless, Singh Sr. had put the Tokyo debacle behind him.
He was ready for Rome, and more than ready to make history.
He'd grown tired of newspapers omitting his goals, of all the
squabbling that took place at each tournament, where political
and religious separatism bled onto the field. He was sick of it all,
he just wanted to play.

If his counterparts weren't fit, so be it, but he would be in
the best shape imaginable. Based on merit, he was not only the
most decorated player trying out in the Bombay selection
camp, but also the fittest and the most physically and mentally
prepared.

Mourning the loss of his mother Karam, who had died after
a terrible bout of pneumonia in 1957, Singh Sr. set out to honour
her legacy and his own by doing what no other Indian athlete had
ever done.

In 1960, field hockey was still one of the most watched and
highly regarded sports in the world. Spain, New Zealand,
Australia, Poland, Argentina and Kenya were all producing quality teams as up and coming nations. The landscape at base camp
crowding, other countries' programs gearing up to climb the
mountain to glory.

Singh Sr. was a man on a mission. Fierce and unapologetic in
camp, he'd learned his lesson, this was not the time to rest on his
laurels. He shoved defenders off balls, took no breaks, asked for no
favours. He was the first on the pitch and the last off.

But on the last day of camp, he got the news: he had been cut
from the team.

Rajdeep Singh Gill said this was not only a blow to him, but
a blow to Punjab, and more importantly, a blow to India. Growing
up in the Punjab state during Singh Sr.'s reign, the Sikh was a
household name. He was the area's unchallenged superstar, a shining light amidst a cloudy national scene full of religious dust.

"He had been playing in National Championships still," says
Gill. "It's not that he wasn't fit at all, he should've been leading the
team. He should've been captain."

There was no time to mount an appeal or reinsertion campaign. The IHF had axed Singh Sr. strategically, on the last day, as the team packed up to head to Delhi for their flight to Rome. The team would be coached by K. D. Singh, known to most as Babu. He was vice-captain in London and captain in Helsinki, but was left off the Melbourne squad. The team was selected by him, Kishan Lal (who had to take Singh Sr. off the field twice in London) and Chand. When speaking of this longstanding sore spot, at first Singh Sr. is hesitant. But after a time, he opens up about one of the biggest disappointments of his life, "Babu was clever and crooked. He realized in his mind that I would be elevated above them all."

Dr. Sudesh Gupta, a longtime friend of Singh Sr.'s who also works for the United Nations as a consultant, called the cut a "national tragedy."

Sarpal Singh, who played with and against Singh Sr. from 1948 onwards, but never played for Team India, said "age may have been a factor" in the selection committee's minds, but putting Singh Sr. on the roster regardless, even as a substitution, would've probably been the most practical play. He could be injected into the line-up if the team wasn't scoring, said Sarpal, offering a veteran presence with know-how and practice playing in big games.

"He was still a very good player," Sarpal added. "Leaving him off meant they had no one up front at centre-forward with very much experience. It was not a position to take lightly."

But the die was cast. All Singh Sr. could do was find Leslie Claudius, the only player who'd won three gold medals, like him. Claudius had been named team captain, but was distraught that his usual target, his go-to centre forward, would not be making the trip with him.

Although Claudius was barely over five feet, his ability to disperse the ball throughout his team was invaluable. Chand is noted as saying in a few articles that, "Claudius selects himself, now I have to select the rest of the team."[242] In late 2012, Claudius passed away at the age of 85 due to cirrhosis of the liver.[243]

Singh Sr. and Claudius shook hands as he headed off. There were no words that could do this moment justice, so they simply nodded and looked into each other's eyes, knowing the road ahead for both of them would now be a lot tougher.

Despite Singh Sr.'s exclusion from the roster, India was a powerful team. This was evident in their first game on August 27, 1960 at the Olympic Velodrome when they trounced Denmark 10-0.[244] Three days later they would defeat the Netherlands 4-1, and then three days after that New Zealand 3-0 to finish top in their group.

Prithipal Singh, the "king of the short corners" had amassed five goals throughout the group stage, albeit playing as a defender. Having played with Singh Sr. for the Punjab Police and state squad, he was filling the goal scoring role adequately, but from an unusual position. But Rome was his first Olympics, and his experience against tougher squads was tested in India's first playoff match against a young Australian squad. India squeaked out a 1-0 win, their lone goal finally coming seven minutes into the second extra time period.

Back home, the rumblings began. India did not have a legitimate goal scorer in Rome. Calls went out to fly Singh Sr. to Italy, to charter a private plane so he could jettison in like Superman and save the day. Team India was relying on spot corners, and using set plays to get most of their chances. This worked in the round robin, but against tougher opponents, they didn't have nearly enough time to get Prithipal the ball for a clear shot.

Singh Sr., trying to remain positive, cheered for the team while he listened to the games on the radio back in Patiala. India's next opponent was Great Britain; the team scored sixteen minutes in and hung on for dear life. Once again, they emerged with a nail-biting, nerve-wracking 1-0 win.

Two days later, they faced none other than Pakistan in the final. Singh Sr. and his fellow police officers gathered around the radio at work, listening intently. Their fists clenched, teeth grinding. Each tackle, each penalty stung a little more than usual.

Six minutes in, Ahmad Nasser of Pakistan would score. India would pressure and lay it all on the line, but they had hit a wall. Pakistani goalkeeper Lala Abdul Rashid, who had played for

Punjab University before Partition pushed him and his family west, denied any equalizing tally.

While it was an incredibly anti-climactic win, the 1960 Olympic gold medal match was deeply impactful for both countries. There would be no fourth consecutive gold for India. The streak was over. In *India and the Olympics*, Boria Majumdar and Nalin Mehta observed that, "From the very start, India's campaign at Rome appeared jinxed. Almost all its victories were by narrow margins and on more than a couple of occasions it was plain lucky."

At the police station in Patiala, Singh Sr. sat quietly beside the radio. His co-workers had fallen silent as the final whistle blew. They headed back to their stations, out into the city, leaving their supervisor alone with his thoughts.

"Dame fortune, however, did not smile on Leslie and the 1960 Indians," wrote Singh Sr. in his autobiography. "It was a classic goal by inside-right Naseer Bunda in the 6th minute that relegated India to silver standard. The Indians attacked for all they were worth. Udham, Jaswant, supported by Peter and Bhola worked tirelessly and came near scoring several times. But the tenacious Pakistanis hung on to their slender advantage. The positions had reversed and so had the people's emotions. There was jubilation across the border and gloom in India; they let off crackers and felt on top of the world; we only brooded and shook our heads in disbelief."

Claudius, interviewed by *The Times of India* in 2000, expressed his dismay: "I never thought I would win a silver medal under my captaincy . . . I was so unlucky. I just can't explain it."[245]

Singh Sr. said the team was ripe with managerial errors, a result of infighting, a biased selection process, and a committee that seemed more concerned with who would go to the games than with how the team should be playing. "The news of India's debacle was tragic," he wrote in his autobiography. "Many held newcomer Jhaman Lal Sharma (who would never play for his country again) responsible for the goal—and not without reason. He and Prithipal Singh formed an untried pair of deep defenders . . . The Pakistani inside-right got away, side stepped, charging Laxman and pushed the ball home. That one mistake cost India their seventh gold medal . . . the critics also pointed out that the team had no leader of the attack and observed that I could have made the Rome trip with much better results. I may sound boastful but I do feel that the selectors' axe fell on me rather unceremoniously."

Compounding the stunning defeat, Singh Sr.'s coach and mentor, Harbail, died tragically in a plane crash outside of Moscow shortly after the games. The man who had plucked Singh Sr. from obscurity at Khalsa College in Amritsar; who guided him during the Helsinki and Melbourne Olympics; who gave him the peace of mind to simply do what he did best, was gone. Singh Sr. remembers him as sincere to a fault, selfless and self-effacing. When the IHF decided, for unknown reasons, not to retain Harbail as coach for the 1960 Olympics, the IOC scooped him up in an instant to be an official in Rome.

Singh Sr. walked home to his wife and children after his shift that night. The city was dreary, as if the entire country were mourning India's loss. A sombre mood washed over the streets; the red sun set across the horizon, signalling that the day did in fact transpire, and would stick within history. Singh Sr. untied his police boots and slowly slipped them off as he sat by the stool near the front entrance. Sushil had made him a hearty meal of stuffed paratha, steamed rice and chicken from a local vendor. He untucked his uniform and sat at the table. He was starving, but for some reason, had lost his appetite.

★★★

He took the hint. After the Rome Olympics, Singh Sr. retired from international play, bowed out of the stage upon which he'd won three Olympic gold medals and amassed 22 goals.

There would be no press conference from the IHF, no real notice in the newspapers. It wasn't until 1962 that the IHF finally reached out to Singh Sr., asking him to coach the national squad for the Ahmedabad International, held that year in the western state of Gujarat (the home state of both Modi and Gandhi). India won, crushing their international opponents on home soil, and Singh Sr. proved to be a formidable leader off the field, too. He danced the line between a player's coach, and a tough selector. He had no time for out of shape, potbellied, showboating vagabonds. Skill took a backseat to desire, fitness and accountability. He cast aside players who could display trickery with their sticks for those willing to work their asses off for the team.

Around this time, Singh Sr. left the world of policing, too, coaxed away by A.L. Fletcher, the financial commissioner of development for Punjab. Fletcher—a Christian Indian from Kerala in the south of the country—was creating a new sports department for the state and wanted Singh Sr. to be deputy director. Singh Sr. said Fletcher was a very powerful man, and saying no wasn't really an option. But given that he had literally been handcuffed into becoming a police officer, leaving his first profession wasn't necessarily the occasion for deep mourning.

"I never wanted to be in the police," he tells me multiple times during our interviews. "As deputy director of the Sports Department I had a tremendous amount of administrative work to handle and Fletcher and I literally burned the midnight oil, chasing papers, making some of our semi-literate staff work out plans and begin scientific coaching programmes."

Fletcher took Singh Sr. under his wing; they drove around the Punjab, looking for the best areas to develop playgrounds. The idea was if children had a place to play games like cricket and field hockey from a young age, they would develop a love for such sports right from the get-go. Singh Sr. had seen it in Europe, where local youth leagues were nonprofits run by the government with the sole intention of instilling a love of sport in the nation's adolescence. Singh Sr. wanted badly to emulate this idea.

Together, he and Fletcher were digging roots for the emergence of Punjab's impressive sporting culture, giving kids a chance to enjoy sports with friends before coaches and mentors plucked them from the playgrounds for more serious competition.

"Eventually," Singh Sr. recalls, "things started taking shape. The saplings that we had planted began sprouting new leaves and the department grew in strength."

It was less than six months before Singh Sr. was promoted to director. His grassroots approach was getting green lights from upper management. But, like everything else, picking sites for fields eventually fell prey to corruption; Singh Sr. mentions driving by more than one empty lot sitting unused, too far from clusters of homes for kids to randomly wander on and start a game of cricket or field hockey; picked by local civic leaders with ulterior motives, void of proper community planning.

Singh Sr. kept his eye on the IHF, but stayed out of the politics. After his win in Gujarat, he expected to be offered the coaching assignment for the 1962 Asian Games in Jakarta, Indonesia, but for some reason the IHF went in a new direction. India would subsequently lose 2-0 to Pakistan in the finals. This revolving door of coaches is something that sadly plagues India's field hockey body to this day, Singh Sr. said.

"I am not against the authorities changing coaches—that is their prerogative and they have every right to their choice—but I just do not understand why they throw them out and take them back at will. There is no system, no logic behind their moves—a successful coach should have a longer lien of office; he must be given the benefit of continuity. After my success with the Ahmedabad assignment, I should have had the boys with me. Instead, they threw me out. But the Jakarta reversal opened their eyes; they brought the national camp back to Punjab and got me back to do the coaching hackwork. They inducted Habul Mukherjee as the coaching spokesperson but most of the real work was done by me."

The 1964 Summer Olympics in Tokyo would be Singh Sr.'s chance to gag the critics once and for all. If he could put forth a squad that would topple Pakistan, he thought, he would surely pull out a long leash when it came to coaching the national squad.

Singh Sr. gathered the selectees more than a month before in Chandigarh. He housed his players in dorm rooms, laid down strict curfews and ground rules. He hired a chef to prepare hearty meals of chicken and rice, forgoing sweets and spicy curry. Each day his players went through a finely regimented schedule that included yoga, physical fitness training, mental preparedness and proper rest time. He had them do unusual drills to work on specific skill sets. He constructed set plays and attacking structures that could be interchanged on the fly, based on the opponent's tendencies and weaknesses.

As their flights approached, Singh Sr. picked up his custom-made coach's blazer from the tailors and met with his boys. The mood was tempered this time around; there would be no room for egos, no pig-headed thoughts that India could coast like a bird on a tailwind to the top of the podium.

The day before they were scheduled to fly, Singh Sr. got word: he had been relieved of his coaching duties. Like a broken record, a recurring nightmare, it had happened again. Dharam Singh, deeply connected to IHF leadership, would now suddenly, inexplicably, be coaching the squad. Dharam did not even meet many of the players until they boarded the plane for Europe.

Singh Sr. was furious, and this time, he couldn't contain his anger. He sat down at his desk at work and penned a letter to Ashwini Kumar.

"I wrote a very nasty letter," he recalls, "saying you have used me and abused me, all the time. I wrote, the saying is kind of like what it is like when someone goes to a prostitute. I felt humiliated, I had taken pride in coaching the team and it was taken from me."

Despite Singh Sr.'s physical absence, with his training and guidance, India went on to win their seventh gold, defeating arch rivals Pakistan 1-0 in the finals. Singh Sr. took quiet solace in the fact that this was his squad, his boys that carried his words to Tokyo with them.

The death of Prime Minister Nehru shortly before the games had given Singh Sr. an added charge. He could still hear Nehru's words at the Bhakra Dam; could recall the Prime Minister personally assigning him the duty of maintaining and fostering field hockey glory. While India's version of the Kennedy family would have its share of tragic deaths over the decades, Nehru went quietly, dying of what appeared to be natural causes at the age of 74 in New Delhi. As India's first Prime Minister, he was the last of the founding fathers. His body, draped in the tricolours of the Indian flag, was cremated as per Hindu tradition on the banks of the Yamuna River.

Singh Sr. continued about his life, playing the odd club match with friends, his body at last on the decline. He still loved the game, but was getting more satisfaction from coaching, passing on wisdom to a new generation of youth in whom he saw great promise.

But the IHF did not call. Their high ranking officials were rushing to take credit for the Tokyo gold; some claimed that cutting Singh Sr. as coach and manager was a genius move. For the 1968 Summer Olympics in Mexico, Singh Sr.'s phone didn't ring. The IHF had decided he would take no part in helping the team off the field. India subsequently dropped to bronze even while being coached by Dhyan Chand; Pakistan won gold.

Now the IHF was in disarray. In 1970, they finally reached out to Singh Sr., asking him to manage the team for the 1970 Asian Games in Bangkok, Thailand. Singh Sr. asked if he could coach instead of manage; he felt he was not suited for the politics that came with helping pick the squad. He put forth a plan to bring the team to the Punjab for weeks of training, a similar regime to that he had used before Tokyo.

The IHF denied his request, and he went with the team as an administrator, forced to deal with all the political infighting and favouritism that went on during the selection process. It was an unending headache. Singh Sr. hated every second: "The team had been groomed by other experts, and my talent was wasted."

Once again, India lost 1-0 to Pakistan in the finals.

For the 1971 World Cup in Barcelona, Spain—with Singh Sr. back in the IHF's doghouse—India lost to Pakistan in the semi-finals 2-1, settling for bronze.

After 1971, Singh Sr. wrote an open letter to the IHF, politely suggesting a few changes to the team's preparation tactics. Foregoing personal pride, he put forth the ideas he had used for Tokyo, hoping the IHF would steal and take credit for his concepts. At least the squads they put forth would be properly prepared, he thought.

He wrote that the team needed more training before tournaments which would include yoga for stretching and relaxing, proper meals prepared by chefs, and an emphasis on speed and endurance rather than ball-handling skills. He also suggested a new set of drills every day at camp, to help keep the players from training in a monotonous way, and having a team doctor travel with the team to help with illnesses and injuries. He added a small paragraph about how the IHF could select the team better; hold camps around the country rather than use a small selection committee to make the decisions from a high level.

The IHF did not respond to his letter, and when the 1972 Olympics in Munich, Germany came around, Singh Sr. was not called to help out. India won bronze, its performance, like all else, overshadowed by the harrowing Munich Massacre. Singh Sr. said he noticed many of his suggestions in play (a team doctor made the trip with the squad; fitness was a high priority), but gold still eluded Team India.

The IHF's inexplicable disdain for Singh Sr. continued through the next two international engagements—the Amsterdam World Cup in 1972, in which India would lose to the Netherlands in heartbreaking fashion on penalty strokes, and the Tehran Asian Games in 1974, in which India would once again lose to Pakistan in the finals.

Back home, the Punjab Sports Department was crumbling from the inside out due to favouritism, nepotism, greed and corruption. Singh Sr., never one to play office politics, soon had a target on his back for a number of reasons: jealousy, religion, groupism. Many were gunning for his spot; power hungry colleagues made backroom deals to circumvent and dive bomb his suggested programs. It wasn't long before any administrative task put forth by Singh Sr. on paper was nothing more than tissue for the lavatories.

"Emotionally and psychologically, I had a harrowing time" he said. "There were many hands working at cross-purposes and I wasn't satisfied with what I was doing. The department had no direction and my schemes and plans tended to drift about."

He needed a break, a vacation. He was coming home at night to the loving embrace of Sushil and his children, his only solace in a world that seemed to be turning its back on him every chance it got. At work, Singh Sr. watched as people were hired and promoted solely on personal connections and religious lines. Under-qualified candidates were now running departments and overseeing dozens of employees. Money was wasted, and the people who suffered the most were the athletes.

Everyone was to blame, Singh Sr. said—Sikhs, Hindus and Muslims. He adds, "I could only shake my head."

Then an invitation came in the mail, from Senator James C. Corman, the chair of the J.F.K. Memorial International Hockey Tournament in Washington. D.C. Ganga Singh Dhillon, a Sikh who had immigrated to the US and was a out-spoken leader of the Khalistan movement, lobbied Corman to get Singh Sr. as chief guest. One of Randhir Singh Gentle's four brothers had also moved to the US and helped get Singh Sr. invited as a VIP as well. While Singh Sr. says he was not a sup-porter of the Khalistan movement, a chance to get away and watch some field hockey without the politics was incredibly enticing.

Having accumulated a number of holidays (enough for six months leave), Singh Sr. decided to make a trip of the event, tak-ing a half-year break from work to attend the tournament in Washington and visit his son Kanwalbir (Ken), who had settled in Vancouver. Singh Sr. and Sushil left their two youngest sons Karanbir (Ringo) and Gurbir (Gugu) back at home with his father and packed their bags for America.

Ganga greeted Singh Sr. at the airport in typical American fashion: with a hug and a hearty handshake. He'd set up a num-ber of speeches for Singh Sr. at universities across the country with burgeoning field hockey programs. He wanted him to spread the "gospel of hockey" around the United States, some-thing Singh Sr. took great pride in.

"This was a celebration of hockey, both men's and women's teams," says Singh Sr. "It was so great to see the game played in such a spirit, for the love of the game."

By this time, Singh Sr. was seriously considering leaving India altogether. The politics and corruption had become too much. He wanted to start anew, in a fresh country, and Canada appeared to be the perfect fit, given that one of his children had already settled there.

In 1971, Canadian Prime Minister Pierre Trudeau had declared Canada open to immigration, laying the seeds for a climate of multiculturalism that runs through the country's veins to this day. The subsequent 1976 Immigration Act[246] drew a swath of immigrants from all over the world looking for a new way of life. Many Sikhs settled in the Fraser Valley of British Columbia, east of Vancouver, gravitating towards the agricultural land base as a way to etch out a new existence.[247]

Ringo spoke about how the Sikhs' history in Canada pre-dates the Trudeau era, running far back in the country's history.

"Indo-Canadians were here in numbers much farther back than [Trudeau's immigration push]," said Ringo. "My two maternal uncles came a generation before and sponsored Ken. One of them is married into a family which had the first female Indo-Canadian allowed to immigrate to Canada. That family came a generation or two even before that via ship from Hong Kong."

Ken talked glowingly of Canada in the 1970s over the phone. There was no corruption, work was relatively calm and void of favouritism, and sporting heroes were national stars. Gordie Howe, Bobby Orr, Maurice "The Rocket" Richard, all highly decorated ice hockey players, were treated like gods across the country. Richard in particular, as a man of French Canadian descent, had gone through strife akin to Singh Sr.'s during his career, but was now widely regarded as one of the game's greatest goal scorers and competitors.

Singh Sr. liked what he was hearing.

US officials were also trying to coax him into a coaching role. They wanted his expertise and prestige to help them grow support for field hockey in their country. The offers were tempting, but Singh Sr. struggled with the thought of abandoning the nation he'd loved so much. India was his homeland, however tattered and bruised she appeared to him.

Tragedy struck before decisions could be made. While in Washington watching the matches, Singh Sr. and Sushil got word that Singh Sr.'s father had fallen ill and been taken to the hospital. The news hit Sushil particularly hard, as Dalip had spent a lot of time with her while Singh Sr. was out playing field hockey and working. Without a patriarchal figure of her own, she had developed a close relationship to Dalip, and she headed back to their hotel in tears.

The room phone rang again. Luckily, it wasn't further bad news. An IHF administrator was calling. They wanted Singh Sr. to lead Team India to the 1975 World Cup in Kuala Lumpur, Malaysia. India's field hockey elite wanted so badly to beat Pakistan that they were willing to give the reins of the team to their proverbial Sikh whipping boy.

It was perplexing, but Singh Sr. was excited nonetheless. "I did not find out the reasons until later," he said. "At that moment I felt as if I had been given another chance."

He'd been given carte blanche to both manage and coach the squad. Singh Sr. knew the Montreal Summer Olympics would follow immediately after the World Cup; a win in Kuala Lumpur would guarantee him the chance to lead the squad at the 1976 games, and offer him a chance to win a gold medal as a coach. Thrilled and excited, Singh Sr. started planning for the job while still in Canada, even touring the pitch in Montreal to inspect it.

Mike Toth, a Canadian journalist living in Mississauga at the time, sought out Singh Sr. and published a piece on him, excerpted below, which touched on his Rome exclusion:

"Glance as far and wide as you wish, there are not too many stars of the stick (or any other sport, for that matter) whose neck muscles strain under the weight of three Olympic gold medals. Balbir Singh is such a three-carat star. The reason he hasn't got a fourth is something he's a bit reluctant to discuss. You see, he was left out of the team that represented India in the 1960 cavalcade of amateur athletics in the ancient splendour of Rome . . .

"Many people still believe that India would have had its seventh straight gold—a landmark no other country has ever achieved in any sport since the best of the world started gathering in earnest in the historic setting of Athens in 1896—had Balbir Singh been in the line up instead of sitting a few thousand slapshots away from the shadow of the bench."

Singh Sr. and Sushil headed home that December, and within a day Singh Sr. was setting up camp while attending to his father in the hospital. His chance had come to reclaim his role within India's hockey world.

Answers to the mystery of the IHF's behaviour soon proffered themselves. Due to infighting and corruption, the IHF had splintered into two groups behind P.N. Sahni, a Punjab from the north, and executive M. K. K. Ramaswamy, a millionaire industrialist from the south of the country. Ramaswamy, a pudgy, plump Hindu with furled, mischievous eyebrows, was an influential Madras businessman, with backing from high ranking members of the Delhi government. He wanted to return power to the south of the country, away from Ashwini and the Punjabis in the north.

Tensions grew so extreme that the Switzerland-based Federation Internationale de Hockey was forced to dissolve the IHF; taking over the organization briefly, and then handing the reins to the Indian Olympic Association. Kuala Lumpur's coaching and administrative staff was thus chosen by outside forces, which meant the decision was set in stone.

For what looked like a brief, fleeting moment, the road to victory was clear of corruption, and nothing stood in Singh Sr.'s way. Kuala Lumpur would be a chance for redemption, a chance for him to pull his coaching career from the mud, wash it off and shine it golden.

MAGIC IN KUALA LUMPUR

"I say "our" because I write as an Indian man born and bred, who loves India deeply and knows that what one of us does today, any of us is potentially capable of doing tomorrow. If I take pride in India's strengths, then India's sins must be mine as well."

~ Salman Rushdie

The whistle blows.

Players jog to the line, huffing and puffing. One of them stops at the end of the field, bends over, and vomits up a lunch of chicken and rice made by the team chef. He wipes his mouth and stands upright, already prepared for the next wind sprint.

Singh Sr., whistle in hand, walks past his players along the side of the pitch, inspecting their physical state. They're panting like dogs, sweating buckets, legs afire and lungs ready to burst like overfilling balloons.

"Again!" Yells Singh Sr., then blows his whistle. His boys do not hesitate. They start running the length of the field, across and back. "C'mon, c'mon, *c'mon!*" Singh Sr. yells, forcing them to pick up speed.

They return, even more wiped. One drops to a knee in exhaustion, but his teammates pick him up. They stand, like soldiers, waiting for further instruction. Singh Sr.'s whistle gets incredibly close to his mouth, the players cringe, not sure how much more they can take.

Singh Sr. walks up, looking his boys over. He knows they have been fraternizing with female students, taking phone calls late at night while housed at Punjab University in Chandigarh in Hostel 4, right beside the girl's Hostel 3. He understands the temptation, he is not a robot, he is not void of sympathy when it comes to their youthful exuberance. But he does not want his boys distracted. His players are here for one thing, and one thing only, to win gold at the 1975 World Cup in Kuala Lumpur and then carry on to Montreal for the 1976 Summer Olympics.

"Do you think the Pakistani players are out fraternizing with females?" says Singh Sr., knowing strict Muslim rules means there is little chance of this. "Do you think any of the English players are out boozing it up? Or the Dutch? Or the Spanish?"

His players shake their heads, beads of sweat whisk off them like lawn sprinklers.

He stands, an unsympathetic drill sergeant. Then his tone becomes more forgiving. He relents, just for a moment.

"Look I am no fool. But we must win in Kuala Lumpur. You all have the great task of restoring India to field hockey glory. You must become saints of the game, tireless, your passion unending, your focus unwavering . . . I understand these girls you are talking to are very pretty."

Some of the players chuckle.

"So here's the deal," he continues, walking back and forth. "After we win the World Cup. I will take you back here for a few days and you can spend as much time with the pretty ladies as you like. How does that sound?"

His players perk up, injected with a new sense of vigour. Singh Sr. looks them over. They look ready—for a few more lines.

Tweeeeeeeeet!

***

Singh Sr.'s eyes grow sore from looking over piles of files: reports, accounts, stipends and contracts. Spread across his desk like bland peacock feathers, the manila folders are a daunting managerial mountain to climb. Given the rampant corruption in the IHF, Singh Sr. cannot afford any more scandals. He's chosen to take the entire administrative wing of the team under his watch, so nobody can syphon funds, take bribes or cook the books.

As a result, he is mentally exhausted, goggle-eyed from trying to match up expense sheets and sort out travel paperwork and flight itineraries. But it is a necessary evil.

A university administrator comes up to Singh Sr., knocks on his office door. He looks up, bleary and tired.

"Yes?"

"Sir, your wife has called, she said you must return home. Your father has taken a turn for the worse."

Singh Sr. stands up, drops his pencil and rushes out the door. He's home in record time, his wife by his father's bedside, crying.

"He is bleeding," she says, pointing to a pool of blood on the ground.

Singh Sr. rushes to the phone and calls an ambulance. He has only been running the camp for three days, but now the hospital is the number one priority.

His father, the stern, strict man who instilled so much discipline and pride in his boy, helping him build a foundation that would bring three gold medals to himself and his nation, is dying.

Singh Sr. sits outside in the waiting room, his wife crying into his arms. She is not handling his dad's condition well. Dalip has become a real father in her life. Now he is lying in bed, unconscious; his long, lean body frail, like a weathered twig that was once a mighty tree.

After he speaks to the doctor, Singh Sr. takes his wife home. There is nothing they can do. The hospital said they would send word immediately if Dalip's condition got better—or worse. Singh Sr. sits Sushil down, wiping tears from her swollen cheeks. She is still crying.

"You need to eat," he tells her.

She does not respond, but continues sobbing into her hands.

Singh Sr. summons his two youngest sons, telling them to watch over their mother. They nod accordingly as he tries to get some sleep.

"Yes, father."

With so much on his mind, sleep comes at a tossing and turning cost. Another long night of sorting out thoughts, pushing them aside as his mind tries, and fails, to find peace.

He stands up early that morning, stretching his back, which aches from hours in a hospital chair and an office desk. He has to go, he has a training session to run with his players in less than a few minutes. He closes the door, sets out on a jog to the university grounds. His father's words, spoken to him before he had taken a turn for the worse, echo through his skull:

Duty first. Self and everything else afterwards, son.

They repeat over and over as he runs through the city, cutting across streets, maintaining an efficient pace. He pushes the emotions down and away, so he can focus on the task at hand. There is no time for mourning.

Singh Sr. arrives at the pitch, catches his breath. Gurcharan Singh Bodhi, the co-coach and trainer V.J. Peter are waiting. S.S. Gill, on staff at the university's physical education department, comes up to Singh Sr.

"How is your father?" he asks.

"Not well."

"You should be with him, at his side."

Singh Sr. shakes his head. In his autobiography, though, he laments his decision to continue running the team despite his father's condition: "I often repent having not cared for father and Sushil as much as I should have . . . I tell myself he could have not misunderstood me. I was only doing my duty by the nation."

Some of the players make their way onto the pitch for training. Singh Sr. looks over at his fellow staff, takes a deep breath in, then blows his whistle to start practice.

★★★

Dhyan Chand was supposed to head the Selection Committee for Team India at the World Cup, having been appointed by the Indian Olympic Association. However, oddly, Chand was "not available" and thus the entire roster fell into the lap of Singh Sr. The other remaining members of the selection committee—which included one of Singh Sr.'s nemeses, Nandi Singh—could try to influence his decision, but the final call would be his.

Singh Sr. had been lining up matches for the original roster, which was composed of 42 players including Ashok Kumar, Dhyan Chand's son, who would go on to make the team. Singh Sr. had been alternating training sessions with tough matches against some of the country's elite club teams—Corps of Signals, Eastern Command and the Haryana State Electricity Board. The squad would end up playing 35 matches over the span of two months.

Each night after the game, Singh Sr. would host an informal round table with his players and serve specifically prepared recovery meals. The group would mull over the mistakes of the day's match, then set out to correct those errors at practice the next day. Players were also undergoing bio-medical testing, fitness and physical examinations. A team of doctors from the Christian Medical College of Ludhiana were paying close attention to all of them, fine-tuning them into field hockey machines.

"It can now be said without fear of contradiction that our team was the fittest in the tournament at Kuala Lumpur," he wrote in his autobiography, "and continued playing attacking hockey throughout the tournament, and showed no sign of fatigue as well."

Singh Sr. had amassed a platoon of players that included five Sikhs out of the 24 from the Punjab area. This number was extremely high, and he made no bones about why he picked them.

"While selecting players for Punjab Police, Punjab State or India I never thought of the religion, only merit."

The IHF leftovers, still embroiled in a contentious legal battle, were furious. This was far from the squad they wanted, and they continued their lobbying efforts to bring their personal favourites into camp.

While Singh Sr. was poring over the files associated with running the team, his phone rang again, and he was vaulted back to the present tense.

His father had passed away.

At the hospital, he found his wife crying, his sons distraught. Gugu came up to him, eyes watering over.

"Dad, mom has not eaten all day. I am worried about her."

Singh Sr. walked over to his wife. Her eyes were swollen shut with tears, her body wavering. She fell into his arms, fainting, and was rushed to the Post Graduate Institute of Medical Education and Research in Chandigarh. Singh Sr. waited patiently outside her room while the doctors looked her over. One came out, holding a chart, adjusting his glasses. With no time to mourn his father's sudden and abrupt passing, he was now forced to contend with the love of his life falling ill.

"Sir, your wife has had a brain hemorrhage. She is in a coma."

All Singh Sr. could do was nod. The world crumbling around him; the Gods were surely testing him now. There would be no exhale, no rest, no time to think. If he gave up running the squad so close to the games, it would tarnish his image and reduce his chances of ever coaching for India again.

He had to make a choice—family or country.

"Will she be okay?" he asked quietly.

The doctor looked over his notes.

"Yes I believe so. She just needs to rest and gather her strength back up, she was very frail from not eating."

Singh Sr. drew in a deep breath. Training was about to start again.

"What can I do to help her?"

The doctor looked at him, a sense of compassion over his face.

"She is okay here for now. She needs to rest."

"Okay," says Singh Sr. He shook the doctor's hand, and started to walk to his sons.

"Excuse me sir. I am sorry to do this to you at this time, but I must tell you something."

Singh Sr. looked back at the doctor, fear written on his face. The doctor put his hand up in a calming manner.

"Please do not worry Balbir, your wife is fine." Singh Sr. looked confused, the doctor continued. "My name is Dr. P.N. Chuttani. You do not know me, but I know you. In 1948 I was studying at medical school in London. I was one of the medical students who helped convince V.K. Krishna Menon, India's first High Commissioner in London, for you to play in the final against Great Britain."

Singh Sr. didn't know how to react. He was shocked, flabbergasted. Such an odd time to cross such a path, almost an angelic figure returning once again to watch over him.

"I know you are training the team at the university. I promise you: I will watch over your wife with all my strength and energy. You have done so much for our country, it is the least I can do. I also have a good doctor who can come to Kuala Lumpur with you as well, if you so see him fit."

Singh Sr. nodded, still perplexed. Here was a man who was worlds away with him in London. A man he could credit with helping start his amazing legacy, who was now overseeing the care of his beloved wife. Dr. Chuttani put his hand on Singh Sr.'s shoulder.

"Please sir, do not worry about your wife. I will oversee her personally at every step of her recovery."

Throughout his life, Singh Sr. has had little in terms of allies. Now he had one, at the most opportune time.

"Thank you," he says, still half in disbelief, furiously shaking the doctor's hand.

At the training camp, Singh Sr. knew he had to change things up. The leftover schemers and corrupt officials from the IHF were still trying to influence his decision-making process. They pestered him with suggestions, telling him if he selected certain players, sums of money would be given to the team and him personally.

Singh Sr. had had enough. He ended training camp, declaring the team's roster well ahead of schedule. He continued to line up matches with teams from across the country—Indian Airlines, Air India, the Punjab Police squad.

After the game each day he raced to the hospital. He hoped his father would understand his spastic schedule, that his duty would not dishonour his legacy.

His wife was recovering, lifting a burden off his weary shoulders. He sat on the edge of his bed, his father's ghost by his side.

"Duty first, son."

The phone rang. He was half afraid to pick it up.

On the other end of the line was Indira Gandhi, the only child of Nehru, who had been elected India's Prime Minister in 1966. She was an unwavering, calculating ruler who in June 1975, after the World Cup, would declare the Indian Emergency, during which the press was censored and more than 100,000 Indians jailed due to their opposition of the government.[248]

Indira's son Sanjay Gandhi also imposed a forced mass-sterilization campaign during this period, and Indira herself was accused of many crimes, including electoral fraud and the controversial 24th

Amendment, passed by a Indira-led Congress, which enabled Parliament to dilute fundamental rights of the country's citizens through amendments of the Constitution.[249]

Singh Sr. was taken aback by the phone call, unsure of how to respond. He figured Nehru had spoke of him throughout the years to his daughter, and she was reaching out to carry on the relationship to the next generation.

"Hello." Indira did not mince words. She had no time for building any kind of a friendship. Her country was threatening to give out beneath her feet.

Was Singh Sr. ceding his will to the "politics of the game?"

"No," said Singh Sr., responding just as sharply. "I have chosen them on merit alone," he added.

Taking a call from the Prime Minister used to be a treat. Now it was something else, he knew the conversation would be rife with political implications. He feared becoming a pawn in Indira's chess game.

Still, he told her he would be taking 18 players to Kuala Lumpur, the oldest of them 29, the average age 24. His squad was young, and the papers scolded him for this decision. They lacked experience, reporters groused; they lacked character. But Singh Sr. believed they had two aces up their sleeves: youth and speed, with just a sprinkle of veteran leadership. And he was more than ready to unleash his boys on the world.

Indira accepted his answer, and the conversation was over as quickly as it had begun.

He stood up in the living room, looked around.

Then promptly headed to the wall and unplugged the phone.

★★★

The Hockey World Cup was first played in 1971, Pakistan winning the inaugural tournament. India had come second in 1973 to the Netherlands; now there was a chance for a first place finish. The tournament would also serve as the perfect warm-up for the 1976 Summer Games.

For Singh Sr. it was many things: redemption, a chance to silence the critics, a chance to honour the death of his father and a chance to honour India during its time of need. From the second he learned he would be spearheading the squad, no detail was too small. No stone would go unturned.

But corruption knew no bounds. It followed the team across the continent as they headed toward World Cup glory. In *India and the Olympics*, Majumdar and Mehta outline what transpired within the IHF's ranks in the 1970s, the Sahni/Ramaswamy feud that would literally plague the IHF for the next decade.

Again, with the dispute at its heights in 1974, the IOA cancelled the affiliation of the IHF and took over the administration of hockey in India. But Ramaswamy was ultimately given leadership power, and he tried everything he could to wrest power from Singh Sr. As a result, the team arrived in Kuala Lumpur only a day before the opening ceremonies.

Luckily Singh Sr. had gotten the team to Singapore first where they could escape the mess and play a few matches to stretch out their legs. And once the tournament started, Ramaswamy stepped back from the spotlight knowing interference at this time would do no one any good, even himself in his lustful pursuit of power.

One of Singh Sr.'s closest confidants during the tournament was Dr. Rajender Kalra, the team's physician referred by Dr. Chuttani. Dr. Kalra would become a close ally in the eye of the storm, and the two remain friends to this day, with the physician coming to Singh Sr.'s living room to be interviewed by me over tea and cookies.

Malaysia shares a history of British colonization with India. The country itself went through years of tumultuous rule by various factions and external countries' interests before finally achieving independence.[250]

Japanese fighters invaded Malaya and the Borneo territories in late 1941, during the Second World War. Within a year of Japan's surrender in September 1945, the British formed the Malayan Union, then dealt with an ongoing communist push for self-governance. Malaya was restructured as the Federation of

Malaya in 1948, and achieved independence in August of 1957, a decade after India. In 1963, Malaya united with North Borneo, Sarawak, and Singapore. Less than two years later, however, Singapore was expelled from the federation and established an independent republic.

Internal hostilities between Chinese and Malay factions in Kuala Lumpur disrupted the 1969 national elections, prompting the declaration of a state of emergency which ran from 1969 to 1971 when the country's political turmoil finally started to settle down.

The country itself is a mishmash of cultures and religions, divided primarily along ethnic lines. Most Malays (who make up the majority) are Muslims, most Indians are Hindus with a minority being Muslims, Sikhs, or Parsees; and most Chinese are Buddhists with a minority Muslim representation. Christianity has bled into some of those who are of Chinese and Indian descent. Much like India, Malaysia is a melting pot of multiculturalism where things like race and creed still heavily divide most facets of society.

Staying at the Merlin Hotel in Kuala Lumpur—a bland looking building with rows of windowed rooms aligned in a box-like formation—Singh Sr. quickly quarantined his boys. He had the entire section of their floor cornered off; no guests, especially females, were allowed anywhere near team members. One had already tried to board the team bus to the opening ceremonies, the players trying desperately to invite the pretty girl on before Singh Sr. intercepted her and shooed her off.

He had the floor guarded by security personnel to make sure nobody slipped through. No phone privileges after 9PM, as some of the players were apparently receiving "sexy" calls from unknown ladies. No one was to leave their rooms without specific consent from the coaches. Also no player would be permitted to drink alcohol. Singh Sr. outlined some of the tendencies and unusual quirks of his boys in his autobiography, showcasing how close attention he paid to each player on his squad:

"Ajit Pal and Varinder shared one room and what a combination they made—one quiet, the other sober and very respectful. At times Ajit Pal was tense for obvious reasons and even missed his meals before matches. His fears stemmed from his previous experiences. He was scared of the reception he would get back home if India lost again. We had to give his morale a boost from instances in India's ancient history; this worked with him very well and by the end of the tournament he was more confident of himself. Varinder, a sound player, unfortunately developed a severe viral infection which Dr. Kalra controlled with strong psychological treatments besides proper medicines and he was able to play regularly. He did not feel any weakness. Leslie Fernandes and Ashok Dewan chose to stay together. Leslie, though an intelligent player, was found to be a little too quiet, even off-mood at times. And Dr. Kalra felt that he used to tire himself with too many warming-up exercises. He was forever asking for Glucose-D. At times he would look depressed or too deep in thought. Bad performance depressed him easily. Dewan, a newcomer to the international scene, just would not enter into any discussion. His early nervousness vanished with good achievements on the field.

"Phillips and Kindo stayed together and they understood each other very well. They were forever discussing hockey and seemed to be fully aware of the fact that they were in Kuala Lumpur to play for India and give their best. Phillips had problems with his gastro-intestinal system and was treated accordingly; he developed muscular strains and a sprain in the ankle and suffered from painful corns on his little toes. Corn caps did the job. Pain in the abdomen was his constant complaint. After the final match he fell unconscious due to exhaustion. A player of strong will and guts, he punished his body very hard and never gave up trying. Psychologically he was sound and confident of himself and looked upon Kindo as his conscious keeper. And Kindo was the least complaining type. He endeared himself to everyone with his ever smiling and sporting disposition."

One of the most intriguing players on Singh Sr.'s squad was a quiet yet fierce 21-year-old defender named Aslam Sher Khan, the only Muslim on the roster. Aslam's father had played with Chand in the 1936 Olympics, but Aslam was not expected to crack the starting line-up in Malaysia. Singh Sr. said Aslam mostly kept to himself, and Singh Sr. kept a close eye on him, knowing he might need him in relief.

Before the games started, Singh Sr. took Aslam to a mosque along with Dr. Kalra and assistant coach Bodhi. Once there, the *imam*, an Islamic worship leader, noticed Singh Sr. instantly because of his distinctly Sikh turban.

The imam looked puzzled. "Are you a Sikh?" he asked.

"I am a Guru Nanak Sikh," replied Singh Sr. "And for Guru Nanak mosque, mandir, church and gurdwara are the same."

The imam nodded, non-confrontational in his response.

"May Allah give you success," he replied, placing his palms together, then showed him and Aslam the way in.

Behind him, Singh Sr. says, was the entire Pakistani team. As he left the mosque with Aslam, he overheard one of the players say something to him in passing.

"You stole our blessing."

Aslam was still not included on the opening game roster, and he spoke about his exclusion from the starting 11 in his autobiography *To Hell With Hockey:*[251]

"I could not sleep that first night in Kuala Lumpur, like on all other nights during our stay. The night before the World Cup tournament was about to begin, I prayed to God to help me prove myself worthy of representing my country ... The next day, instead of playing for India, I was once again relegated to the sidelines. . . . I burnt with rage and shame. Much as I tried, I could not understand the reason for my disgrace. Why was I considered an anathema? What the hell was wrong in being Aslam Sher Khan? . . . I cursed the chauvinistic bastards who had selected the playing team. Those people were only concerned with themselves, and could not think beyond the first person singular or plural."

While field hockey was like religion in India during this time, it was pretty clear religion also played a massive part in Indian field hockey.

India's first match was against England on March 2 at Stadium Merdeka. Right from the get-go, Singh Sr. said his players appeared sluggish. Phillips would score 12 minutes in, but the Brits quickly equalized. Phillips scored again on a penalty corner, but then India couldn't muster anything else and were forced to claw their way to a 2–1 win.

"We were not happy with how we were doing at that point," says Singh Sr. "We expected more."

With five days rest in between games, Singh Sr. said morale was a serious issue. He worried he had run his players too hard in training, that all the field hockey had fatigued them mentally and physically. Great Britain, although still a formidable opponent, was not the team it had been in 1948. The country had gone soccer mad, and field hockey had drifted from the limelight. Thus they were no longer a perennial powerhouse.

"We had to keep the boy's spirits high," Singh Sr. said. "I kept them on the pitch for fun games as much as possible. I think they felt more at home there."

Next was Australia, and India would score three minutes into the contest. However, the Aussies equalized nine minutes later on a penalty corner, and the Indians became their own worst enemy.

"We stopped playing our game," Singh Sr. recalled. "Our guys were fighting the ball. They were being tested. I think the adversity was getting to them."

India would have to settle for a tie. Many of the administrators traveling with the team wanted to ring every alarm bell imaginable, but Singh Sr. decided to stick to his guns. Two days later, it was Argentina, and the wheels came right off. India scored first, but the Argentinians scored two unanswered goals and went into a machine-like defensive lockdown. Trapping their opponents with a slew of defenders, they dropped their forwards back to midfield and clogged the scoring areas with human shields. India lost, and was in serious danger of not making it out of the group stage. They had to win their final pool match against a tough West German squad, or risk elimination.

When they got to the hotel, Singh Sr. broke one of his own rules. After the players had sullenly entered their rooms, he called the front desk.

"I said to them that our players could order as much beer as they want. I wanted them to get drunk so they would forget the loss to Argentina and go to sleep."

Dr. Kalra said this became the purpose of the trip, to turn this group of men into a cohesive team, he wanted them to booze it up together in their rooms and bond, tell stories and find out who their teammates were so they could gel.

"We visited churches together as a team because there were Christians on the team. We went to a mosque for Aslam. He said it does not matter what religion you are all from, we are one team, here together," said Dr. Kalra.

The next evening, they headed back to the stadium to play West Germany on a slippery pitch drizzled with intermittent rain. The match itself had been pushed back as the Pakistan-New Zealand game that started earlier that day was postponed—with Pakistan winning at the time of delay—and moved to a new pitch, the one where India and West Germany were supposed to play.

As a result, India's game didn't start until the early evening; when they scored a goal the West German goaltender protested that the lighting was too bad. The officials actually called the game and scheduled a rematch for the next day, even though there were only a few minutes left and India was leading; earlier, Pakistan's game with New Zealand had been replayed from the precise point of rain stoppage. Singh Sr. and his team launched a formal appeal, but it didn't matter. They would not resume the match, but replay it in its entirety, two days later.

India won 3-1, but now Singh Sr.'s players were exhausted, having played one extra game. This World Cup was not going as he had hoped, and he was sure the local Muslim-led organizing committee were going to do his boys no favours.

Dr. Kalra was doing everything he could to jumpstart the players. Defender Surjit Singh sought out the physician, outlining a problem he had that was eating him alive. "He said the number he was wearing, number four, was unlucky and he wanted to change it," Dr. Kalra said, smiling.

Knowing this was not allowed in the rules, Dr. Kalra got a local Indian man to make him some *til* and *gur*, a simple concoction of sesame seeds and jaggery, and told Surjit the snack would wash away his bad luck.

Dr. Kalra said Aslam came to him the night before their scheduled match against Malaysia, asking for a sleeping pill as he was restless about not being chosen for the starting 11.

"I did not give it to him," says Dr. Kalra.

Instead the doctor took him down to the lounge for a coffee, and Aslam confided in him that he thought he was being left off the starting 11 because he was Muslim.

"I told him Allah might have a play for him," says Dr. Kalra.

The doctor headed to his room where he was staying with Singh Sr. and told him of the Muslim's regression. If anyone knew of religious favouritism, it was this Sikh. Singh Sr. decided he needed to do something.

"The truth was I played (Michael) Kindo because he was better than him."

Kindo was a 27-year-old deep defender with a lot more international experience, but Singh Sr. understands why Aslam thought he was playing religious favourites given the country's circumstances.

The next day, Stadium Merdeka was packed with raucous fans. About 25,000 screaming Malaysian fans to be specific. The stadium was located in the heart of the city, and many locals climbed the walls of the structure to get a better view, hanging from bannisters and perching atop rooftops. Security forces had their hands full.

Like many matches in the tournament, the game was delayed due to a torrential downpour. Players had to wait, pumped full of adrenaline, then play on sluggish fields bogged down by water. This World Cup would clearly demonstrate the need to move field hockey to artificial surfaces, as the small white ball would literally stop mid-strike, making for a comical elbow in play.

Malaysia scored 32 minutes in, boosting the home crowd. India equalized eight minutes later, but then the Malaysians converted on a penalty corner.

It was 2-1 and time was running out. Singh Sr. needed a spark. Defender Surjit Singh had been taking a number of penalty corners, but was coming up empty.

"He couldn't score," Singh Sr. recalled. He looked to his bench. "Aslam!"

The quiet defender darted up from his seat, completely taken aback. In a crowd of screaming Muslim fans, Singh Sr. wanted his young Muslim defender in the eye of the storm.

Singh Sr. did something a bit out of character as he signed the substitution card. He hugged Aslam, then planted a kiss on his cheek. Aslam darted onto the field, so excited he was almost unsure where to run.

In the 65th minute, with a loss staring them in the face, India was awarded a penalty corner. Aslam was known for having a wicked, but unpredictable, shot—either right on target, or flying wildly off into the stands. Now the circular bullet whipped out to his spot, and India's only Muslim player loaded his chamber, eager to etch his name into the history books with one slice of his wooden blade.

"My entire life changed that day," Aslam told me in the lobby of the Park Royal Hotel in downtown Delhi.

Though he would go on to a long career in politics, his auto-biography title, *To Hell With Hockey,* speaks volumes about what happened to his love of the game after that crucial match, as he retired from play shortly after Kuala Lumpur. In the book, he speaks about the goal, writing that racism partly fuelled his iconic shot: "*Mian* is a strange word. While it is a nomenclature for a Muslim gentleman, depending on its pronunciation, it can also be used to convey ridicule. Suddenly I found no ridicule in the way I was called *Mian*. The faces of my colleagues showed helpless pleas.

"For a fleeting moment, I felt like teaching Indian hockey the lesson it deserved," he continued in his autobiography. "However, my pain was insignificant when compared to my loyalty for my country. I would teach Indian hockey the lesson it deserved by bringing it back from defeat and helping it win . . . Something in me told to hit into the right corner of the goal, in spite of my stance and the loss of leverage.

"I hit the ball to the right, and a poor carpet shot entered the goal. The stadium erupted into silence. Suddenly, my teammates were kissing me . . ."

Balbir was weeping hysterically like a child. 'I hope I did not let you down,' I said. 'Don't make me feel small. You have lifted us all up today,' Balbir replied, wrapping me in his arms."

India had drawn blood—and drawn even in the process. The momentum shifted like a sea tide, and soon the pitch had tilted in their favour. In the 79th minute, into golden goal territory, Harcharan Singh delivered the final dagger. The home crowd fell silent. The Indians jumped for joy amidst a sea of boos and cat-calls.

After the match, the whole team crowded around Aslam, patting him on the back and hugging him. Little did he know that back home he was now a national hero, igniting parades in city streets across the country after the win.

Singh Sr. headed back to his room with Dr. Kalra. They hugged, trying to contain their excitement. Much like in London, they'd walked into a country worlds away, and won. The Muslim faith has long been at odds with many other religions on the Indian subcontinent, dating back the reign of the Mughal Empire.[252]

The night before the final, as Singh Sr. and Dr. Kalra sat on their beds, a strange man appeared at security, demanding to speak to the coach of the team. He came late at night, telling Singh Sr. and Dr. Kalra he had a very important letter to give them. "He said inside it was the result of the final match, that he had predicted it," says Singh Sr.

Both Singh Sr. and Dr. Kalra refused the letter, knowing it might bring them bad luck. But this man, who Singh Sr. said was clean shaven and obviously of Indian descent, looked completely inconspicuous and far from crazy.

The man continued, further outlining his theory. Being the third day of the third month in the third World Cup, the final game would have three goals. Singh Sr. agreed to take the letter so the man would leave and not disturb his team, but kept it secret from the players, as "We were worried it would bother them."

Pakistan had had two full days rest after beating West Germany to book the other slot in the final; in contrast, India was forced to suit up the day after their win against Malaysia. But the team did not care about outside influence or political trickery.

They had their swagger back, courtesy of their Muslim defend-er—now on the starting 11.

Singh Sr. wanted his players to focus on field hockey, but he knew a sense of unity with their opponents might help human-ize the situation. Inside the dressing room he set up his usual prayer table, incorporating symbols from each religion represent-ed by his team. Knowing how divisive the subject had been dur-ing his playing career, he was preaching harmony, solidarity. His boys understood the immense pressure of the game. To win, Singh Sr. wanted them to come together as one.

It was a sunny day in Kuala Lumpur, Singh Sr. recalls. The stands were once again packed for the opposing team, though the crowd was now interspersed with pockets of Indian supporters. Team India, in their baby blue jerseys and white shorts, and Team Pakistan, in dark green and white, took to the field cautiously. The game was rough and tumble from the opening whistle.[253] The Pakistanis had developed a reputation for playing tough, whacking opponents with their sticks and ramming into players at any chance. But Pakistani star Samiullah Khan—who tried to slam into an Indian player—got the worst of it; he was forced to leave with an injury almost as quickly as the game had started.

Seventeen minutes in, Mohammad Saeed Khan struck and scored, sending the crowd into a frenzy. India's forward Phillips, who was trying his utmost to emulate Singh Sr., kept valiantly going for goal, but met the wrath of the defenders' sticks over and over. After the match, his legs were littered with cuts and bruises.

The game was filled with stoppages from penalties, slogging out the minutes in a see-saw back and forth, with most of the play congregating in the neutral zone. Aslam got a chance just before half to replicate his penalty corner triumph, but the opposing keeper made a diving save to keep Pakistan up 1-0 heading into halftime.

Singh Sr. knew this was India's time. All those perspiring days of training at the university in Chandigarh were going to pay off. He told his boys the second half would be theirs, that the Pakistanis would be tired, and this would be their chance to deliv-er a decisive strike. He delivered a rousing speech in the dressing room, channeling his mentor Harbail, telling his boys they had a chance to etch their place in field hockey history. All the sweat, blood and tears would mean nothing if they lost. They did not want this legendary tournament to be forgotten. "Leave it all out on the field," he thundered. "For your country and for your God."

The heart of India's attacking plan was midfielder Ashok Kumar. Though he wasn't a scorer like his father, he was a tireless disperser—a central highway through which all of India's chances ran. In the forty-fourth minute, one of his balls squeaked through to Phillips, who beat two defenders and started to enter the Pakistani circle before being fouled. India received a penalty corner, and defender Surjit, wearing his new "lucky" number four, courtesy of Dr. Kalra's *til* and *gur*, netted the defining equalizer to the crowd's dismay.

In the 51st minute, after a scramble in front, none other than Dhyan Chand's son came crashing in. Although the Pakistani players protested, the referee stood by his decision that the ball crossed the line. 2-1 India.

The final whistle sounded; the Indians leapt for joy. Their first and only World Cup. *Sportsweek*, a long-defunct Indian sports magazine, wrote in a piece that ran shortly after the final: "Thirty-five minutes to glory: in those wondrous, many splendored moments of magic, India provided the frosting for the cake baked in the fiery furnaces of Kuala Lumpur, and got right back where she belonged—back on the top of the hockey world."

A *The Hindu* article, which quotes Kumar and Aslam, notes that the victory has been relegated to the unremembered over the years. Aslam says theirs was the last gasp of Indian hockey supremacy, noting, "They switched to artificial turf after that game. It changed the game so much, we never saw glory like that again. It is sad how it has been forgotten over the years."

However, at that moment in time, with India about to embark on its own emergency, the victory was a welcome distraction. "There was tremendous excitement in India," says Singh Sr. "Our national hockey team had won a world level tournament after eleven years. Unprecedented crowds thronged to greet the team wherever the boys went."

The *Indian Express* ran a piece outlining the impact of the victory on the nation: "It would be pleasant to dwell on India's magnificent 2-1 victory over Pakistan and relive every moment of that epic struggle for supremacy, a real hockey classic . . . It was the ultimate test of skill, speed, stamina, mental and physical conditioning. India seemed to have reserved their best form for the final showdown with Pakistan. Pre-match tactics were studiously rehearsed overnight. The morning was spent in visiting a church, a temple, a Gurdwara and a mosque: a reminder of the secular nature of our society and the composition of our team."

Aslam spoke about being coaxed back onto the pitch after the game to wave to the Muslim fans, an experience that typified his tough existence as a religious minority in India.

"My heart choked with tears as I waved to the crowd," he wrote in his autobiography. "Little did they know that I had no one to wave to. Father was dead. Amma was back home in Bhopal. The little girl who felt that I would become a great player one day had crossed into the shadows of death. There was no one to share this moment with me. I brushed away the thought, and the tears that came with it."

When Singh Sr. got back to the hotel room, his phone rang. He stood in the room like a statue, shoulders covered in garlands. Dr. Kalra looked at him, still as stone. The phone echoed loudly in the quiet confines of the space. Singh Sr. slowly walked towards it, picked it up as if it might be spring-loaded with explosives.

"—Hello . . ."

It was Indira, calling to congratulate him on his team's victory. A gallon of oxygen exited Singh Sr.'s lungs in one push. Dr. Kalra wiped his hand across his face. Singh Sr. thanked Indira, and hung up politely. He looked at Dr. Kalra, who held his hand up in a "Eureka!" moment.

"Ah!" He headed to the nightstand, opening the supposedly fortuitous envelope from the mysterious man. Both men looked over the note simultaneously, written in pen.

"India will win, three goals will be scored."

★★★

After the celebrations died down, the IHF's new head, Ramaswamy—who had won power from Sahni and then cut all his ties to the organization—set up a private meeting with Singh Sr. Ramaswamy sat down in his office and literally handed him a bag of cash. He would not say who or where he got it from, but that it was for Singh Sr. and that was all that mattered.

Singh Sr. shakes his head recalling this moment. "I said 'I don't need that'," he recalls. "He said 'take if you have some expenditures' and he put it on the table. I kept telling him I didn't want it but he ended up leaving it with me."

Not sure what to do with the cash, Singh Sr. decided to hand it out to each of his players. Ramaswamy found out, and was furious that his bribe had failed to achieve its goal of buying the coach specifically. He was trying to buy Singh Sr., but all he did was give the money to his boys.

Ramaswamy had also promised the players that they could bring a large amount of items and goods back through customs if they flew in through Madras—he said he had connections at the airport. However when they arrived, customs seized most of their goods for violations. Singh Sr. ended up paying the fines out of his own manager's salary. Then, good to his word, he took his players back to the dormitory in Chandigarh and let his boys hang out with all the girls on campus. Much like Harbail, he'd enticed his players perfectly, and rewarded them accordingly.

However Ramaswamy's new IHF leadership brass were out to sully him. Singh Sr. was expecting a formal bonus for his work in Kuala Lumpur, which would barely cover the wages he lost at work during the tournament and training. The players had received some money unofficially, what they called "diet money", which helped circumvent the amateur IOC code. Each player and sub-coach Gurcharan Bodhi received 15,000 rupees.

Singh Sr. waited patiently for his cheque, but it never came. While some of his players were being illegally gifted plots of land and brand-new scooters, Singh Sr. got nothing but silence and a cold shoulder.

Samuel Banerjee, who helped Singh Sr. write his autobiography and publish it (in 1977) through Vikas Publishing House in

New Delhi, which still operates to this day, said the Sikh has reason to be upset about his handling.

"He has not been treated kindly by the Indian Hockey Federation," says Banerjee. "He has had only one independent national coaching assignment. That was when he prepared the Indian team for the 1975 World Cup Hockey Tournament at Kuala Lumpur. What his team did is now part of the glorious history of Indian hockey. Yet his reward was an unwarranted rebuff from the federation. He was ignored, but he preferred to keep quiet rather than indulge in counter-attacking. Certain incidents have made him bitter, but not angry. All Balbir thinks about is hockey. It is a pity that the Federation has not bothered to give him due recognition."

Singh Sr. brushed the incident off, focusing on preparations for the 1976 Montreal Summer Olympics, now only a few months away. He wanted the team back in Chandigarh to train, to get his boys back on track after a few months of leisure.

What happened to him next is something Singh Sr. says he still can't totally comprehend.

"Despite the success at the 1975 World Cup, I was unceremoniously censured by the Indian Hockey Federation and dropped. I still do not know officially what my fault was. I may be mistaken but I guess the men in power do not like people who have been, at any stage, associated with Ashwini Kumar. If this is true, they must be narrow minded people."

Ashwini had been outed by the IHF leadership, however Singh Sr. was seen as a product of his time in power. Thus after gold was won, Singh Sr. once again became replaceable in the eyes of the IHF.

"I hope my fears are incorrect," Singh Sr. wrote in his autobiography. "If the IHF bosses want me to prove to them that I do not belong to any camp they are mistaken. I can never do that. My actions should speak for myself. Where were they when I lost my dear father in the early days of the Chandigarh camp for the preparation of the 1975 World Cup team? They never bothered to know that I neglected my seriously sick wife while the camp was on. I stuck to my duty. Personal loss and mental anguish meant nothing to me. I lived with the boys, treated them as friends and acted as their mentor and guide. And what did I get in return? The sack: a big humiliation for some obscure reference I had made in my report to the IHF. Was it justified? I did everything in the interest of Indian hockey."

Singh Sr. contests to this day that his Kuala Lumpur Report (each coach is required to file a post-tournament report) was simply an accounting of the events that had transpired. The IHF alleges he leaked it to the media as part of some type of smear campaign.

Ramaswamy had outed Ashwini and Sahri, blacklisted Singh Sr. and fired another official named R.S. Bhola for apparent corruption. An entirely new set of coaches and administrators were now sent to look after the team for the Montreal Olympics. The team was handpicked by Ramaswamy and some of his closest confidants within the IHF—and by anyone who might be willing to "donate" to the team, or offer some cash to get their son or nephew on the World Cup winning roster.

Their blindness to the outside world proved costly. Meanwhile the FIH had traveled to Montreal and declared the grass pitches unfit for play after a harsh Canadian winter. The Montreal Olympic Organizing Committee, along with Montreal mayor Jean Drapeau, suggested hosting the field hockey matches on astroturf instead. The FIH, along with the Montreal organizers, headed to Toronto and borrowed a field usually reserved for American football games. The test matches were a success: the game became quicker; passes were sharper. The decision was easy to make—and since Montreal all international games have been held on either artificial turf or astroturf.

Ramaswamy ignored the switch, apparently assuming his team would adjust easily to the new playing surface seamlessly. He was wrong. India went 3-2 in the group stage, ultimately finishing seventh.

OLYMPIC CIVILIAN

"The disappearance of the British Raj in India is at present, and must for a long time be, simply inconceivable. That it should be replaced by a native Government or Governments is the wildest of wild dreams . . . As soon as the last British soldier sailed from Bombay or Karachi, India would become the battlefield of antagonistic racial and religious forces . . . [and] the peaceful and progressive civilization, which Great Britain has slowly but surely brought into India, would shrivel up in a night."

~ J. E. Welldon,
former Bishop of Calcutta

"Sir, it is not safe to leave the airport."

He stands, defiant, in the long hallway of the Palam Airport in Delhi. After everything he's endured, a young aviation employee is telling him not to set foot in his own country. The nation for which he bled and won three Olympic gold medals and a World Cup for, the country he policed with bare hands, the country over which he lost endless nights of sleep.

"I will not wait here," he says in an argumentative tone. "This is my homeland."

The airline attendant holds his hands up, trying to reason with this defiant, stubborn man.

"Sir, it is not safe for Sikhs to go outside right now. They are killing them in the streets."

He walks by the airport employee, moving towards the exit. "I will go out," he says. "I will take the risk."

More airline employees step in, each one desperately attempting to reason with him. "Sir," one cries. "If you must go out, may you remove your turban so they do not know you are Sikh?"

The insult a punch in the gut. Now he's even more enraged. He's a proud Indian citizen, born in the dusty mud huts of Haripur and raised in the tiny village of Moga. This scene is sacrilegious, absurd, almost comical.

He keeps walking. He can see through the airport windows into the streets now, make out plumes of smoke lifting into the air from various points around the city. Sirens wail in the distance. He looks over to the holding area, where groups of wide-eyed Sikhs are huddled with their baggage behind groups of heavily armed airport security guards.

Gurinderjit Singh Bhomia, Sushbir's husband's brother—a deputy inspector general with the Border Security Force—rushes onto the scene, utterly relieved to see him. He's been abruptly tasked with an important duty: pick up the decorated Olympian and ensure his safety.

"Balbir, oh thank you! You are okay!" He hugs Singh Sr. hard, embracing him like he's about to tackle him to the ground. Then he holds him at arm's length, inspecting him for wounds. "Are you okay?"

"Yes, I am fine," says Singh Sr., slightly aggravated.

In 1984, Indira Gandhi had been assassinated by her Sikh bodyguards, shooting her, point-blank, in retaliation for Operation Blue Star. Singh Sr. had initially heard of the news while on a layover in Germany. He refused the German airport's offer of a free hotel until the riots died down. All around him passengers came off their planes from across the planet, saw the news, and covered their mouths in horror, tears streaming down their faces; but all this man wanted to do was go home.

In the aftermath of the assassination, Hindus took to the streets. The march turned ugly fast, with Sikhs around the city running for cover, hiding in basements and shacks, holding their children tight as the bloodthirsty mob came looking for them. The assassination had blindsided the nation, but now the verdict was in: the Sikhs were to blame, and revenge would be had.

After Singh Sr. registered the familiar face, he returned to his rigid state, started again for the glass doors. Gurinderjit, flabbergasted, physically stopped him, gesturing frantically out into the riotous day.

"Balbir! You must stop; you mustn't go outside. They are killing Sikhs, dragging them into the streets and beating them to death with rods and stabbing them with knives. They are hunting them down and murdering them. It is revenge for Gandhi's assassination."

"If I die," says Singh Sr., moving beyond him, "I die a Sikh, so be it."

Gurinderjit takes a deep breath. His head swivels around to the airport officials, holding their hands up in confusion.

"Okay," he says. "Will you at least take off the turban?"

Singh Sr. blows air out of his mouth. He took his turban off for no one, for God alone.

"I did not kill Indira. Why should I be a target?"

Gurinderjit wipes sweat from his brow. He is in no position to debate the finer points of mob rule and religious intolerance. Every step Singh Sr. takes brings him closer to the door. He has to act fast; find a plan, a quick thinking strategy.

"Okay, okay, okay," he says, unholstering his firearm.

There are security guards with guns everywhere, blocking the airport entrances. He walks up to them, off duty but looking particularly militaristic. His voice is loud, bombastically authoritative, leaving no room for dissent.

"I am a deputy inspector general for the Border Security Forces," he says as he pulls the hammer back on his pistol. "We are going to escort this man to his car. This is Balbir Singh Sr., winner of three Olympic gold medals for India. Do you want him to die on your watch?"

The security workers cock their weapons and oblige, standing at attention. Gurinderjit checks to ensure that he has a round in the chamber. If things get hairy, it will happen quickly.

Outside, he wastes no time, hurrying Singh Sr. into his car with two other members of the security force. Singh Sr. gets into the backseat, but does not duck.

"Balbir, would you hide below the seats for me?" Gurinderjit asks, his tone as polite as can be.

Singh Sr. shakes his head, crosses his arms, defiant to the last request. "No."

Gurinderjit nods, knowing there will be no discussion. He closes the door, shifts into gear, and zooms out of the parking lot, right through the pay service window's wooden divider. They hit Delhi, and he starts running red lights, weaving in and out of traffic. If he stops, trouble might come. If he can keep moving, there is less chance someone will spot Singh Sr.'s turban and try to ambush the vehicle. Traffic starts to bottleneck; he honks his horn furiously, shoulder checking for both cars and venomous Hindu rioters.

Out the side windows, Singh Sr. can see the horror. Burnt bodies lying in smouldering, smoking messes. Sikhs dragged into the Delhi streets, beaten to death with whatever people can get their hands on. Their Hindu counterparts pouring kerosene over their heads and throwing matches at them. Women and children dragged from their homes screaming and crying, lit afire with no remorse. Gurdwaras burned, stormed by angry rioters. Absolute chaos, mob rule pushing society to the lowest common denominator. It is Hell on earth.

He remembers the smell of burning flesh from Partition. Three decades later, the unforgettable stench is back in his nose.

"Have we not made any progress as a nation?" he thinks to himself. He holds his breath, covers his nose, turns his eyes forward. He has seen enough violence for a million lifetimes.

At last, they retreat to quieter streets.

★★★

Though Ramaswamy and his deep industrialist pockets now ran the IHF outright, the Montreal Olympics in 1976 were a complete debacle, a much-publicized embarrassment and another black smear across India's field hockey resume.

The IHF was completely unprepared for the switch to astroturf, neglecting to get the squad any contests on the new style of pitch before the Olympics. At times they looked silly, making plays designed for thick grass. Other teams such as Australia and Argentina, now fully adapted to the new setting that allowed long passes on a consistent surface, took the Indians by complete surprise. They looked like spectators at a tennis match, watching the ball go back and forth across their vision, hopeless, unable to cope, failing victim to the oddest of opponents—the playing surface.

Ramaswamy had cast off Singh Sr. for his Kuala Lumpur Report that somehow leaked to the media. Drama-loving journalists ate it up, ran it through the wire as far away as Malaysia. It pointed out the officiating and administration errors at the 1975 World Cup, infuriating the organizing committee who threw mountainous waves of backlash at the IHF. Singh Sr. attests to this day he never released it publicly, and wanted nothing more than for it to remain internal. His biggest mistake was thinking the people he handed it off to would remain honest, even for a split second.

The conniving Ramaswamy had bribed any dissent, and fired any leftovers against his rule despite Montreal's terrible outcome. His sole purpose was to run the IHF unchallenged; power hungry, his lust for control fed by his fortune. But it had little to do with putting the best field hockey squad on the pitch. Ramaswamy had an official gag order placed on Singh Sr. to censure him, denying any chance to plead his case in public, or private. He cast him from the island, and it appeared now as long as Ramaswamy was in charge, Singh Sr. would not be a part of Indian field hockey in any manner.

However the 1975 World Cup win created one windfall, Punjab Chief Minister Giani Zail Singh promoted Singh Sr. to director of the Sports Department, a post Singh Sr. had been working towards for 13 years. But this too came with its own backlash and baggage.

Milkha Singh, a track and field star who had competed for India at the 1958 British Empire and Commonwealth Games in Cardiff, Wales, was furious at Singh Sr.'s appointment, and demanded the promotion be struck from the record and the job be given to him. He attested he'd been hired a day before Singh Sr., therefore should be promoted ahead of him, even though he clearly lacked experience as a director as his reading and writing skills were novice at best. Singh Sr. was chosen by Fletcher based on merit, but Milkha wanted the position on chronology, favouritism and groupism.

The whole thing spiralled out of control, leading to charges of theft of personal files and ended up in the Indian courts. After a lengthy battle that made it all the way to the Punjab High Court, they ruled in favour of Singh Sr., but he had long since lost any standing within the department as the debacle smeared his image, tarnishing him as a supervisor.

"It's not the country doing it to me," says Singh Sr. when asked about the issues he faced professionally. "It's the people."

It was another blow to the chest of a very proud man. One now utterly exhausted and looking like he may never regain his footing on the canvas.

The days turned into months and the months into years, and Singh Sr. figured his coaching career with India had passed him by. He was no longer even considered for tournaments, the new regime had moved on, scratched him permanently from their list, he thought. By now his career with the Punjab Sports Department was also winding down. He'd given up on a lot of his projects, to build playgrounds around the state, to offer cash incentives to athletes for training and to set up scholarship funds.

The Punjab Sports Department was so disjointed, so splintered, so ripe with corruption like a labourious, dying animal, it was no wonder India stopped sending any real threats to the Olympic games. Singh Sr.'s initiatives were dive-bombed, kamikaze-killed by his colleagues upon departmental approval.

Although India would win gold at the 1980 Olympics in Moscow, at that time part of the Soviet Union, the games were largely boycotted by other nations—65 in total. The boycott was in protest due to the Soviet war in Afghanistan, one of the major conflicts of the Cold War.[254] The Americans led the revolt, taking most of the perennial powerhouse countries along with them as strategic allies. Only six teams competed in the field hockey tournament—no Pakistan, no Great Britain, no Netherlands. India suited up against teams like Tanzania and Cuba who had no business competing on the world stage.

Of course, the jealousy back home continued to follow Singh Sr. Milka Singh, now high up with the Punjab Sports Department despite his blatant misgivings, was furious again he did not receive an invite to Moscow. He lobbied Indira, trying to put pressure on the government to send him to Moscow, swapping him out for Singh Sr.

"He called her. She said this is their doing, there is nothing I can do for you," says Singh Sr. "Her hands were tied, the IOC would do what it wanted to."

Milka ended up going, however had to stay at the Indian embassy and was not given official delegate status.

Singh Sr. however was an official guest of the USSR. During the Cold War, India was much closer to the Soviet Union than the United States. He was subsequently treated like a VIP, an honorary visitor in the Communist nation. He said at the time it felt like any other games, but looking back on it now, strikes an odd tone in his memory.

"I did not know it at the time, but the politics were very powerful."

The USSR rolled out the red carpet at the Moscow airport, literally. He was ushered into a special convoy and limousine, given a team of handlers and personal bodyguards. After so many years of being snubbed, the consolation of finally becoming an Olympic delegate, however skewed by international politics, was flattering.

Two years later, the windfall from his Soviet appearance bore another extraordinary opportunity, another chance to coach and manage the team; but once again it was forces outside the IHF taking power. It was 1982 and political tensions between the Sikhs and ruling Hindu majority had been strained. Indira Gandhi wanted to shore up relationships with the minority group.

She had eked her way back to power through a political splinter faction, and now needed all the allies she could muster to retain power. Her Congress Party had lost the general election in 1977 after the Indian Emergency and its fallout, but she was back in power. A collective sigh had engulfed the nation, they had voted for change, but somehow ended up with the same thing. She'd heard conversations her father Nehru had about the Sikh athlete, and knew she needed to rekindle the relationship, so while the IHF was disbanded, she picked the coach and manager herself.

Singh Sr. was also chosen to light the sacred flame at the 1982 Asian Games with long jumper Deanna Tewari. Indira watched intently from the stands above the crowd. Singh Sr. wonders now if he was also chosen to light the flame along with Tewari as a political play—Indira trying to quell the Sikh uprising and dissent that was growing everyday.

"It was a very tense time," says Singh Sr. "You could see that something was not right, that the country was not the same. Everyday Sikhs called for their own nation, they had had enough of the government."

Regardless, when it came to running the men's field hockey squad, not much had changed. Rajinder Singh Jr., a well-connected player from Punjab, was in favour with Ramaswamy and the IHF. Ramaswamy forced Singh Sr. to not only add him to the roster for the tournament, to play him as defender even though he had a badly injured knee and couldn't partake in any training sessions. It was one of many roster decisions Singh Sr. disagreed with, and while Indira had given him the power, the IHF quickly took over the process, forcing Singh Sr.'s hand on a number of occasions.

India would get thumped by Pakistan in the final 7-1, Indira herself storming out midway through the match in disgust, exiting the stadium in a huff before she was supposed to hand out the medals to the winners.

"I kind of suffered a bit of a heart attack during that game," says Singh Sr. "I was pretty tired of all the politics by then. It was too much."

After the tournament, Rajiv Gandhi, Indira's son and successor, reached out to Singh Sr. He asked him to take the team to Melbourne for the Essanda Cup—a prestigious club tournament that regularly drew heavyweight teams from around the world— to wash away the stink of the 1982 games, offering to pay for the team's travel expenses. Singh Sr. said the tournament was fun, and the team captured silver beating Pakistan, however by this time, he'd now completely soured to the idea of having anything to do with the IHF, officially retiring from coaching upon his return.

"I couldn't take it anymore," he says, shaking his head in memory. "I was done, that was it."

It was a solemn denouement, and there would be no press coverage, the IHF once again took his gesture as a personal shot, and placed him back in their doghouse.

Now back home with Sushil, it was largely a quiet time, Singh Sr. left with little escapism now that field hockey had formally left his world. His sons had left for Canada looking for a better life themselves, and Singh Sr. found himself increasingly isolated from the sporting community. The IHF had blackballed him, his name meant nothing now when it came to Indian field hockey. The Punjab Sports Department's cronyism had left him on the outside looking in, and new managers did everything they could to deny him promotions now that Fletcher had retired.

"I wanted to do something else with my life. I was tired, I wanted to be a grandfather and watch the kids grow up."

The entire situation came to a head, and Singh Sr. announced his retirement from the Punjab Sports Department. He'd had enough of India, all the fighting, the killing, all the injustice done in the name of religion and divineness. The corruption, the politics, it had permanently soured his palate, a stain across his tongue. At the end of 1982, Singh Sr. would punch in for his last day at the Punjab Sports Authority, another proud whimper. He filed his letter of retirement, and was ready to head to Canada to focus on being a grandfather.

The only remaining duty was to attend a Public Accounts Committee in Ludhiana, an exit interview of sorts, largely a formality. The meeting was scheduled for noon, and Singh Sr., ever the punctual being in a country of tardiness, was five minutes early.

However the chairperson of the Public Accounts Committee had long since cast Singh Sr. aside as a malcontent, and informed Singh Sr. that he was late, and therefore his pension would be revoked. Close to two decades of service flushed down the drain for apparently being tardy to his final meeting. It was a slap in the face, a stab in the back and a illegal hit all rolled into one callous gesture.

"He stopped my pension," says Singh Sr., still flabbergasted to this day at what transpired. "I served the department for so many years, but this was what they were doing to me?"

Singh Sr. did not know what to do, he had no authority anymore, he was supposed to be retired.

Sushil gathered the courage to phone their sons in Canada, and asked them for $100 Canadian each month to squeeze by. It was a small pittance, but he was determined not to cause too much stress to his sons living their own lives on the other side of the planet. But he knew this couldn't go on for long, he was draining the resources of his offspring and goodwill of his community.

Finally he couldn't take it anymore. He mustered up the courage and called Jawaharlal Gupta, a renowned lawyer in India who would later become a chief justice for the Indian High Court. Singh Sr. walked into his Delhi residence, embarrassed he had nothing in his pockets to offer this high-priced, high powered attorney but a daunting case of corruption in a land chock full of it.

"I said to him, I cannot pay you much. But he refused to take any money from me. He said to me 'Balbir you are a celebrated sportsperson of this country, it is my duty to help you and represent you.'"

Once again, Singh Sr. would have to go to court, and once again, the law would rule in his favour.

"They gave me my pension back, with interest," he exclaims, a smile across his face.

Despite the court ruling, neither the Public Accounts Committee chairperson nor anyone with the department ended up facing any type of punishment, or even a disciplinary hearing. Singh Sr. scrounged up some cash, mostly backpay from his pension, and headed to Gupta's office. As soon as the lawyer saw the money, he pushed it back into Singh Sr.'s coat pocket, refusing to accept a dime.

"Your money is no good here," said Gupta. "You have done so much for this country."

Another angel had swooped in, saving Singh Sr. in his gravest time of need.

Singh Sr. and Sushil headed to Canada to visit their sons. They talked on the plane ride about moving overseas permanently. The Canadian government was still welcoming refugees and immigrants with open arms. Pierre Trudeau, a left-leaning Liberal and former Prime Minister, had regained power and wanted Canada to remain open to the world.

Singh Sr. and Sushil struggled with the decision. He felt as if he was turning his back on his country, but what kind of life could he expect back home? The IHF wanted nothing to do with him, his career had been tarnished by a series of controversial encounters. He held hope he might be invited to the 1984 Los Angeles Olympics as an official dignitary, possibly another chance to rebuild his name that had been dragged through the mud, but other than that, what did he have to look forward to?

"We did not know what to do," says Singh Sr. "I wanted to stay in my country. But I don't think Sushil agreed with me. She had taken a great liking to Canada."

Then in November of 1983, tragedy struck at the heart of this man, a knockout blow to his core, knocking him to his knees more fiercely than he had ever felt on the field.

Sushil suddenly fell ill. Singh Sr. called his neighbour who was an Army doctor, however as the two drove her to the Post Graduate Institute of Medical Education and Research, she passed away in the car of a heart attack.

When asked to describe the feeling of losing the love of his life, Singh Sr. falls silent, tripping over his words. There is no explanation, no consolation for this blow. At a time when he was feeling punished simply for living, God drew him another setback, this one more monumental than all the others combined. Sushil, the only thing he loved more than field hockey.

An all-encompassing dark cloud rolled atop Singh Sr., washing over him. His closest confidant, his partner in life, was now off to the next life.

"I was very sad," he musters, before trailing off.

After he regains his mental footing, he regales in a few light-hearted stories about Sushil. He tells me of how they used to play table tennis in their Chandigarh home. Sushil, having played badminton all her life, regularly mopped the floor with the three time Olympic gold medalist. He snickers when speaking about it.

"Outside I was a great athlete. When we played together, she was better than me."

The 1984 Los Angeles Olympics[255] drew near and the Sikh community in Los Angeles reached out to him. He'd also been granted permanent resident status in Canada, on account of his lawyer's suggestion given he was traveling to the country so much to visit his sons.

The field hockey matches were to be held at Weingart Stadium, part of East Los Angeles College in Monterey Park, California. Singh Sr. attended each game, but below the surface nothing was okay. Still reeling from the passing of Sushil, back home Indira Gandhi and her ruling party had given the green light for Operation Blue Star. She'd tired of trying to patch the relationship up with the Sikhs, and brought the heavy hand of rule down on them in one mighty blow.

Los Angeles itself was dealing with its own internal dilemma at the time. Racial tensions within the African-American community were slowly bubbling to the surface. High unemployment and crime, rampant drug use; the city's inner ghettos were slowly inching towards a breaking point. A flood of crack cocaine brought with it a wave of gang violence, and an infamous nickname—The Gang Capital of the Country.[256]

Back home in India, the Khalistan movement had been gaining steam under Indira's rule, and many Sikhs were now pushing for full independence. Outside the stadium, Sikhs who had immigrated to the United States protested during India's games, yelling and screaming obscenities at the players as they entered and left.

They had tried to lobby Singh Sr. to come to one of their rallies to make a statement for the Khalistan movement—part of the reason he'd been invited—but Singh Sr. says he remained true to one cause his whole life.

"I am a nationalist, I played for the country always," he says defiantly. "It was not in my heart to do this."

The American Sikh population in Los Angeles quickly soured towards him. They saw him as a traitor, and regularly waited for him to arrive at the stadium and tossed sour food at him.

"They would yell, 'Balbir go home! Balbir go home!' "

Before one of the matches, as Singh Sr. entered the pitch, he noticed a Sikh man had stolen an Indian flag from a teenager and was ripping it up in a sign of protest. Singh Sr. broke from his entourage and ran over to the burly figure who towered over him, who now had the flag in his mouth as he tore it to pieces.

"I took the flag from him," says Singh Sr. sternly. "I took it from his mouth."

Los Angeles police came and had to break up the whole scene, and now Singh Sr. had been seen publicly defending India in the eyes of the Los Angeles Sikh community.

Singh Sr. was forced to enter the stadium in secret, away from the protest and the chants of "traitor" being thrown at him along with rotting fruit.

"I remembered my father, he sacrificed his young life as a freedom fighter. And at that time I realized the importance of the national flag and what it truly meant to be an Indian."

It was on his way home from Los Angeles that Indira would be assassinated by her Sikh bodyguards and the whole ordeal would come to a frothing head.

After his narrow escape with Gurinderjit from the airport, Singh Sr. holed up in a house in Delhi for about ten days. He could not go outside for fear he would be murdered. Singh Sr. protested every day, wanting to resume his normal life. He felt like a caged animal in his own country, outsiders rattling the bars and poking sticks through at him. His agitation almost got him burned alive.

"I said 'Why can't I go outside? People know me, they know who I am.'" He protested one day, standing at the door as his family tried to hold him back.

The Bhomia family quarantined him for his own safety. Regardless of his gold medals, regardless of everything he had done for his nation, carrying India to the top of the sporting world, if he were to set foot in the streets in Delhi, he would be a target.

The number of deaths incurred in the anti–Sikh riots is still widely contested. Official government reports state somewhere around 2,700, while other reports claim as high as 30,000 were murdered over the span of about four days.[257] In 2015, the California state assembly went as far to pass a resolution which labeled the riots an act of "genocide",[258] however the US government refused an official petition on the same issue.[259]

One of the most harrowing and chilling stories of the riots is outlined in Rahul Bedi's retrospective article for the BBC.[260] During the riots, the journalist was posted in Delhi, and witnessed firsthand some of the atrocities that took place.

"Two inquiry commissions and seven investigative committees into the 1984 Sikh riots later, no one has been held guilty for the Trilokpuri killings," he wrote. "Of the 2,733 officially admitted murders, only nine cases have so far led to the conviction of 20 people in 25 years; a conviction rate of less than 1%."

Holed up in his daughter's house, Singh Sr. had been forced into hiding in the same city where he'd won national field hockey championships and had at one time been carried around on admirers' shoulders like a hero.

Once an Olympian, now a civilian, he was a traitor; an accomplice to murder because of his religion, a scapegoat, a troublemaker. His country had turned its back on him, shoving him around, pushing him down into the muddy dirt with no apology.

★★★

In 1985 the Air India bombings sent concussive shockwaves through the world's media headlines, bringing attention to the Khalistan movement for all the wrong reasons. Only one man—Inderjit Singh Reyat, who lived in British Columbia—has ever been convicted in relation to the mass murder. It is widely believed the terrorist attack that claimed the lives of 329, most of them Canadian citizens of Hindu-Indian descent, was retaliation by Sikh militants for the storming of the Golden Temple in Amritsar, also known as Operation Blue Star.[261,262,263] The plane, which originally took off from Toronto, had a bomb placed in one of its bags due to odd security lapses. While it was flying over the Atlantic, southwest of Ireland, the Boeing 747 exploded mid-air. Many passengers exhibited "flail pattern signs" which means their bodies had been thrown from the plane into a free fall of some 9,400 metres.[264]

To this date, it stands as Canada's largest mass murder—a gruesome, pre-meditated act of violence in revenge for a religious spat between two groups who had been feuding for decades.

The bombing placed an asterisk over the Sikh community in Canada, a horrible event they would be tagged with, in a country known for its political and religious tolerance for all under the stipulation of peaceful living and a law-abiding lifestyle. Ujjal Dosanjh, the 33rd premier of British Columbia who immigrated from Jullundur, first to the UK and then to Canada in his early 20s, was interviewed by CBC for their documentary on the terrorist attack. Dosanjh outlined how the tragic event caught not only Canadian citizens, but Canadian law enforcement agencies too, by complete surprise.[265]

"I felt, and others felt that the government of the day, the political establishment of the day, even the law enforcement establishment, not the people on beat, on the ground, the actual established leadership did not feel that there was a problem. You know there's some brown guys, some with turbans, some without turbans, killing each other or hurting each other, making fiery speeches about something that was 15,000 miles away. It didn't effect anybody else in the society, it doesn't matter."

Luckily Singh Sr. had been granted permanent resident status the year before, and unlike other countries, the political backlash towards Sikhs in Canada was virtually non-existent. Canada was showing its true colours, a nation of tolerance under the banner of multiculturalism. Singh Sr. decided the best thing to do was to stay out of India, so he accepted any offer he could—London for the 1986 Field Hockey World Cup, 1995 to Berlin for the Champions Trophy tournament. In between he visited his family in Vancouver, playing with his grandchildren, avoiding any tension back home by simply inhabiting another country across the Pacific Ocean.

By the time the 90s rolled around, Singh Sr. was spending as much time in Vancouver as he was in India. Back home he'd sold his house in Chandigarh, a reminder of his wife, her energy now gone, leaving a gaping void in the place they resided. However he could not afford to purchase a home of his own anymore, so he was forced to move in with his daughter Sushbir and her husband.

In British Columbia he hooked up with the Vancouver Hawks, a longstanding field hockey club established way back in 1895. The team welcomed him with open arms, asking him to coach and offer advice to their many male and female teams. Singh Sr. relished at the chance to pass some of his knowledge onto the next generation, he was like a kid again. In 1988, Singh

Sr. was made a lifetime honorary member of the club. John McBryde, a longstanding executive member of the Hawks said Singh Sr. became a catalyst for his players to strive towards over the years.

"During the last decade, since construction of the synthetic hockey pitches at Tamanawis in Surrey, Balbir has been invited, as guest of honour, to present gold medals to the winners at the international competitions held annually at that facility," wrote McBryde in an email. "Balbir is an enthusiast who has always been supportive of hockey at every level over many decades, internationally as well as locally. In addition, and equally important, Balbir is universally acknowledged as a true sportsman and perfect gentleman who demonstrates the very highest ideals of the game, and a person whom we would wish all our participant members to emulate."

Hawks players and coaches were constantly asking Singh Sr.'s advice on tactics and plays. He was a special advisor, watching games and taking notes. Although he had long since retired from coaching and managing, being around the game drew a smile across his face again. He signed autographs and sticks, Canadian kids of all descents asking him to take pictures with him. In India, he was a nobody, but here in this community, he was a rightful star.

By 2000, Singh Sr. had spent so much time in Canada his lawyer advised him to apply for citizenship. "He said to me it would be a good idea, given the circumstances. It would make traveling there much easier."

During an official induction ceremony in Vancouver a few months later, he became a Canadian. He looks back on the event with great pride, almost like an award or medal he'd won. While back home it was if they were trying to rip citizenship from his hands, here he was being offered it like a gift.

"Canada has always been such a great country to me. The people here are different, everyone is welcome, everyone is happy. There is no fighting."

★★★

It's the first day of the London 2012 Olympics. Queen Elizabeth II officially opened the games during a colourful, four-hour extravaganza conceived by *Slumdog Millionaire* director Danny Boyle. The mood is electric, there's something in the air, a crackle of energy running through the country's electrified condition. The city had become the first ever to host the event three times, the last being the Austerity Games in 1948. They'd been pining to bring them back, and now the time had come, the waiting was over.

Sitting on a plush red couch in the BBC studios overlooking Olympic Park is Balbir Singh Sr.[266] He's dressed in a navy blue blazer, baby blue shirt, and a red and white striped tie. On his right lapel sits a pin of the Indian flag. Atop his head is a bright red turban, literally the exact colour of the couch he's inhabiting, almost as if selected to fit perfectly together.

To his right is Naga Munchetty, a British journalist. Singh Sr. smiles at the camera, and at his interviewer, endlessly polite, warm and ultimately modest above all else. This is his second interview on the BBC in the past month, having been profiled on *The Hub* before the games started, outlining his iconic career.[267] But now, on opening day, he sits statue still in his seat, but inside an upstart boy from Moga is dancing around his brain, hockey stick in hand.

"Every Olympics brings with it amazing stories of sporting success," says Munchetty. "Now one man who knows all about that is Indian hockey player Balbir Singh. He won gold medals at the 1948 games, the '52 games in Helsinki, the Melbourne games in 1956. Balbir Singh thank you so much for joining me. I hope I don't offend you by saying you're what, 87 years old and still passionate about sport, I'm sure?"

"Well thank you," responds Singh Sr. with an infectious smile. "I am very happy to be here for the second time."

A few months before the games, Singh Sr. was walking in the Fragrance Gardens when his cell phone rang. It was Eilidh Dawson, the head of Marketing for iLUKA Ltd., whose company had been contracted out to handle public relations for the iconic event. She was informing Singh Sr. that he had been chosen for a special exhibit titled *The Olympic Journey: The Story of the Games*.[268,269,270,271,272]

Held at the Royal Opera House, and co-sponsored by BP (then named British Petroleum), the event hand-picked 16 athletes to tell the story of the modern day Olympics. The IOC wanted to capture the spirit of the games, choosing athletes who not only won medals, but invariably made political and social statements in the process.

There's Jesse Owens and his four gold medals at the 1936 Olympics in Berlin under Nazi Germany's rule, sending a defiant message during a time of international strife. There's Australian Aboriginal track and field star Cathy Freeman, whose gold at the 2000 Sydney Olympics was a lightning bolt bulletin for her nation and the world, shining a light on the struggles of Aboriginal people across the planet. There's the "Russian Bear" Aleksandr Karelin, named the greatest Greco-Roman wrestler of all time after amassing countless medals at the world championships, European Championships and Olympics.

Finally, it's Balbir Singh Sr., the only athlete of South Asian descent, and the only field hockey player on the list. The 16 chosen and subsequent exhibition is not simply a list, but a worldly chronology of the games since it began in modern times. From 1896, through two world wars, a Cold War and over a hundred years of tumultuous history, the International Olympic Committee picked just 16 to represent the entire lineage.

As he listened to Dawson on the other end of the line, Singh Sr. had to sit down on a park bench. The emotion too much for his knees, the thoughts became overwhelming. London wanted him to come represent India, the world, and the Olympic Games, the most illustrious sporting event ever produced as a species. While many Olympics of the modern era have held special clout, weight or infamy—1972 in Munich, 2004 in Athens; London in 2012 was a return to the city that saw the games through the Second World War and Hitler's tyrannical grasp at world domination. London, to Indians, is the world's city, the centrifugal centre of cultural, economic and societal life. Indians have become the largest foreign-born group in the city and the country, gravitating to it since the days of Partition.[273]

"Yes, I think I can make it," says Singh Sr., holding his hand on the park bench to sturdy himself.

After his interview with Munchetty on opening day, the whirlwind continued. On August 5th at the Riverbank Arena in London, Singh Sr. was a special guest at the India vs. South Korea game.[274,275] Sadly, India would lose 4-1, however before the match Singh Sr. was brought out onto the pitch for an interview in front of the crowd alongside FIH president Leandro Negre.

"Now you're a bit of a hockey legend aren't you?" asked the announcer. "Three gold medals from three Olympic games, an amazing achievement and something you must be very proud of?"

"Well I share that honour along with my teammates," answered Singh Sr. "Because hockey is a team game and I was one of them, and the entire team did very well and I was part of that team."

He would attend multiple matches throughout the tournament, sitting with a who's who of field hockey dignitaries and administrators.

A few days later, Dil Bahra—who lobbied to get his Guinness World Record—toured Singh Sr. around the city and took the Sikh to meet Brit John Peake at an event hosted by Mike Smith of the National Sports Museum. Singh Sr. and Peake played against each other at the 1948 Olympics, and now, decades later, could shake hands and share some stories of their time during 1948.[276]

Singh Sr. says Peake was a lovable, affable character, and he quite enjoyed sharing a moment or two with the Brit. "We shared a laugh and a chuckle talking about the pitch conditions in London and how terrible they were."

It was one event after another, handshakes, hugs and accolades. Singh Sr. was an international hero, a VIP, atop the sporting world's history books where he belonged. The IOC had put him up in a plush hotel in London along with members of the International Hockey Federation, and he regularly chatted with administrators who were still apologizing for their championship goal count gaffe, proudly corrected by Bahra. While attending the event at the Royal Opera House, Singh Sr. said his hand got tired from signing so many autographs. He posed for hundreds of photos, people asking him questions about what the games were like back in 1948. Asking him what it was like to win three gold medals, back to back to back.

"It was such an honour to go to London, the people there treated me so well, with so much respect."

Singh Sr. also met former Australian team captain Colin Wansbrough, who played against him and India in a practice match before the 1956 Olympics in Melbourne, which Wansbrough outlined in an email.

"I took the day off work, illegally, to play at Elsternwick Park, and they beat us 13-0. I was centre-half, and Balbir was centre-forward and he hit eight goals with the Indian goalie playing for us in the second half. He presented me with his stick after the game—how good was that! That night the team were the guests of the Indian team for dinner at the Olympic Village in Heidelberg—my first very hot curry."

Bahra also informed Singh Sr. that he had found a stamp of him from the Dominica Republic, a 16 cent stamp issued in 1958 that commemorated India's three gold medals and clearly features a picture of the Sikh.[277] It was like Diwali every day, a new event, a new chakra within his energy. He wondered if he'd somehow fallen asleep, drifting off into a dream after so many nightmares back home.

But something was off, something wasn't right. Back in India his appearance was almost non-existent in the newspapers and national media. Here was one of their own, basking in the glow of the most hyped Olympics in decades, and its poster boy was being almost completely ignored.

Singh Sr. says he did no interviews via phone for outlets back home, or even receive any emails asking for quotes. Oddly, it was as if he wasn't even there.

A missed opportunity to promote one of their own, a glaring oversight for India's sporting culture. Alone, surrounded by dignitaries and admirers in London, Singh Sr. was somehow still being forgotten in his homeland. He shrugs when asked why he thinks this happened.

"I do not know, it is a mystery to me," he says, trying to keep his words positive. "I had such a good time over there though, it was so great to visit the city once again during that time. The Olympics were so magical the second time around."

THE GREAT INDIAN CIRCUS

"Tell me, why is the media here so negative? Why are we in India so embarrassed to recognize our own strengths, our achievements? We are such a great nation. We have so many amazing success stories but we refuse to acknowledge them. Why?"

~ P. J. Abdul Kalam,
former Indian President

My final interview before Kabir and I embark on the labourious, vehicular journey south to Delhi—for more interviews—is with Sanjiv Dosanjh, the programme executive for All India Radio based out of Chandigarh. He's also a friend of Singh Sr.'s, and I'm excited to get the chance to speak to a fellow journalist, maybe talk shop or exchange a few war stories. All India Radio is the country's public broadcaster, much like the National Public Radio in the United States or the Canadian Broadcasting Corporation in Canada; both publicly funded organizations which are known to have high journalistic standards.

Dosanjh is rigidly polite, a slender, lanky man with wire-rimmed glasses who has a distinctly radio-friendly voice. He is in interview mode from the moment I sit down, which means having any type of casual chat about the profession is off the table. His silky smooth, nicely primped voice glows in a flowing tone about Singh Sr. throughout our talk. He admits he has not been given ample due when it comes to the pages of the country's history book. When asked if this is because of his religious background—he offers this response.

"India is very proud of being a secular nation. We award our citizens and figures based on merit, and I don't think something like this would come into play at all."

I ask him why he thinks Singh Sr. has not been given his due, and he says India has somehow forgotten its older generation of heroes, which appears to contradict Chand's fame. With Singh Sr. in the room, it becomes clear this is an uncomfortable line of questioning over tea and cookies, so I divert the talk back to how amazing Singh Sr. is, and we roll back into a healthy, radio-friendly back and forth flow.

Kabir has a novel idea. By now we're both utterly sick of the traffic, and getting into Delhi via car during the day is probably one of the worst ideas ever for two sneezing, coughing, ill and tired individuals. It's estimated each year 1,600 people die in Delhi traffic accidents during the rush hours which runs from about 7AM to midnight,[278] so Kabir wants us to leave Chandigarh around 12AM.

First I have to obtain an exit Visa from the Chandigarh Police Station—a tall, dusty building that houses many families of rhesus macaque monkeys in the parking lot trees. I'm oddly excited I may get a chance to view India's notorious corruption up close, and I bring $20 American along with me to the police station, tucking it in my back pocket. Sadly, after about two hours, tons of paperwork, a lot of Punjabi and one pink receipt that cost about $1 US, I get my exit Visa quietly without incident. Kabir says the fact that I'm white and am traveling on a Journalist Visa means government officials are especially careful of my presence.

"They may be corrupt—but they're not stupid."

Before I leave the Bhomia residence, Sushbir hands me a copy of a 2000 thesis titled *Balbir Singh Legendary Hockey Player: A Case Study*. Written by Doctor of Philosophy candidate Maninder Dhillon for the University of Chandigarh, it outlines Singh Sr.'s life in basic form. The thesis does at one point tackle the subject of why Singh is not famous or more celebrated in his homeland, and what he can do to improve his stature. However never once does it mention religion as playing any part in any of this.

As we leave the Bhomia residence at night, I say my good-byes to Sushbir and Singh Sr. He hands me a teal green patterned scarf made by a local vendor, and wishes me a safe journey back to Delhi. He mentions he plans on coming to Vancouver the following fall, and I tell him I'd love to catch a field hockey game with him to chat strategy and maybe share another whisky night. It's a date. When I try to touch his feet, a sign of respect for elders in Indian society, he stops me immediately.

"I will see you again," he says in his warm tone.

Dank smog smears the headlights; street-lamps dim amber yellow as we make our way south. Brightly coloured, rustic trucks with the word 'honk' painted all over them scatter the National Highway 1. We pass dilapidated bus stops by the overpasses, where overflow passengers come dangerously close to us while we hit

speeds of up to 60 kilometres. In the dark, everything is blanket-
ed with a sullen, eerie mist; a showering rainfall of pollution. By
now I'm pretty much able to sleep in any condition, so I doze off
in the passenger seat, jerked awake periodically as Kabir is forced
to dart and dive between meandering buses and trucks like a race
car driver.

We get stuck at one bottleneck behind a massive truck with
a comically oversized bale of hay tied to its flatbed. It showers so
much hay onto the car Kabir is forced to turn on the wiper
blades, and we both reach out the front window to free strands
from the windshield.

The Delhi outskirts appear as a community hastily rebuilt in
the wake of an atomic bomb. Stripped of colour, void of paint as
if a cleansing agent ripped through and hot washed three quarters
of the structures from decoration. Corporate logos are hand-
painted, warped first world symbols now bastardized and flooded
with Hindi slogans. Around 4AM, when India finally sleeps for a
brief, fleeting moment, the Delhi sprawl feels like the zombie
apocalypse. The odd gruff straggler cuts across the highway, wild
dogs run parallel with us in packs, and the lights from the city
slowly burn off in the peripheral, a candlelit brushstroke behind a
wafted, fogged out window.

About 5AM traffic fills out around Noida, a city in which
many are pegging development hopes as call centres and software
technologists have flocked to the area.[279] It's seen as part of *new*
India's "middle class", the spoils of consumerist capitalism trick-
ling down to the peasants. Noida Authority chairman and CEO
Rama Raman recently also declared his home "India's greenest
city",[280] to which Kabir lets an exhausted sigh out of his mouth.
Since Modi took office, he's paved the way for economic growth,
largely at the expense of environmental regulations and sustainable growth.[281] I ask Kabir if there's any community planners in
this country, to which he laughs.

"The developers are the community planners."

The plethora of construction sites and cranes are hard to
ignore, but it's on the roads where you really notice the city's distinct civilians.

White minivans and buses stream by, packed to the brim with sleepy workers on their way to shifts at call centres and technology companies—the zombies of this apocalypse. They lean against the windows, eyes shut, mouths open, catching any form of sleep they can. Kabir says they work long, gruelling, quota filled hours; most of them have three or four jobs. They forgo sleep, vacation and a life outside work for the chance at economic prosperity amidst the new Indian economy, but Kabir says most of them just end up working themselves to death, or burning out of the industry.[282]

The freshest oxygen you will ever breathe anywhere near Delhi is the air-conditioning in your car. Kabir and I wrap ourselves in blankets and crank the A/C so we get something other than the most polluted oxygen on the planet.[283] Kabir takes a small detour so we can drive by Major Dhyan Chand National Stadium;[284] outside is a large, 20 foot iron coloured statue of Chand holding a hockey stick, and in the dark, amplified by ground lighting, he looks God-like and irregularly beige. He towers over the entranceway as an imposing figure of stature, an icon for all to see and worship in a country stuffed full of deities.

We pass the All India Institute of Medical Sciences' hospital, a publicly funded medical college. Outside, laying on the ground are countless sleeping bodies. People enduring months of delays and backlogs for treatment for various illnesses in this makeshift waiting room. Kabir says a security guard regularly makes rounds with a stick, poking bodies and removing the dead who've passed away. While Indians are supposed to have public healthcare, it's no surprise the private sector is the only place you can guarantee treatment, for a price, be it a local or as a medical tourist.[285] The World Health Organization ranked India 112th out of 190 counties, beating China and Brazil but finishing worse than Iraq and Syria.[286]

In *Why Nations Fail: The Origins of Power, Prosperity, and Poverty,* writers Daron Acemoglu and James A. Robinson outline the odd state of the sector's system:

"The story of health care delivery in India is one of deep-rooted inefficiency and failure," they write. "Government-provided health care is, at least in theory, widely available and cheap, and the personnel are generally qualified. But even the poorest Indians do not use government health care facilities, opting instead for the much more expensive, unregulated, and sometimes even deficient private providers. This is not because of some type of irrationality: people are unable to get any care from government facilities, which are plagued by absenteeism. If an Indian visited his government-run facility, not only would there be no nurses there, but he would probably not even be able to get in the building, because health care facilities are closed most of the time."

We arrive at Kabir's apartment in the Shribadrinath complex in a state of functioning delirium, and both immediately pass out. We have to get up early the next day for an interview with Ashwini Kumar on the other side of Delhi in the New Friends Colony. Kabir's been massaging his contacts all week, and I'm excited to talk to someone so close to Singh Sr. through many crucial parts of his life.

When I awake on my makeshift cot, Kabir informs me we have overslept and are already now an hour late for our interview. We run out to the car, only to be met by a vicious foe—Delhi rush hour. With all our previous planning now blowing up in our face like a bad science experiment, Kabir tries to get us across the madness while calling Ashwini's handlers to tell him we're going to be quite tardy.

By the time we reach his house in a gated community and find parking, Ashwini is so upset he doesn't leave his bedroom or agree to an interview, which is understandable. He's well into his 90s and his handlers say he is hard of hearing and tires easily, so the best I get is walking around his living room looking over a few trophies and awards.

I hear Ashwini call from his room at one point, his voice hoarse and tired.

"Where is Balbir? I want to talk to Balbir."

In October of 2015, around a year after I stood in his living room, Ashwini passed away at the age of 94.[287] The following SportsKeeda article outlined his career, however did not pass on the chance to take a shot at one of India's most celebrated field hockey administrators, outlining how tough the country is on its heroes and notable figures even in death.

"A careful perusal of Ashwini Kumar's reign as the helmsman of Indian hockey reveals several contradictions. Undoubtedly India still got medals in international competitions but mainly silver and bronze."

Kabir has another interview scheduled for us, but we are now late for that one, and can't even find a parking in a nearby mall to grab Subway sandwiches to fill our grumbling stomachs. It's at this point Kabir reaches some type of metaphysical wall; the honking, breaking, shifting madness that is Delhi's traffic gridlock chaos has overwhelmed even him. We get stuck at one light in a rather exposed position, almost impeding traffic flow on two sides of the road. But no one will let us right the car, instead they drive up on the curb to get around us, Kabir profusely swearing at them as they pass.

India, it appears, has a chokehold on both of us.

We find another Subway at the Khan market, a western style outdoor mall in central Delhi, and a valet parking attendant plays some kind of hybrid form of Tetris and musical chairs to park our vehicle. I suggest we bypass the clog by getting a hotel room in downtown Delhi, and see if any interviewees will come to us. Criss-crossing this city over and over on four wheels would be asking for a self-induced panic attack.

The Park Hotel on Parliament street in downtown Delhi ends up being our quickest, safest and cheapest bet as Kabir haggles on the phone for a few hours. The city has no distinct downtown core or strip, the area crammed together with large gated buildings, concrete high rises and wide streets flooded with pedestrians. Luckily the Park Hotel is somewhat in the middle of Delhi and close to a highway, meaning we might be able to ask a few people to come to us.

While the outside of the building is bland—faded white blocks of stained concrete and curtained windows which look more like a uniform bureaucratic building—inside, past the security check, the lobby looks like something out of a 70s Hollywood movie: pink circular couches, fuschia carpeting, white opaque beads running down from the ceiling. I've walked from dusty third world metropolis to the set of Match Game in a matter of seconds.

After settling in I make the mistake of gorging on the hotel's buffet, and spend the rest of the evening on the toilet with the infamous Delhi belly while Kabir tries to set up as many interviews as he can in my final two days. I have the longest shower I've ever had, falling asleep in the tub, Kabir knocking on the door, wondering if I'm still breathing.

I lie down on the plush bed after another exhausting day; wiped, cleansed, drained completely of energy. I am a vase of a body, flush from hours on the toilet, pores opened and seeping from a long, hot wash. I pass out again, asking the front desk for a wake-up call as Kabir snores away on the bed beside me, phone in his hand, shoes and glasses still on.

***

It's the morning of Thursday, November 20, 2014. I head to the lobby and grab two newspapers to read with breakfast—*The Times of India* and the *Delhi Times*. The front page of the *Delhi Times* is an advertisement for the opening of two new Khazana jewelry showrooms. I switch to the *The Times of India*, scanning headlines for something to read:

"An attacker opened fire from an AK-47 as he tried to kidnap pharma tycoon K. Nityanada Reddy in Hyderabad's upscale Banjara Hills on Wednesday . . . PM Narendra Modi reached out to Fiji on Wednesday, trying to make up for the three-decade-long indifference towards the South Pacific nation which is home to a big population of ethnic Indians and is of strategic importance to India because of its location . . . Thousands of followers of Rampal were told to attend a 'satsang' at Satlok Ashram, then used as human shields as his 'commandos' fought pitched battles with cops . . . In a horrific case of 'honour killing' in the capital, a 21-year-old final year student of Sri Venkateswara, a leading college in Delhi University's south campus, was allegedly murdered by her family because she had married a boy from another caste and region . . .

The body of the 13-year-old son of an east Delhi jeweller was found near a drain in Geeta Colony Wednesday morning, a day after the boy was abducted while walking home from school and the family received a ransom demand of Rs 1 crore."

Inside *The Times of India* on page two is a full page piece called "The Great Indian Laugh Riot".[288] The article is part of a series in which writers, journalists and comedians delve into "some of the stereotypes that define the nation." Done tongue in cheek, it takes aim at such cultural faux-pas as "traffic Tarzans, with an allergy to helmets" and "The omnipresent lech on the Indian road". Writer Manas Gupta has a column at the bottom of the page, titled "Made in India: Spot your Stereotype".

"It is indisputable. The subtext of the life of a billion Indians is the great circus—colourful, chaotic, cacophonous, and corrupt. We fling muck on the road and blame the government for it. We produce children faster than Japan produces cars. Our railway tracks are the world's largest public toilet. We equate our guests to Narayana, the God. That's our motto. But we specialize in fleecing tourists. The only thing longer than the Indian traffic jam is the classic Indian power-cut. Elsewhere in the world they cast their vote. In our land we vote our caste."

Gupta goes on to secede that Indians are stereotypes at times, much like anywhere in the world—the overtly polite, über boring Canadian, the gun-toting American, the bad Asian driver, the drunk Irishman. Gutpa acknowledges the fact that Indians have a lot of negative qualities that manifest themselves through unhealthy stereotypes, but that this is their country and they should continue to love it regardless—because, well, there really is no other option.

"So yes, aside from our obsession with cricket, Bollywood and politics, the unapologetic Indian caricature is a reality. He lives life on his own terms, however unreasonable. Join us on this walk on the wild side, as we bring you the trapeze artists, jokers and ringmasters of this Great Indian Circus, act by act."

Security at the Park Royal is tight, leftovers from the 2008 Mumbai terrorist attack in which a handful military trained extremists brutally mowed down close to two hundred civilians with high-powered assault rifles. Most recently, Pakistan released the man who allegedly masterminded the plot that killed approximately 166 people, many of them foreigners and tourists.[289] The sight of hotel workers with Uzis and AK-47s is a little bit unnerving, but as I gorge on the buffet breakfast with the other Anglo-Saxon nondescript Westerners, I'll take whatever falsified sense of safety I can scrounge together at this point.

My first interview ends up being one of the most intriguing chats of my trip. Aslam Sher Khan, the enigmatic Muslim defender who became a national hero overnight for his penalty corner goal in the semifinal against Malaysia at the 1975 World Cup. He's dressed in a brown suit, open shirt, and he sits casually against the screaming blue spaceman couches in the lobby. Aslam hands me his business card, he's a former union minister with the government of India.

Aslam parlayed his game-tying goal into a lengthy political career, and he offers a wide variety of candid, unrehearsed opinions, something I'm not used to hearing exit a politician's mouth. I can't help but ask him about his biography, *To Hell With Hockey*, published in 1982. Some of the chapter titles speak volumes about the book's content alone: Old, Dark, Slimy, Balding Homosexual; Politics, Dirty Politics; The Pick-Up Girls; Juvenile Hockey Officials; Crucifixion at Montreal.

"You like the title?" he asks as I chuckle at its abrasiveness.

We talk about the 1975 World Cup, in which he was the only Muslim player on the squad. He no longer agrees with his younger self that Singh Sr. didn't play him because he was of a minority faith, but understands why he thought this during that period of time.

"It becomes so much of what you believe and understand to be true, you assume it to be true."

I ask him about Singh Sr. and his subjugated legacy, and if religion plays a part in Chand's elevation as a Hindu when it comes to field hockey supremacy.

"I could not see why it wouldn't be."

Khan tells me India is so splintered into factions, it's not simply religious divides, but family, social, regional, and political as well. I ask him why Chand has risen above all the rest, unearthed from the mass of infighting. He shrugs, like the answer is blaring out through loud speakers across the streets of the nation and not hidden in nuanced dirt.

"He is of the majority."

We talk about Modi, a subject Aslam approaches much like many Indians do: skepticism. He says politicians in India always promise the world knowing little actually changes, this is the way things have always been. When reality reappears as the norm after the hot-air dust settles, the public gets angry and then unapologetically moves onto the next saviour. He says even if Modi did want to bring about legitimate change, which he doesn't believe is entirely true, there would be no way to do it in India. The country is too disjointed, too bureaucratic, too fragmented, too poor and too illiterate, he says.

"India *is* India."

I ask him whether Modi could actually finally be that lightning bolt of change, to set the nation ablaze on a fresh path towards a new India, righting the course of the nation once and for all.

"I wouldn't hold your breath," he replies with a smirk.

It's nice to have a less veiled conversation with someone. I can prod gently without feeling incredibly socially awkward. Aslam holds no spite or malice, in fact he appears calm and at peace with the way his life played out. Having experienced harsh religious intolerance throughout his existence, all the while fighting for his playing career on the pitch, one might conclude a cushy life as a politician and respected delegate is a welcome consolation prize.

When I get home to Vancouver I read his biography, and it plays out strikingly similar to Singh Sr.'s life. A stern father, buckets of obstacles to overcome like corruption, greed, jealousy, religious bigotry. He even points the finger at Sikhs in a portion of his book titled "End of Punjabi Domination" after Ashwini was outed and replaced by the millionaire Ramaswamy.

Later in the day I speak to K. Arumugam, a slender man with dark, greying hair and glasses who lives in Delhi. He is a field hockey historian and writer, having published a few books on Indian Olympics and India field hockey. In 2008 Arumugam started One Thousand Hockey Legs,[290] a non-governmental organization that helps kids pick up the sport around the country. Arumugam shows me photos of the writers' room where he is working on the biopic of Dhyan Chand, currently still in development but with rumours swirling that Indian mega film star Shah Rukh Khan might play the lead.[291]

Arumugam is most definitely a Chand supporter, saying he is undeniably the greatest player of all time, and that his achievement in Berlin was greater than Singh Sr.'s in London.

"It was such an accomplishment for South Asia, to beat Germany at that time, there is no greater conquest for this nation."

I ask him why Chand was left off the IOC's list of 16 iconic Olympians, and why Singh Sr. was included.

"This is a bias list, they did not choose it based upon merit."

I ask him then if there is any religious favouritism in play when it comes to Chand's elevated stature and Singh Sr.'s anonymity on a national scale.

"No this is not the case, not at all. Chand was a better hockey player, he was more skilled and his ball-handling abilities were far superb. And his achievements were of much greater benefit to India."

After I return home, he reiterates his position to me via email.

"I wish to share one thing with you. If a player is not popular in India it is certainly NOT because of once [sic] class, caste, region or religion. I heard it so first time in my long association with hockey as journalist, author, researcher and promoter through NGO. Indian public is above all such petty things."

★★★

My final day in Delhi will include a trip to the Press Trust of India's offices. It's a short walk from our hotel through the crowded streets, and once again I'm excited to chat with some of my counterparts on the other side of the planet.

My first interview is with M.K. Razdan, the editor in chief and chief executive officer of the news agency, which employs more than 400 journalists and some 500 stringers (correspondents) across the world. Razdan's office is plush with stained wooden blinds, a small palm tree in the corner and a big screen television playing the news channel on mute.

Razdan talks of the rise and ascent to power of Modi, and the Prime Minister's lofty expectations. Like any executive, his answers are well-crafted, conservative and always on point.

"The people have great hope for him. What remains to be seen is whether or not he can deliver or follow through on what he has promised the people."

Razdan denies that Singh Sr. has been subjugated due to his Sikh roots, offering a typical response around the idea of "merit" and "secularism".

"In India's founding documents it outlines we are governed as a secular nation, and we take great pride in upholding this in every regard."

As a journalist back home, I can't help but want to poke around the beehive-like newsroom. The clatter of keyboards, the heated phone interviews, the daily deadlines, the hustle and the bustle are intoxicating anywhere on the globe. With Razdan's blessing, I speak to G. Sudhakar Nair, a longstanding editor with The Press Trust of India who just got back from a trip with Modi to Australia as part of the PM's press convoy. His answers about the populous Prime Minister are similar, one of guarded optimism and a journalist's skepticism of fiery election campaign promises amounting to nothing more than smoke drifting into the atmosphere. I ask him about Singh Sr., the one question that has now defined my trip. Is he not famous because he is Sikh and Chand is of Hindu majority?

"It could be, I am not sure."

My final chat is with a young journalist, Mona Parthasarathi, a senior correspondent. When I ask her about India's global identity, and the increased spotlight that's come along as a carriage to Modi's horse given his much publicized speeches in New York and Australia, she says one thing irks many Indians.

"I think it is important people realize we are not a nation of snake-charmers," she says. "We are very spiritual, but not to this level. We are grounded, rooted in science and fact."

The "snake-charmers" stereotype is one I've heard more than half a dozen times in interviews, giving a candid glimpse into the Indian psyche and how its people view itself through the outside world's eyes.

Parthasarathi has covered field hockey extensively, however she does not agree that Chand is more famous than Singh Sr. because of faith-based reasons, brushing aside the question.

When we return to the hotel that evening, Kabir coaxes me out for a dinner to celebrate my last night in India. We head to the Laughing Monkey, a trendy restaurant in a funky enclave of the city. The patrons are equal parts middle class locals who dress like Westerners and young Western travellers trying to dress like locals. We share a few imported beers and a shot or two over American styled burgers and fries.

When we get back to the hotel, I'm coaxed again to the lounge area where they're playing pulse-pounding club music, but it's barren and sparsely inhabited. Kabir says he wants to take me to a real nightclub, so we set out back in his car looking for a place to indulge in the city's after hours curriculum. Sadly we fall victim to Delhi's vehicular madness, getting cut off by various concrete dividers and maze-like roundabouts. Part of me is secretly relieved, I'm not sure I'm in the best physical and mental state to walk around drunk and medicated with pulsing house music as my personal soundtrack.

On our way home we pass a police roadblock which features army-like fencing. Two officers are stopping cars periodically; and we're pulled over and Kabir is told to get out of the car as he smells like alcohol, and I'm told to stay in the vehicle. I look back as he talks, then argues, then starts yelling at the officer. The two are having a heated discussion in Hindi, as I look around to see if anyone is watching. After about 15 minutes Kabir comes back to the car, looking rather relaxed considering what just transpired, while I'm sweating bullets.

"What happened?!" I ask immediately as we zoom back to the hotel.

"He was trying to get a bribe from me for drinking and driving, but he didn't have a breathalyzer."

I'm a bit stunned. The officers so poorly equipped and funded, they try to extract bribes without adequate bribery tools. Kabir says this is common, and that if you just argue with them for a bit, they give up and let you go.

I fly out on a red-eye from the Indira Gandhi Airport, Kabir and I exchanging sleepy goodbyes in the parking lot. He said he hopes to come to Canada one day, however the Visa process can be quite difficult and cumbersome these days if you don't have an immigration lawyer on payroll.

On the flight home the movies are piercingly ironic—*The Darjeeling Limited* in which three white brothers bond on a train traveling across India while going to see their mother for the first time after their father's funeral. The streets are void of traffic jams, the trains nominally populated, and little is said about the country's culture other than its unabashed spiritualism. Then its *Life of Pi*, the movie Jyoti Singh Pandey watched before she was gang-raped on a Delhi bus and left for dead. I turn it off, sprawl out across some empty seats. I've had enough editorializing about the rooster coop and just want to sleep.

The cough and cold I picked up travelling to India has followed me home like an unwanted pet, and I have to get a series of x-rays on my chest and lungs to check for infections. I'm cleared of tuberculosis by a doctor, the disease that has reached epidemic levels in India according to the World Health Organization.[292] But it will be six months before my cough finally subsides, India's smog and pollution hanging onto my lungs for dear life.

I chat with Wendy Doniger via email, a University of Chicago professor who also wrote the book *The Hindus: An Alternative History* which came out in 2009 and was later pulled by Penguin Press in 2014 due to controversy in India.[293] Doniger is an internationally renowned and respected Indologist, and I ask her if Indians in general tend to mythologize their figures more so than any other modern culture.

"No more than anyone else. Everyone does that."

I ask her if I can chat to her about the controversy around *The Hindus*, in which Hindi-hardliner group Shiksha Bachao Andolan Samiti filed civil and criminal cases over her work in India.

"I've said all I want to say about that right now."

Doniger is, however, willing to put me in touch with Nikky-Guninder Kaur Singh, a Crawford Family professor in the Department of Religious Studies at Colby College in Maine. She teaches a Global Sikhism class and puts me in touch with her brother Nripinder "Mika" Singh, a retired Sikh living in Palm Springs, California. Mika was born in India in 1945, and his father and Harbail were colleagues at Khalsa College growing up, plus he loves field hockey.

Mika moved to the United States in 1968 to purse his education, obtaining a Master's Degree and a PhD from Harvard University in the fields of religion, society and ethics. Mika and I have a lengthy discussion about the Sikhs' long history within India, and the diaspora movement throughout the years. I ask Mika if the reason Singh Sr. is not famous is because he is Sikh, and that Chand is famous because he is Hindu. His tone is relaxed, but the point comes across with a crystal clarity.

"It is not one of the reasons, it *is* the reason."

★★★

On May 15, 2003 *The Washington Post* ran an article titled "A Fascinating Map of the World's Most and Least Racially Tolerant Countries".[294] The piece, by writer Max Fisher, delves deep into data collected from the World Values Survey[295] which examines cultural beliefs across the planet. Fisher outlines what he did with the source material, creating a infographic map of the results and digging up some compelling evidence in the process:

"When two Swedish economists set out to examine whether economic freedom made people any more or less racist, they knew how they would gauge economic freedom, but they needed to find a way to measure a country's level of racial tolerance. So they turned to something called the World Values Survey, which has been measuring global attitudes and opinions for decades.

"Among the dozens of questions that World Values asks, the Swedish economists found one that, they believe, could be a pretty good indicator of tolerance for other races. The survey asked respondents in more than 80 different countries to identify kinds of people they would not want as neighbors. Some respondents, picking from a list, chose "people of a different race." The more frequently that people in a given country say they don't want neighbors from other races, the economists reasoned, the less racially tolerant you could call that society."

Two countries stick out like sore thumbs on the map:

"In only two of 81 surveyed countries, more than 40 percent of respondents said they would not want a neighbor of a different race. This included 43.5 percent of Indians and 51.4 percent of Jordanians (Jordan is 98% Arabic, and 97% Sunni Muslim)."[296]

While Jordan is a relatively small country with a population of under seven million people, India is not. India makes up more than a sixth of the world's population, so the scalability of the World Values Survey's results should hold serious gravitational force in its findings. To put in laymen's terms, 43.5 percent of 1.25 billion is a lot of people that don't want ethnically diverse neighbours.

Whether we choose to divide racism and religious intolerance is irrelevant. Discrimination is discrimination, be it skin colour, creed or ethnicity. One could never fathom a racist somehow tolerating other religions as neighbours, but not a different shade of skin colour. Ignorance goes hand in hand across the spectrum of divineness, running rampant through various aspects of a person's derogatory mindset. The whole experience of my trip starts to descend upon me like an emptying sea, revealing the bedrock for what it actually is.

If an Arab is Muslim, or an Indian is Hindu or Christian, the segregating nature of labels brought forth by the ignorant mind remain unabashedly wrong and detrimental to society's growth. Persecuting or subjugating someone because they are black and you are white, regardless of a shared Christian faith, does not excuse or downplay how horrible it is; for a Hindu Indian to demean a Sikh Indian, or a Muslim Indian to demean a Buddhist Indian, it remains a deep form of oppression. Call it what you want: racism, intolerance, ignorance; the work of separatism, of groupism based on anything as nominal as geography is the virus that infects and inflicts irreparable damage on mankind's prosperity. We thus remain an anaemic sloth as we lurch forward into a new world, one where fast-paced modernity and 21st century globalization has the potential to bring us together like no other time in recorded history.

Intolerance, be it of race or faith, is the disease for which we have yet to discover a vaccine. Until then, truths, however ugly, callous or personally embarrassing they may be, should always be sought out and uncovered. The World Values Survey, and countless other articles and studies, points out a rampant intolerance of one's fellow citizens that runs through India's psychological core. How it got there remains debatable, the fact that it is there is unquestionable. The Indian complex is a nation that sees itself as secular; however, it is deeply, cavernously divided and ruled by religious dogmatism.

In December of 2014, militant Hindu-nationalist supporters of Narendra Modi allegedly underwent a campaign of mass conversion meetings through intimidation and bribery in the states of Kerala and Gujarat where Modi hails from.[297] In August of 2015, an Indian rationalist scholar was shot dead inside his house in Delhi for speaking out against "idol worship."[298] On October 12 of 2015, Hindu hardliners in Mumbai poured ink over Indian activist and former BJP politician Sudheendra Kulkarni during a meeting of an Indian think tank.[299] The United States Commission on International Religious Freedom Annual Report for 2015 outlined a clear link between the rise of incidents of racial intolerance and the election of Modi in 2014:[300]

"Despite the country's status as a pluralistic, secular democracy, India has long struggled to protect minority religious communities or provide justice when crimes occur, which perpetuates a climate of impunity. Incidents of religiously-motivated and

communal violence have reportedly increased for three consecutive years. The states of Andhra Pradesh, Uttar Pradesh, Bihar,
Chattisgarhi, Gujarat, Odisha, Karnataka, Madhya Pradesh,
Maharashtra, and Rajasthan tend to have the greatest number of
religiously-motivated attacks and communal violence incidents.
Non-governmental organizations (NGOs) and religious leaders,
including from the Muslim, Christian, and Sikh communities,
attributed the initial increase to religiously-divisive campaigning
in advance of the country's 2014 general election. Since the election, religious minority communities have been subject to
derogatory comments by politicians linked to the ruling Bharatiya
Janata Party (BJP) and numerous violent attacks and forced con-
versions by Hindu nationalist groups, such as Rashtriya
Swayamsevak Sangh (RSS) and Vishva Hindu Parishad (VHP)."

The report further outlines specific issues concerning religious intolerance towards Sikhs:

"India's Sikh community has long pursued a change to
Article 25 of India's constitution which states, "Hindus shall be
construed as including a reference to persons professing the Sikh,
Jain or Buddhist religion, and the reference to Hindu religious
institutions shall be construed accordingly. The lack of recognition of Sikhism as a distinct religion denies Sikhs access to social
services or employment and educational preferences that are
available to other religious minority communities and to scheduled caste Hindus. (This is also true for the other faiths listed in
Article 25.) Sikhs are often harassed and pressured to reject religious practices and beliefs that are distinct to Sikhism, such as
dress, unshorn hair, and the carrying of religious items, including
the kirpan."

In February of 2015, Modi spoke at an event honouring
Indian Catholic saints, acknowledging religious intolerance in
India by pledging to defeat it much like many of his lofty elec-
tion campaign promises:[301]

"My government will ensure that there is complete freedom
of faith and that everyone has the undeniable right to retain or
adopt the religion of his or her choice without coercion or undue
influence. My government will not allow any religious group,

belonging to the majority or the minority, to incite hatred against others, overtly or covertly."

They say acceptance or admittance is the first step toward recovery, that acknowledging you have a problem can lead down a road to enlightenment. Denial, some say, is in its own way, a form of cowardice. Tolerating intolerance is its own form of societal sin. If we are to ever reach a globalized, all-encompassing nature as a species, religion may very well cease to occupy a place in our collective mindset for the very reason that it is the ultimate divider.

Spirituality is a necessity amidst today's hyper-modern agnostic societal machine, but at what cost are we willing to achieve global enlightenment? If it means burning someone to death in the streets of Delhi, or putting a bomb on a plane to kill innocent civilians, we are poor habitants of this gift we call earth. If we choose to divide, our cells remain indifferent to the biology of change. The notion of 'I am' therefore 'you are not' is the tether that ties us to the mud like wild dogs. If one man can achieve greatness despite extreme adversity—some of the greatest a nation has, and will ever see—but then becomes forgotten because he wears a turban atop his head, we do not deserve to evolve into something greater as a species. The weight of this problem cannot be understated, the gravity of this error we continuously commit cannot be brushed aside or downplayed. It is woven into the fabric of who we are as people, it infects every aspect of life; its detriment, however casually passed around, speaks volumes against progress as a community, nation and planet.

In May of 2009, Rahila Gupta penned a column for *The Guardian* is response to Hinduism's apparent all-encompassing mandate titled "The myth of Hindu Tolerance".[302]

"There is a profoundly disquieting myth about Hinduism which has been put about by its adherents so often and so successfully that it is in danger of crystalizing into a truth—that of its essentially pluralistic and tolerant traditions."

Gupta goes on to explain this is not just a Hindu problem, or Islam problem, it is a problem with religion as a whole that Sikhs are just as guilty of:

"Sikhism, when it was founded by Guru Nanak, was an explicit rejection of both Hinduism and Islam, especially the caste system. Yet Sikhism is also polluted by the strictures of caste, not just in India but the world over. Gurdwaras or Sikh temples serving various Sikh castes have been flourishing in the UK from the time that Sikhs began settling here."

I'm reminded of a quote by internationally renowned author—Hindi-Indian and noted atheist Salman Rushdie—in a 2002 column he wrote for *The Guardian*. Rushdie had previously received a fatwa from Ayatollah Khomeini, the Supreme Leader of Iran, who ordered Muslims to kill him due the "blasphemy" of his 1988 book *The Satanic Verses*. In his piece, which is titled "Religion, as ever, is the poison in India's blood",[303] the Booker Prize winning writer is lucently clear concerning India's plague-like virus in his closing paragraph:

"So India's problem turns out to be the world's problem. What happened in India has happened in God's name. The problem's name is God."

★★★

Sharp, crisp air on this autumn Saturday afternoon. West out of downtown Vancouver sits the idyllic campus of the University of British Columbia, full of drifting fall leaves that crunch under the student bodies' shoes as they make their way to class. The peninsula lined by the lush, dew-dripping evergreens of the Pacific Spirit Regional Park, it is a bastion of educational structures buried in the forests of some heavenly enclave. It's late October, 2015, and the Vancouver Hawks are about to take on the UBC Thunderbirds in the Vancouver Men's Premier Field Hockey League. The artificial turf of Wright Field lined with a thin layer of water which gives the ball a zip and a tail as it skims across the surface. The crackle of sticks like kindling on a burning fire, calling out the play, teammates shouting directions to each other as the game traverses back and forth.

Singh Sr., myself and Ringo sit in the stands on cold metal benches, wrapped in jackets and winter wear as the icy oxygen catches our breath. From the outset of the game, it's clear the Hawks, Vancouver's longest running club team, are a better squad than the youthful exuberance exhibited by the Thunderbirds. Experience winning over speed, passing over running, the elder statesmen of the game are showing the kids up.

The three of us sit watching, talking strategy. Singh Sr. goes over many different styles of play and formations. His hand draws a line back and forth across the pitch as he rolls out different strategies.

"Such a different game now," he admits, noting the turf has made long passes much more accessible. "When we played, you could not make a pass like that at all," he says with a chuckle.

By halftime it's already 3-0 for the Hawks, a few nifty goals from some gloriously perfect shots and well-timed runs. Singh Sr. commends each tally with a simple statement: "good goal."

We chat about opponents, coaches and teammates: Singh Sr. used to love playing with Udham Singh, one of his fellow Sikh players who won gold with him at Helsinki and Melbourne.

"His passes were always perfect, he always knew where I wanted to go."

He still loves to talk about the good ol' days on the pitch. The week before, after he'd arrived in Vancouver to spend a month with Ringo at his Burnaby home, getting some much needed medical tests in the process, we sat down for one final talk. Whisky was replaced with craft beer and Panago pizza this time, and we filled in some blanks I'd missed while interviewing him in Chandigarh.

It's odd to see this man outside of the rooster coop, walking slowly in the brisk, ocean air of the Canadian hinterlands. He still smiles every time I see him; happy to chat, always eager to accommodate, endlessly modest, to a fault.

As the game winds down, the Hawks pot a few more goals for good measure, and we continue to talk about the nuances of the sport—the weight of sticks, pushing a bully-off through the legs (one of Singh Sr.'s favourite moves), and what the best type of footwear to wear is, if any at all. Love still overflows this man's heart, despite everything he has endured on and off the pitch. But part of me can't help but want to criminalize this scene. Here is one of the sport's greatest players of all time, and after we leave the stands and walk back to Ringo's car, not a single person notices, or even knows, who he is.

I imagine if Wayne Gretzky or Gordie Howe happened to pop in to one of my rec' ice hockey games. I wonder if Steffi Graf ever snuck in to watch some girls practice their tennis swings. I wonder if any of the players on the pitch, be it a Hawk or Thunderbird, even knew they were in the presence of unprecedented greatness. Most of these players only dream about playing for their country, let alone leading their squad to three gold medals for it.

As we stroll back to the car through the university grounds, I'm left with little to go on when it comes to encapsulating this man's extraordinary life. Words do create justice, but do little here in this exact moment of space and time. In my presence, a pure champion, anonymous to his peers, who if they truly knew what he'd accomplished playing the game they love, would be clamouring around him; a giddy mob of adoration and affection. But today, this man in a turban walks unidentified, unavowed once again.

In a world of idyllic perfection, no legend would remain forgotten. But in our stark reality, inside the bustling coops we inhabit and continue to call home—here, in this air, this man remains a ghost of days gone past.

NOTES

[1] http://www.nytimes.com/2015/10/02/world/asia/india-announces-plan-to-lower-rate-of-greenhouse-gas-emissions.html

[2] http://data.worldbank.org/country/india

[3] http://www.nytimes.com/2014/11/17/opinion/in-india-growth-breeds-waste.html?_r=0

[4] http://www.apsmfc.com/ministry-population-cenus.html

[5] https://www.biv.com/article/2014/7/doctor-has-prescription-for-surrey-health-care/

[6] https://www.biv.com/article/2014/9/lumber-companies-surrey-and-white-rock-struggle-ma/

[7] https://www.biv.com/article/2014/9/surrey-could-be-key-unlocking-trade-india/

[8] https://www.biv.com/article/2014/10/got-milk-indias-dairy-market-largely-limits/

[9] http://www.telegraph.co.uk/news/worldnews/al-qaeda/11213127/Al-Qaeda-preparing-for-major-attack-in-India.html

[10] http://www.washingtonpost.com/world/india-pakistan-trade-blame-over-border-clashes/2014/10/09/9f382cc1-8af0-472c-9b1d-9e35be577704_story.html

[11] http://www.cbc.ca/news2/interactives/travel-warnings/

[12] http://fr.rsf.org/IMG/pdf/classement_2013_gb-bd.pdf

[13] http://www.worldatlas.com/citypops.htm

[14] http://timesofindia.indiatimes.com/sports/hockey/hockey-india-league/venues/Major-Dhyan-Chand-National-Stadium-Delhi/articleshow/18009072.cms

[15] http://timesofindia.indiatimes.com/sports/hockey/hockey-india-league/venues/Dhyan-Chand-Sports-College-Lucknow/articleshow/18009841.cms

[16] http://timesofindia.indiatimes.com/sports/more-sports/others/Bharat-Ratna-finally-for-Dhyan-Chand/articleshow/40160849.cms

[17] http://timesofindia.indiatimes.com/entertainment/hindi/bollywood/news/Karan-Johar-to-co-produce-Dhyan-Chand-biopic/articleshow/44604083.cms

[18] http://www.thehindu.com/sport/other-sports/sp-misra-among-three-recommended-for-dhyan-chand-award/article7550997.ece

[19] http://hockeyindia.org/hall-of-fame-dhyan-chand-award-2

[20] http://timesofindia.indiatimes.com/home/infographics/Infographic-Remembering-Dhyan-Chand-on-National-Sports-Day/articleshow/48718785.cms

[21] http://www.bbc.co.uk/programmes/b01jcdg1

[22] http://www.dnaindia.com/india/report-prime-minister-narendra-modi-pays-tribute-to-hockey-wizard-dhyan-chand-2014650

[23] http://www.wsj.com/articles/SB10001424052748703735804575536213214113710

[24] http://www.indiastat.com/demographics/7/population/217/populationasper2011census/527359/stats.aspx

[25] https://stats.oecd.org/Index.aspx?DataSetCode=AV_AN_WAGE

[26] https://www.cia.gov/library/publications/the-world-factbook/rankorder/2102rank.html

[27] http://data.worldbank.org/indicator/VC.IHR.PSRC.P5

[28] http://www.who.int/violence_injury_prevention/road_safety_status/country_profiles/india.pdf

[29] http://file.scirp.org/Html/12-9401064_1806.htm

[30] http://blogs.wsj.com/indiarealtime/2014/10/29/pollution-levels-prompt-u-s-embassy-in-delhi-to-tell-children-not-to-play-outdoors/

[31] http://www.delhi.gov.in/DoIT/DoIT_Transport/trrs29.pdf

[32] http://www.theguardian.com/commentisfree/2011/oct/11/delhi-traffic-chaos-jason-burke

[33] http://www.npr.org/2010/05/19/126395475/along-the-grand-trunk-road-coming-of-age-in-india-and-pakistan

[34] http://archive.indianexpress.com/news/govt-to-hand-ownership-rights-in-resettlement-colonies/1164870/

[35] http://www.vanityfair.com/society/2012/06/ambani-residence-photos-inside-architecture

[36] http://www.dnaindia.com/money/money-mukesh-ambani-is-india-s-richest-man-world-s-richest-billionaires-list-1966260

[37] http://www.telegraph.co.uk/news/worldnews/asia/india/10003228/India-has-one-third-of-worlds-poorest-says-World-Bank.html

[38] http://www.nbr.org/research/activity.aspx?id=356

[39] https://www.washingtonpost.com/world/asia_pacific/indias-huge-need-for-electricity-is-a-problem-for-the-planet/2015/11/06/a9e004e6-622d-11e5-8475-781cc9851652_story.html

[40] http://www.technologyreview.com/featuredstory/542091/indias-energy-crisis/

[41] http://www.thehindu.com/news/national/modi-launches-my-clean-india-campaign/article6468047.ece

[42] http://www.nytimes.com/2014/11/17/opinion/in-india-growth-breeds-waste.html?_r=0

43 http://www.economist.com/news/asia/21607837-fixing-dreadful-sanitation-india-requires-not-just-building-lavatories-also-changing

44 http://chandigarh.gov.in/knowchd_gen_plan.htm

45 http://www.theglobeandmail.com/news/world/dozens-killed-in-suicide-bombing-near-eastern-pakistani-border-with-india/article21419344/

46 http://www.business-standard.com/article/management/building-a-sports-culture-in-india-114042700608_1.html

47 http://www.businessinsider.com/commonwealth-games-bridge-disaster-2010-9?op=1

48 http://www.bbc.com/news/world-south-asia-11101288

49 http://www.biography.com/people/bhagat-singh

50 http://www.culturalindia.net/leaders/bhagat-singh.html

51 http://www.gatewayforindia.com/history/british_history2.htm

52 http://www.theglobeandmail.com/globe-debate/columnists/sikhs-have-been-living-in-fear-of-hate-crimes-since-911/article4468643/

53 http://www.cnn.com/2012/08/06/us/wisconsin-temple-shooting/index.html?hpt=hp_t1

54 http://www.cbc.ca/news/trending/paris-attacks-canadian-sikh-selfie-photoshop-1.3320327

55 https://www.cia.gov/library/publications/the-world-factbook/geos/in.html

56 http://books.google.ca/books?id=3mE04D9PMpAC&pg=PA361&dq=india+world+war+2+million&client=firefox-a&redir_esc=y#v=onepage&q=india%20world%20war%202%20million&f=false

57 http://books.google.ca/books?id=Po-8Pxqvy_cC&pg=PA33&dq=india+world+war+2&lr=&as_brr=3&client=firefox-a&redir_esc=y#v=onepage&q=india%20world%20war%202&f=false

58 http://www.open.ac.uk/researchprojects/makingbritain/content/1942-quit-india-movement

59 http://www.khalsacollegeamritsar.org

60 http://www.thefreedictionary.com/Pakistan

61 http://www.britannica.com/EBchecked/topic/285841/Indian-National-Congress

62 http://storyofpakistan.com/lahore-resolution/

63 https://index.rsf.org/#!/

64 http://indianexpress.com/article/explained/explained-its-a-secret/

65 http://faculty.washington.edu/brass/Partition.pdf

66 http://www.theatlantic.com/international/archive/2014/08/the-fading-memory-of-partition-india-pakistan-bangladesh/376120/

67 http://www.cancerresearchuk.org/about-cancer/type/liver-cancer/about/risks-and-causes-of-liver-cancer

68 http://www.ndtv.com

69 http://www.cnn.com/2014/11/13/world/asia/india-sterilization-deaths-arrest/

70 http://www.worldometers.info/world-population/india-population/

71 http://www.thehindu.com/opinion/lead/indias-godman-syndrome/article6633497.ece

72 http://www.indiatimes.com/news/india/7-indian-godmen-with-super-powers-who-god-couldnt-save-from-prison-228504.html

73 http://www.punjabiinholland.com/news/10342-chandigarh-politicians-hijack-event-to-honour-sports-medallists-.aspx

74 http://www.sukhbirbadal.com

75 http://punjabgovt.nic.in/governor.html

76 http://www.business-standard.com/article/pti-stories/badal-recommends-balbir-singh-s-sr-name-for-bharat-ratna-114091901024_1.html

77 http://www.huffingtonpost.in/2015/07/23/dhyan-chand-british-parli_n_7854178.html

78 http://www.biography.com/people/jawaharlal-nehru-9421253

79 http://www.economist.com/blogs/economist-explains/2014/05/economist-explains-8

80 http://www.aljazeera.com/indepth/opinion/2015/09/modi-india-emerges-150922085537654.html

81 http://www.economist.com/specialreport/india2015

82 http://www.hindustantimes.com/india/rss-s-strategy-to-spread-hindu-first-ideology-to-all-corners-of-india/story-bVZIYrp9gPWbT62hRbIp4K.html

83 http://www.theglobeandmail.com/globe-debate/dont-let-hindu-fanatics-dictate-indias-future/article26709705/

84 http://timesofindia.indiatimes.com/india/RSS-Indias-number-1-terror-group-Former-Mumbai-police-officer/articleshow/49943534.cms

85 http://www.nytimes.com/2014/05/11/world/asia/in-indian-candidate-hindu-right-sees-a-reawakening.html?_r=0

86 http://www.nytimes.com/2015/11/05/world/asia/hindu-mob-kills-another-indian-muslim-accused-of-harming-cows.html

87 http://www.theguardian.com/world/2015/oct/16/indian-muslim-accused-beef-smuggling-beaten-to-death

88 http://www.theguardian.com/commentisfree/2014/apr/14/narendra-modi-extremism-india

89 http://articles.economictimes.indiatimes.com/2015-03-08/news/59894217_1_jawaharlal-nehru-jairam-ramesh-narendra-modi

90 http://www.thefreedictionary.com/Hindustan

91 http://www.theguardian.com/world/2015/nov/09/narendra-modi-the-divisive-manipulator-who-charmed-the-world

92 http://indiafacts.co.in/the-story-behind-nehru-indira-gandhis-bharat-ratna/

93 http://www.espncricinfo.com/canada/content/player/35320.html

94 http://www.espncricinfo.com/canada/content/player/35320.html

95 http://www.espncricinfo.com/sachinfarewell/content/story/689963.html

96 http://www.newindianexpress.com/states/karnataka/article371972.ece

97 http://www.dnaindia.com/india/report-prime-minister-narendra-modi-pays-tribute-to-hockey-wizard-dhyan-chand-2014650

98 https://twitter.com/narendramodi/status/505236135035944961

99 http://indiatoday.intoday.in/story/dhyan-chand-vs-sachin-tendulkar-who-is-the-greatest/1/325341.html

100 http://www.sportskeeda.com/archery/new-born-faces-of-india-archery-trisha-deb-and-abhishek-verma

101 http://www.economist.com/news/briefing/21598967-graft-india-damaging-economy-country-needs-get-serious-about-dealing-it

102 http://www.shiromaniakalidal.net

103 http://indianexpress.com/article/india/india-news-india/sukhbir-singh-badal-punjab-bjp-chief-condemn-desecrations/

104 http://www.telegraph.co.uk/sport/olympics/hockey/10858313/Top-10-greatest-field-hockey-players.html

105 http://www.sportskeeda.com/hockey/myth-major-dhyanchands-statue-vienna-real-story

106 http://pib.nic.in/newsite/erelease.aspx?relid=55452

107 http://news.bbc.co.uk/sportacademy/hi/sa/hockey/features/newsid_3490000/3490504.stm

108 http://www.sports-reference.com/olympics/athletes/si/balbir-singh-sr-1.html

109 http://www.guinnessworldrecords.com/world-records/most-goals-scored-by-an-individual-in-an-olympic-hockey-final-(male)

110 http://www.wsj.com/articles/SB10001424052748703735804575536213214113710

111 http://www.britannica.com/biography/Dhyan-Chand

112 https://en.wikipedia.org/wiki/Dhyan_Chand#cite_note-Brittanica-1

113 http://www.sports-reference.com/olympics/athletes/ch/dhyan-chand-1.html

114 http://indiatoday.intoday.in/story/dhyan-chand-vs-sachin-tendulkar-who-is-the-greatest/1/325341.html

115 http://timesofindia.indiatimes.com/sports/hockey/top-stories/HI-wishes-Dhyan-Chand-on-his-109th-birth-anniversary/articleshow/41094690.cms

116 http://www.ndtv.com/topic/dhyan-chand

[117] http://timesofindia.indiatimes.com/sports/hockey/top-stories/Hockey-is-a-poor-mans-game-says-Balbir-Singh-Sr/articleshow/35120661.cms

[118] http://www.thehindu.com/sport/hockey/balbir-sr-a-class-act/article3635470.ece

[119] http://timesofindia.indiatimes.com/sports/hockey/top-stories/Of-Dhyan-Chands-wizardry-and-Hitler/articleshow/18289193.cms

[120] http://www.sportskeeda.com/hockey/major-dhyan-chand-singh-the-story-of-a-legend

[121] http://timesofindia.indiatimes.com/sports/hockey/top-stories/Of-Dhyan-Chands-wizardry-and-Hitler/articleshow/18289193.cms

[122] http://majordhyanchand.blogspot.in/2013/05/hitler-and-major-dhyan-chand-ancounter.html

[123] http://www.history.com/this-day-in-history/indian-field-hockey-gold-medalist-dhyan-chand-dies/print

[124] http://www.rediff.com/sports/2003/aug/29dhyan1.htm

[125] http://www.huffingtonpost.in/2015/07/23/dhyan-chand-british-parli_n_7854178.html

[126] http://timesofindia.indiatimes.com/sports/hockey/top-stories/Of-Dhyan-Chands-wizardry-and-Hitler/articleshow/18289193.cms

[127] https://books.google.ca/books?id=L-S5lduNeJcC&pg=PP59&lpg=PP59&dq=the+olympics:+the+india+story+chand+hitler&source=bl&ots=G_-3rZg6VB&sig=WwPzcnQZ_CKGQiG7BfunBlRPm6k&hl=en&sa=X&ved=0CB4Q6AEwAGoVChMIxrqe_JvyxgIVA1c-Ch3r0AP4#v=onepage&q=the%20olympics%3A%20the%20india%20story%20chand%20hitler&f=false

[128] https://www.youtube.com/watch?v=Kp5BIHbZJwU

[129] https://www.youtube.com/watch?v=IO3f0NDlnYI

[130] http://www.bharatiyahockey.org/granthalaya/legend/encounters/page1.htm

[131] http://www.hindustantimes.com/brunch-stories/dhyan-chand-hockey-s-original-he-man/article1-1212474.aspx

[132] http://www.rediff.com/sports/2001/aug/28dyan.htm

[133] http://www.bharatiyahockey.org/granthalaya/legend/encounters/page1.htm

[134] http://www.dailymail.co.uk/news/article-1205572/Hitler-shook-hands-black-1936-Olympic-hero-Jesse-Owens.html

[135] http://www.bharatiyahockey.org/granthalaya/goal/1936/

[136] https://www.google.de/maps/place/Roopsingh-Bais-Weg,+80809+München/@48.1730927,11.5531072,17z/data=!3m1!4b1!4m2!3m1!1s0x479e767c156d1121:0x979fec8713ae125

137 http://blogs.timesofindia.indiatimes.com/ronojay-sens-blog/london-1948-india-s-first-olympics-as-an-independent-nation/

138 http://www.thehindu.com/sport/hockey/1948-olympics-record-fourth-gold-medal-for-india/article3620679.ece

139 https://www.youtube.com/watch?v=WG9dOelkiLk

140 http://timesofindia.indiatimes.com/sports/hockey/top-stories/Hockey-is-a-poor-mans-game-says-Balbir-Singh-Sr/articleshow/35120661.cms

141 http://timesofindia.indiatimes.com/interviews/Balbir-Singh-Senior-The-performance-of-the-Indian-hockey-team-has-shocked-me/articleshow/15424409.cms?

142 http://www.mirror.co.uk/sport/other-sports/londons-underground-map-renamed-to-feature-775032

143 http://timesofindia.indiatimes.com/news/hockey-legends-make-london-tube-station-list/articleshow/12552565.cms

144 http://www.theguardian.com/books/2015/apr/15/top-10-books-about-the-british-in-india

145 http://www.telegraph.co.uk/news/worldnews/asia/india/11415532/The-imperial-nostalgia-of-Indian-Summers-should-not-blind-us-to-the-free-prosperous-India-of-today.html

146 http://timesofindia.indiatimes.com/sports/hockey/Dhyan-Chand-to-be-honoured-in-British-Parliament/articleshow/48176699.cms

147 http://www.thehindu.com/sport/hockey/1948-olympics-record-fourth-gold-medal-for-india/article3620679.ece

148 http://time.com/3655351/india-pakistan-kashmir-border-clashes-flee/

149 http://www.quora.com/History/Why-is-the-National-Emergency-of-1975-seen-as-one-of-the-most-controversial-times-in-the-History-of-India

150 http://dailysikhupdates.com/70000-sikhs-became-arrested-save-india-1975-emergency/

151 http://www.rediff.com/news/2004/jun/03spec.htm

152 http://www.khalistan.net

153 http://www.theglobeandmail.com/news/national/rcmp-says-1985-air-india-bombing-investigation-active-and-ongoing/article25071447/

154 http://www.nytimes.com/interactive/2014/04/06/world/asia/modi-gujarat-riots-timeline.html

155 https://www.biv.com/article/2015/4/modis-visit-divides-vancouver-indo-canadian-commun/

156 https://www.biv.com/article/2015/4/indian-pms-visit-promises-raise-surreys-profile/

157 http://www.thehindu.com/sport/hockey/1928-olympics-indias-first-step-towards-ascending-hockey-throne/article3613550.ece

158 http://www.sportstaronnet.com/tss2920/stories/20060520011904700.htm

159 http://www.newyorker.com/magazine/2015/06/29/the-great-divide-books-dalrymple

160 http://www.bbc.co.uk/archive/olympics_1948/

161 http://www.theguardian.com/sport/2012/mar/30/london-1948-olympics-austerity-games

162 http://www.dailymail.co.uk/news/article-2134920/The-Austerity-Games-1948-Olympics-athlete-reveals-caught-tube-compete-5000m-event-half-day-s-work-building-site.html

163 http://blogs.timesofindia.indiatimes.com/ronojay-sens-blog/london-1948-india-s-first-olympics-as-an-independent-nation/

164 http://library.la84.org/6oic/OfficialReports/1948/OR1948.pdf

165 https://news.google.com/newspapers?id=s9I-AAAAIBAJ&sjid=k0wMAAAAIBAJ&pg=3938,4176353&hl=en

166 http://library.la84.org/6oic/OfficialReports/1952/OR1952.pdf

167 http://www.britannica.com/event/Helsinki-1952-Olympic-Games

168 https://www.youtube.com/watch?v=VeYF9PLHGQ4

169 http://www.guinnessworldrecords.com/world-records/most-goals-scored-by-an-individual-in-an-olympic-hockey-final-(male)

170 http://bbmb.gov.in/english/history_nangal_dam.asp

171 http://www.emelbourne.net.au/biogs/EM01090b.htm

172 http://olympic-museum.de/john_wing/jwing.html

173 https://news.google.com/newspapers?nid=P90YG7HA76QC&dat=19561207&printsec=frontpage&hl=en

174 http://indianexpress.com/article/sports/hockey/its-official-hi-says-it-does-not-want-walsh-as-coach/

175 http://timesofindia.indiatimes.com/sports/hockey/top-stories/Terry-Walsh-quits-as-chief-coach-of-Indian-hockey-team/articleshow/45191370.cms

176 http://www.firstpost.com/sports/hockey-india-doesnt-need-terry-walsh-narinder-batra-1822113.html

177 http://www.dnaindia.com/sport/report-frequent-change-of-coaches-destabilising-indian-hockey-terry-walsh-2109833

178 http://www.dnaindia.com/sport/report-frequent-change-of-coaches-destabilising-indian-hockey-terry-walsh-2109833

179 https://in.news.yahoo.com/former-coach-terry-walsh-criticises-184522427.html

180 http://www.firstpost.com/sports/hockey-india-suspends-indisciplined-gurbaj-singh-9-months-2386380.html

181 http://nsnis.org

182 http://www.allaboutsikhs.com/sikh-warriors/the-great-sikh-warriors

183 https://books.google.co.uk/books?id=2_nryFANsoYC&printsec=front

cover&dq=isbn%3D0521637643&hl=en&sa=X&ei=yKFPU_76KoaEO5blgY
gH&ved=0CEwQ6AEwAQ#v=onepage&q=isbn%3D0521637643&f=false

184 http://www.bbc.com/news/world-asia-26235314

185 http://time.com/3545867/india-1984-sikh-genocide-anniversary/

186 http://www.britannica.com/EBchecked/topic/285248/India/47070/
Emergency-rule

187 http://www.britannica.com/place/India

188 http://www.bbc.co.uk/religion/religions/sikhism/

189 http://edition.cnn.com/2009/WORLD/asiapcf/05/18/sri.lanka.con-
flict.explainer/index.html?iref=24hours

190 http://abcnews.go.com/International/story?id=82216&page=1

191 http://www.roh.org.uk/news/16-great-olympians-profiled-in-the-
olympic-journey

192 http://www.hindustantimes.com/punjab/chandigarh/balbir-singh-sen-
ior-s-olympic-blazer-missing-from-nis-museum/article1-1266322.aspx

193 http://www.englandhockey.co.uk/page.asp?section=1357&sectionTitle
=National+Hockey+Museum

194 http://sports.ndtv.com/hockey/news/246620-treasure-trove-of-indian-
hockey-s-olympic-history-lost

195 http://www.deccanherald.com/content/493653/treasure-trove-indian-
hockeys-olympic.html

196 http://www.fih.ch/rankings/outdoor/

197 http://www.thehindu.com/opinion/op-ed/in-search-of-the-elusive-
goal/article3765528.ece

198 http://blogs.timesofindia.indiatimes.com/headon/the-untold-story-of-
how-india-lost-hockey-supremacy/

199 http://zeenews.india.com/sports/others/kps-gill-ousted-ioa-suspends-
indian-hockey-federation_439551.html

200 http://news.bbc.co.uk/2/hi/south_asia/7371799.stm

201 http://www.hindustantimes.com/news-feed/hockey/kps-gill-sacked-
as-indian-hockey-chief/article1-307479.aspx

202 http://www.hrw.org/en/news/2007/10/17/india-time-deliver-justice-
atrocities-punjab

203 http://indiankanoon.org/doc/579822/

204 http://www.tribuneindia.com/2005/20050728/main5.htm

205 http://hockeyindia.org/

206 http://sports.ndtv.com/hockey/news/239820-balbir-singh-senior-con-
ferred-lifetime-achievement-award-by-hockey-india

207 http://www.hindustantimes.com/brunch/brunch-stories/dhyan-
chand-hockey-s-original-he-man/article1-1212474.aspx

208 http://www.hindustantimes.com/brunch/dhyan-chand-hockey-s-orig-
inal-he-man/story-MNtKHOJpsKbSvkvLzbm2hK.html

209 http://timesofindia.indiatimes.com/sports/hockey/top-stories/Dhyan-Chand-never-expected-anything-Ashok-Kumar/articleshow/9791417.cms
210 http://sports.ndtv.com/hockey/news/246079-indian-hockey-legend-late-dhyan-chand-awarded-bharat-gaurav
211 http://www.thefamouspeople.com/profiles/dhyan-chand-5335.php
212 http://www.tribuneindia.com/news/chandigarh/community/pgi-to-screen-film-on-life-of-dr-chuttani/46517.html
213 http://www.hindustantimes.com/chandigarh/how-chuttani-built-a-grand-institution-block-by-block/story-iA1OujeRW04nK3QxzzFtkO.html
214 http://www.fih.ch/rankings/outdoor/
215 http://www.bloomberg.com/infographics/2013-12-27/nine-decades-of-subjugation.html
216 http://indiatoday.intoday.in/story/amu-vice-chancellor-zameeruddin-shah-sexist-female-student-smriti-irani-hrd-ministry/1/400299.html
217 http://www.nytimes.com/interactive/2015/03/04/world/asia/india-delhi-gang-rape-documentary.html?_r=0
218 http://www.theguardian.com/film/2015/mar/12/delhi-high-court-indias-daughter-film
219 http://www.cbc.ca/passionateeye/episodes/indias-daughter
220 http://www.huffingtonpost.com/huff-wires/20130913/as-india-gang-rape/
221 http://www.theatlantic.com/international/archive/2014/11/the-politics-of-pda-in-india-kiss-protest/382877/
222 https://www.washingtonpost.com/news/worldviews/wp/2015/02/12/why-theres-a-war-on-valentines-day-in-india/
223 http://www.nytimes.com/2013/02/14/world/asia/in-india-kisses-are-on-rise-even-in-public.html?partner=rssnyt&emc=rss
224 http://www.cnn.com/2007/LIVING/wayoflife/09/27/public.display/
225 http://www.indohistory.com/kamasutra.html
226 http://blogs.reuters.com/india/2013/03/07/happily-single-in-india-dont-count-on-it/
227 http://www.wsj.com/articles/the-politicsl-of-gay-rights-in-india-1435854890
228 http://www.independent.co.uk/news/world/asia/indias-gay-community-scrambling-after-court-decision-recriminalises-homosexuality-9146244.html
229 http://www.gulabigang.in
230 http://www.cbc.ca/news/world/sampat-pal-s-gulabi-gang-fights-for-gender-revolution-in-india-1.2926690
231 https://www.imf.org/external/pubs/ft/staffp/2002/03/pdf/cerra.pdf
232 http://news.bbc.co.uk/2/hi/south_asia/55427.stm

233 http://archive.indianexpress.com/news/-youngsters-are-blindly-aping-the-western-culture-/361830/

234 https://www.youtube.com/watch?v=uxzGPQ454BQ

235 http://www.nytimes.com/2015/03/22/opinion/sunday/how-english-ruined-indian-literature.html?_r=0

236 http://www.firstpost.com/india/cleaning-up-indias-police-heres-what-can-remove-corruption-among-top-cops-2260692.html

237 http://www.cfr.org/corruption-and-bribery/governance-india-corruption/p31823

238 http://www.channelnewsasia.com/news/asiapacific/corruption-eating-away-at/2052130.html

239 http://www.britannica.com/event/Massacre-of-Amritsar

240 http://theplanetd.com/the-golden-temple-of-amritsar-indias-shining-star/

241 http://web.worldbank.org/WBSITE/EXTERNAL/COUNTRIES/SOUTHASIAEXT/0,,contentMDK:20916955~pagePK:146736~piPK:146830~theSitePK:223547,00.html

242 http://www.madhyamam.com/en/node/7467

243 http://www.thehindu.com/sport/hockey-legend-leslie-claudius-passes-away/article4222149.ece

244 http://library.la84.org/60ic/OfficialReports/1960/OR1960v2pt1.pdf

245 http://www.livemint.com/Specials/l10hrjkQhPTPaICIgtgbyJ/Leslie-Claudius-hockey-magician-passes-away.html

246 http://www.pier21.ca/research/immigration-history/immigration-act-1976

247 http://www.winnipegfreepress.com/local/across-the-river-286915681.html

248 http://www.thehindu.com/specials/in-depth/the-emergency-imposed-by-indira-gandhi-government/article7357305.ece

249 https://books.google.co.in/books?id=4yp0yhzdKWIC&printsec=frontcover&hl=en#v=onepage&q&f=false

250 http://www.encyclopedia.com/topic/Malaysia.aspx

251 http://www.bharatiyahockey.org/granthalaya/hellwithhockey/

252 http://www.historyworld.net/wrldhis/PlainTextHistories.asp?historyid=ab99

253 https://www.youtube.com/watch?v=kEgtoyVu1IU

254 http://2001-2009.state.gov/r/pa/ho/time/qfp/104481.htm

255 http://library.la84.org/60ic/OfficialReports/1984/1984v1pt1.pdf

256 http://web.archive.org/web/20060823024931/http://www.usdoj.gov/dea/pubs/history/1985-1990.html

257 http://info.indiatimes.com/1984/

258 http://timesofindia.indiatimes.com/india/California-assembly-describes-1984-riots-as-genocide/articleshow/47011681.cms

259 http://www.thehindubusinessline.com/news/world/us-refuses-to-declare-1984-antisikh-riots-as-genocide/article4573340.ece

260 http://news.bbc.co.uk/2/hi/south_asia/8306420.stm

261 http://www.reuters.com/article/2010/09/18/us-airindia-idUSTRE68H1W220100918

262 https://www.youtube.com/watch?v=yS_4ZNa1ByI

263 http://www.theglobeandmail.com/news/national/rcmp-says-1985-air-india-bombing-investigation-active-and-ongoing/article25071447/

264 http://www.montereypeninsulaairport.com/AirIndiareportcontents.html

265 https://www.youtube.com/watch?v=yS_4ZNa1ByI

266 https://www.youtube.com/watch?v=mI48QK-64eU

267 https://www.youtube.com/watch?v=P66mKMDaBtM

268 http://www.roh.org.uk/about/the-olympic-journey

269 http://www.roh.org.uk/news/now-open-free-olympic-experience-at-the-royal-opera-house

270 http://www.roh.org.uk/news/16-great-olympians-profiled-in-the-olympic-journey

271 https://www.youtube.com/watch?v=DgQStAzq6sU

272 http://www.bp.com/en/global/corporate/press/press-releases/the-olympic-journey-the-story-of-the-games.html

273 http://timesofindia.indiatimes.com/nri/other-news/Indians-take-over-London-Census-shows-they-are-largest-foreign-born-group-in-city-now/articleshow/20157057.cms

274 http://www.fih.ch/files/competitions/2012/OG%20London/Men/Day%204/INDvKOR.pdf

275 https://www.youtube.com/watch?v=WG9dOelkiLk

276 http://www.nationalsportsmuseumonline.org.uk/content/collection/hockey-museum

277 http://www.hockeyonstamps.com/Default.aspx?id=600713

278 http://www.theguardian.com/commentisfree/2011/oct/11/delhi-traffic-chaos-jason-burke

279 http://timesofindia.indiatimes.com/city/noida/Infrastructure-projects-to-get-a-boost-with-Noida-Authoritys-Rs-8000-crore-budget/articleshow/29427179.cms

280 http://timesofindia.indiatimes.com/city/noida/Noida-is-countrys-greenest-city-drive-to-push-cover/articleshow/47951562.cms

281 http://www.nytimes.com/2014/12/05/world/indian-leader-favoring-growth-sweeps-away-environmental-rules.html

[282] http://www.forbes.com/sites/morganhartley/2012/12/16/the-culture-shock-of-indias-call-centers/

[283] http://www.ibtimes.co.uk/worlds-most-polluted-city-delhi-now-shows-dangerous-levels-ultra-fine-particles-1508234

[284] http://www.sportsauthorityofindia.nic.in/index1.asp?ls_id=512

[285] http://www.telegraph.co.uk/news/health/expat-health/9017878/Expat-guide-to-India-health-care.html

[286] http://thepatientfactor.com/canadian-health-care-information/world-health-organizations-ranking-of-the-worlds-health-systems/

[287] http://www.sportskeeda.com/hockey/witness-to-an-era-novy-kapadia

[288] http://timesofindia.indiatimes.com/india/The-Great-Indian-Laugh-Riot/articleshow/45209051.cms

[289] http://www.theguardian.com/world/2015/apr/10/mumbai-attacks-suspected-mastermind-freed-bail-pakistan

[290] http://www.onethousandhockeylegs.com

[291] http://indianexpress.com/article/entertainment/bollywood/karan-johar-to-make-biopic-on-hockey-legend-dhyan-chand-will-shah-rukh-khan-play-the-lead/

[292] http://www.who.int/bulletin/volumes/92/11/13-129775/en/

[293] http://qz.com/187020/the-real-reason-wendy-donigers-book-on-hindus-was-banned-in-india-its-not-boring-enough/

[294] https://www.washingtonpost.com/news/worldviews/wp/2013/05/15/a-fascinating-map-of-the-worlds-most-and-least-racially-tolerant-countries/

[295] http://www.worldvaluessurvey.org/wvs.jsp

[296] https://www.cia.gov/library/publications/the-world-factbook/geos/jo.html

[297] http://www.nytimes.com/2014/12/26/opinion/religious-intolerance-in-india.html?_r=0

[298] http://time.com/4016747/mm-kalburgi-india-murder-rationalist-idol-worship-hindu-nationalism/

[299] http://www.bbc.com/news/world-asia-india-34504434

[300] http://www.uscirf.gov/sites/default/files/India%202015.pdf

[301] http://www.theguardian.com/world/2015/feb/24/india-modi-religious-freedom-tolerance

[302] http://www.theguardian.com/commentisfree/belief/2009/may/28/hinduism-tolerance-india

[303] http://www.theguardian.com/books/2002/mar/09/society.salman-rushdie

ACKNOWLEDGMENTS

By no means is this book presented as anything but one person's experience and recollection of India; the author makes no claims of understanding the country (explicitly), its people or its incredibly intricate nature, culture, longstanding history or inner workings. This is but a sliver of time spent by one journalist, and should not be assumed as an overall view. This is simply an outsider's perspective, nothing more, but surely nothing less.

Regarding online footnotes, as most understand the ever-changing beast that is the internet, apologies are made for links that are now broken.

Acknowledgments to all the writers whose work proved invaluable towards this book: *India: A Portrait* by Patrick French; *In Spite of the Gods: The Strange Rise of Modern India* by Edward Luce; *Behind the Beautiful Forevers: Life, Death, and Hope in a Mumbai Undercity* by Katherine Boo; *India After Gandhi: The History of the World's Largest Democracy* by Ramachandra Guha; *A Passage to India* by E.M. Forster; *India Becoming: A Portrait of Life in Modern India* by Akash Kapur; *India: A Million Mutinies Now* by V.S. Naipaul; *The White Tiger* by Aravind Adiga; *Midnight's Children* by Salman Rushdie; *Kim* by Rudyard Kipling; *India: From Midnight to the Millennium and Beyond* by Shashi Tharoor; *Midnight's Furies: The Deadly Legacy of India's Partition* by Nisid Hajari; *Shadows of the Raj: Anglo-Indian visions of empire, the Raj Revival, and the literary crafting of national character* by Genevieve Gagne-Hawes, UBC PhD dissertation.

Genevieve Gagne-Hawes, your edits and insight proved invaluable. You are a writer's dream, a deftly skilled editor, and a true pleasure to work with. To my agent and cornerman, Alec Shane of Writers' House, here's to many more years of triumphs.

To Chris, for once again allowing me to do what I do best, be creative.

To the Bhomia/Dosanjh household, thank you endlessly for letting me pry into your private life. To my mom and dad, and especially little sister Maxine, you are the greatest family a guy could ask for.

Amy, my love bug, thanks for your patience (and final edit!) as I descended into India, and got lost at home in the writing of this book.

Finally, thank you Balbir, for showing me a level of perseverance I thought didn't exist. You are my hero.